TRANSFORMING
SOCIAL WORK
EDUCATION

TRANSFORMING SOCIAL WORK EDUCATION

*The First Decade of the
Hartford Geriatric Social Work Initiative*

EDITED BY

Nancy R. Hooyman

COUNCIL ON SOCIAL WORK EDUCATION
Alexandria, Virginia

Library of Congress Cataloging-in-Publication Data

Transforming social work education : the first decade of the Hartford Geriatric Social Work Initiative / edited by Nancy R. Hooyman.
    p. cm.
    Includes bibliographical references and index.
    ISBN 978-0-87293-134-3
    1. Hartford Geriatric Social Work Initiative. 2. Social work education—United States. 3. Social gerontology—United States. 4. Social service—Scholarships, fellowships, etc.—United States. I. Hooyman, Nancy R. II. Title.

    HV11.7.T73 2009
    362.6—dc22

                                    2009002682

Printed in the United States of America on acid-free paper that meets the American National Standards Institute Z39-48 Standard.

Council on Social Work Education, Inc.
1725 Duke Street, Suite 500
Alexandria, VA 22314-3457
www.cswe.org

Dedication

We dedicate this book to the countless faculty, academic administrators, staff, students, and community partners who enthusiastically participated in the GSWI programs 1998-2008. It is their commitment and hard work that will ensure that all social workers are prepared to enhance the quality of life for older adults and their families.

Contents

Acknowledgments

We are grateful to the many people who have contributed to this book and to the success of the Geriatric Social Work Initiative (GSWI). We begin by acknowledging the board and staff of the John A. Hartford Foundation of New York City, especially Laura Robbins and Jim O'Sullivan, respectively, program officers for the GSWI, and Norman Volk and Corinne Rieder, chairman and executive director, who have all supported this work wholeheartedly for more than a decade.

As noted throughout the book, Hartford's support of social work education, practice, and research through its decade-long investment in the GSWI has had a transformative effect on the field. It has fostered a growing national network of social work faculty, students, academic administrators, and practitioners committed to gerontological social work and the quality of life of older adults and their families. And it has increased the gerontological competencies and content within field and classroom curricula, doctoral dissertations and evidence-based faculty research, and a wide range of national conferences and publications. Most important, the foundation's investment across the past 10 years well positions social work educators, researchers, and practitioners to enhance the health and well-being of older Americans and their families in the coming decades marked by dramatic demographic changes.

This book would not have been possible without the hard work of Kathryn Wilham, editorial assistant. Her high-quality editorial assistance during long evening and weekend hours ensured the timely completion of the book. We thank Julia Watkins, executive director of the Council on Social Work Education (CSWE), for her leadership with the CSWE curriculum development programs. We especially acknowledge the social workers who provided leadership for the first Hartford geriatric social work project, funded in 1998, the Strengthening Aging and Gerontology in Social Work Education Project: Joan Levy Zlotnik, project coordinator, followed by Anita Rosen as project coordinator and Cathy Tompkins as faculty coordinator.

Others who were central to the completion of this book are Varya Gracheva, program assistant, and Jody Meisel, doctoral student at the University of Washington, both with the CSWE Gero-Ed Center, and Jeannine Melly and the Social Work Leadership Institute staff at the New York Academy of Medicine.

Foreword

Corinne H. Rieder and James F. O'Sullivan

The John A. Hartford Foundation of New York City made an unparalleled, sustained private contribution to social work education, authorizing $64.5 million in a 10-year span. Over 1,000 social work faculty have participated in programs funded by Hartford, curriculum development awards have been made to more than 200 social work education programs, and more than 1,000 students have been involved to date. In addition, scores of local foundations and agencies have been recruited to support aspects of social work education as a result of matching requirements attached to the foundation's grants.

The foundation's grants and activities have crossed traditional boundaries of social work education—reaching baccalaureate, master's, and doctoral programs; foundation, generalist, and specialty course work, and field placements; stakeholders from students, faculty, field supervisors, and deans and directors; and micro, mezzo, and macro practice preparation. Notably, the foundation's support for social work education did not come from any historical ties to social work practice or education. Instead, the Hartford's foundation's trustees and staff recognized that social work practice and social work education are critical to its mission of improving health care for older Americans.

This book, written as the foundation's Geriatric Social Work Initiative (GSWI) celebrates its 10th anniversary, reviews the initiative's individual programs and its impact to date. The chapters draw lessons for those who seek additional philanthropic support for social work education and suggest ways that social work educators in all specialty areas can ensure that social work education embraces their area by reviewing the examples of how aging has been infused in almost all aspects of the social work education enterprise.

Corinne H. Rieder is executive director and treasurer of the John A. Hartford Foundation. James F. O'Sullivan, director of Rockefeller Philanthropy Advisors, worked at the foundation from 1998 to 2008, eventually serving as senior program officer and overseeing the Geriatric Social Work Initiative (GSWI) on behalf of the foundation.

Hartford's approach to funding in social work education, from pilot projects to bringing innovations to scale, would work for social work at the intersection of any number of intractable and/or chronic conditions, for example, antipoverty programs, pediatrics, prison-to-community transitions, and interpersonal violence, to name a few.

The John A. Hartford Foundation

From its founding in 1929 the John A. Hartford Foundation has been at the forefront of pioneering advances in medicine and health care, funding research and programs that have revolutionized medicine and helped to shaped the delivery of health care in the United States. In its first 5 decades, Hartford grants funded biomedical research that supported the first kidney transplants, created dialysis equipment, discovered and disseminated electrical therapies for restoring abnormal heart rhythm, set up the first cardiac care units, helped turn cataract surgery into a minimally invasive procedure, and used lasers to treat diabetic retinopathy, among others. Later grants supported demonstration projects and research devoted to innovative local health care financing arrangements, including reimbursement experiments, cost-containment initiatives, efficacy of medical technologies, and public education.

In the 1980s the foundation began to focus on aging and health, recognizing that the success of the public health and medicine systems from 1900 onward had paved the way to an unprecedented growth of the over-65 population. That growth was affecting medicine and health services earlier than it was in almost any other part of American society. Despite expectations that the baby boomers—those born between 1946 and 1963—will be healthier than prior cohorts of retirees, the sheer number of these adults means that it will be the largest group ever of older people with chronic illnesses and functional disability. In addition, projections suggest that the number of older adults with serious psychiatric disorders will climb from 4 million in 1970 to 15 million in 2030 (Jeste et al., 1999), and the number of older adults referred to substance abuse treatment will increase from 1.7 million in 2000 to 4.4 million in 2020 (Office of Applied Studies, 2005). These health issues are typically associated with impairments in function and poorer health outcomes, which suggest that the growth in the numbers of older people with health, mental health, and substance abuse problems will place greater demands on service delivery systems than the statistics alone indicate.

Moreover, the current health care workforce is unprepared to meet the demands of changing demographics in terms of actual numbers of health care workers and adequate training for these workers (Institute of Medicine, 2008). In medicine, for example, only 7,128 U.S. physicians are certified geriatricians, although 36,000 are forecast to be needed by 2030. In social work, only 5% of social workers are trained in aging issues (Caring for an Aging America Act of 2008), and 17% of social workers who work with older adults report that vacancies are common in their agencies, while 21% indicate that vacancies are difficult to fill (Whitaker, Weismiller, & Clark, 2006).

In its education and training efforts, the foundation focuses on three health professions it sees as key to effective, affordable health care for older Americans: medicine, nursing, and social work. Since 1983, Hartford grants in medicine supported projects first to develop geriatrics as an academic discipline, including faculty development awards; programs to increase the number of MD-scientists; and a national network of Centers of Excellence in Geriatric Medicine and Training. In nursing, a 1996 grant led to the creation of curriculum standards and then faculty development programs; both continue today with a national scholars program and a network of Centers of Geriatric Nursing Excellence.

In 1997–98, Hartford staff oversaw a rigorous process to determine how older patients could best be served when traditional medical and nursing care had been provided. The answer was quickly obvious: Social work's contribution to effective care for older patients had already been validated in previous foundation grant programs on geriatric interdisciplinary teams, and the foundation had developed an appreciation of social work's many roles. The function most commonly associated with social workers is case management, but a more complete list also includes interventions for individuals, families, and communities, plus advocacy for the client and for broader changes in nonprofit organizations and at all levels of government. Most important, practice with individuals and families is consumer directed, giving the client dignity and choices in service types, providers, and timing of care. Perhaps most fundamentally, social workers are knowledge workers, requiring the ability to process and use increasing amounts of data to fulfill their professional responsibilities and to act autonomously using judgment and experience to solve problems. They are expected to provide psychosocial assessment, care management, and information and referral services. To be prepared for this large role, social workers require a competency-based professional education and lifelong learning to be able to take advantage of and adjust programming to scientific advances and changes in policies, and to broker opportunities on behalf of clients. Further, in balancing the many potential needs of older adults, social workers are expected to determine the cost-effectiveness of treatment while ensuring support options for their clients.

In health care, social workers are crucial service providers who enable older adults and their families to access the array of health and social services available as part of modern medicine. From Hartford's perspective, geriatric social workers are the professionals trained to help older people and their families capably use the multiple systems of care that provide health and supportive services to older adults. In medical social work, the most frequent question social workers are asked to address on behalf of their clients is "Can this individual return to his or her prior environment?" The goal for services is to support the highest level of client functioning at the safest level of care. When delivered well, social work services have a positive impact on medical systems by reducing the length of stay, or avoiding "bounce-backs" by obtaining benefits and supports for clients and providing consumer and caregiver education. These services are applicable in almost all chronic health care interventions, with examples in mental health, cancer, arthritis, chronic pain, diabetes, HIV/AIDS, substance abuse, Alzheimer's, and with end-of-life care.

Social Work and Aging

In the foundation's view, appropriate, effective social work services contribute to health care in vital ways. The traditional medical model of health care services does not take into account older adults themselves or the necessary details of community-based systems and supports to meet the needs for care of older adults. By contrast, social work assessment and services try to explicitly consider clients' values, history, and desires, which is inappropriate or unrealistic for most services provided by other health professions. Social work training in systems theory thereby provides a window into considering the needs of informal caregivers and recognizes the ongoing personal and economic relationships that affect services provision. Both medical and nonmedical interventions are needed to keep older adults at home and living autonomously for the longest possible period, with social work providing the nonmedical care and often coordinating independent medical services on behalf of clients. The ability to age in place, meaning to live at home and grow old in a familiar environment, must be supported through ecological and systems perspectives, of which medical care is only a part. The competence of an older person is recognized as changing and subject to social and environmental interventions (such as caregiving, activities of daily living supports, and mitigation of environmental barriers). Social workers enhance older people's functioning by tying together formal supports (such as respite care and health care programs) with informal sources (including social networks and personal assets, among others).

Clients, caregivers, and society all benefit from social work's professional perspective on the individual and environment. For older adults, aging in place is often preferable to institutionalization, because environmental and relationship predictability can be maintained while existing social ties help maintain functioning and resiliency. For caregivers, not having to worry about the effects of institutionalization or arrange visits is beneficial. And for society, it is considerably more cost-effective by preventing premature or inappropriate placement.

The need for geriatric social workers to care for our nation's older population is clear. Current projections and workforce data suggest that by 2020 there will be a shortfall of at least 21,000 professional social workers with expertise in aging required to meet the needs of the population (Bureau of Labor Statistics, 2004). Failure to increase geriatric leadership within social work programs will maintain the status quo: a dearth of students—our future leaders—entering careers in gerontological social work and minimal social work research aimed at improving the care of our aging population.

As the profession in health care that is the most concerned with holistic approaches to treating patients, including older ones, social work needs to graduate students ready to enter practice with the ability to create innovative interventions and programs to promote health and autonomy among older adults. Until the advent of the Hartford GSWI, most students received little specific knowledge of the aging process and how to address health and behavioral health issues in diverse locales such as hospitals, doctors' offices, hospices, mental health clinics, community counseling centers, and long-term residential programs for individuals with mental illness. In health care, aging-savvy social workers are crucial service providers who enable older adults and their families to access the array of health and social services available as part of modern medicine.

The GSWI

The GSWI has created a broad base of programs to ensure that all social work graduates are geriatrically prepared, supporting and accelerating the progress of a national gerontology-education (gero-ed) movement. This unparalleled investment began in 1998 with a faculty development project, Strengthening Aging and Gerontology in Social Work Education (SAGE-SW), through the Council on Social Work Education (CSWE). In 1999 the Hartford Faculty Scholars Program was funded with a cohort of 10 scholars. The Practicum Partnership Program (PPP), initiated in 1999 and now called the Hartford Partnership Program for Aging Education (HPPAE), focuses on the advanced field curriculum for MSW students and has implemented a rotational model of field education and innovative partnerships with community agencies. The Hartford Doctoral Fellows program, funded in 2000, provides dissertation support and professional development opportunities. The CSWE Geriatric Enrichment in Social Work Education Project (GeroRich), which emphasized curricular and programmatic change, was funded from 2001 through 2004. The latest initiative, the CSWE National Center for Gerontological Social Work Education (Gero-Ed Center), has been funded for 2004 through 2012 and encompasses a range of programs to train faculty, recruit students, and, through the Master's Advanced Curriculum (MAC) project, design specialized and gero-infused foundation classroom content. These initiatives, with their distinctive but complementary approaches, are described in the following chapters.

Ensuring the needed future increase in gero-competent researchers, educators, and practitioners necessitates strategies to sustain changes made through Hartford funding. Later chapters present the overall communication and dissemination strategies developed by the GSWI programs and discuss the importance of collaboration among social work programs and scholars around the country, as well as among the administrative staff for each of the GSWI programs. Finally, lessons learned related to resource development, marketing, and institutionalization of change that are relevant to all social work educators are discussed, providing reflections on the sustainability of these programs.

As we pause to review the work of the past 10 years, it is clear that many older people will receive better care and will have longer, healthier, and more fulfilled lives because of the work described in this book. A private foundation cannot support change if there is a lack of willing hands, minds, and hearts. Principal investigators, consultants, deans and directors, faculty, students, and community partners have embraced the Hartford foundation's mission of improving health care for our country's older people, and their integrity and commitment has been the underpinning for all the success to date. To all the participants of the GSWI's many programs we offer our sincerest congratulations for the accomplishments described in this book and our gratitude for all your work. Together, the interlocking programs of the GSWI have helped all social work education programs, creating teaching resources, developing tomorrow's gerontologically expert faculty, and launching programs that prepare future social workers to practice successfully with their older clients.

References

Bureau of Labor Statistics. (2004). *Occupational outlook handbook, 2008–09 edition: Social workers.* Retrieved September 15, 2008, from http://stats.bls.gov/oco/ocos060.htm

Caring for an Aging America Act of 2008, H.R. 6637, 110th Cong. (2008).

Institute of Medicine. (2008). *Retooling for an aging America: Building the health care workforce committee on the future health care workforce for older Americans.* Washington, DC: National Academies Press.

Jeste, D. V., Alexopoulos, G. S., Bartels, S. J., Cummings, J. L., Gallo, J. J., Gottlieb, G. L., et al. (1999). Consensus statement on the upcoming crisis in geriatric mental health: Research agenda for the next two decades. *Archives of General Psychiatry, 56*(9), 848–853.

Office of Applied Studies. (2005). *Substance use among older adults: 2002 and 2003 update. The national survey on drug use and health report.* Retrieved April 28, 2006, from http://oas.samhsa.gov/2k5/olderadults/olderadults.htm

Whitaker, T., Weismiller, T., & Clark, E. (2006). *Assuring the sufficiency of a frontline workforce: A national study of licensed social workers.* Retrieved January 25, 2008, from http://workforce.socialworkers.org/studies/aging/aging.pdf

PART I

Bringing New Approaches to Preparing Tomorrow's Social Workers

CHAPTER I

The Need for Gerontological Social Workers

Nancy R. Hooyman and James Lubben

The Demographic Imperative

The primary impetus driving the Geriatric Social Work Initiative (GSWI) to prepare gerontologically competent social work educators, scholars, and practitioners is the rapidly growing population age 65 and older. In the year 2006 alone, 7,918 baby boomers reached age 60 each day, By 2020—only 11 years from now—16% of Americans will be 65 or older; by 2030, 20% will be 65 or older, compared with 12.4% today (Administration on Aging [AOA], 2008; U.S. Census Bureau, 2006). And these senior boomers are expected to live longer than prior generations. Even though the boomers will be healthier on average than prior generations, their sheer numbers will increase the demand for community-based services to prevent and manage chronic illness.

With the aging of the baby boomers, the 65 and older population is projected to increase by 147% between 2000 and 2050, whereas the population as a whole will increase 49% during this same period (U.S. Census Bureau, 2006). These trends are largely driven by increased longevity and lower fertility rates. Increased immigration rates are also an important factor, because immigrants are generally younger than nonimmigrants (Angel & Hogan, 2004). No other demographic shift in recent history is having as profound an impact on every societal institution—workplace, retirement, education, health care, and the family—and accordingly on the social work profession, as the aging imperative.

The greatest population increases will be among those age 85 and older, driven largely by increased longevity, primarily because of improved medical care earlier in the life course. In fact, by 2025 one in 26 Americans can expect to live to age 100 compared to 1 in 500 in 2000 (AOA, 2008). Many of these oldest old will be cognitively impaired; nearly 50% of those age 85 or older now suffer from Alzheimer's disease (Merck Institute & Gerontological Society of America, 2002; National Center for Health Statistics [NCHS], 2006). Those older than age 85 are also more likely than those age 65 to 74 to have chronic illnesses that affect their daily activities and require health care, long-term care, and other support services. Accordingly, this more vulnerable population is likely to need increased social work services. Furthermore, social workers will be critical to promoting and maintaining the well-being of the growing numbers of healthy older adults. Programs that are aimed at delaying the onset of disability and fostering elder-friendly communities to build on elders' resilience and support civic engagement and aging in place will become even more important in the future (AdvantAge Initiative, 2007; AOA, 2008; NCHS, 2006).

Another trend with implications for social work is the increasing diversity and accompanying vulnerability of segments of the aging population. Because of women's longer life expectancy than men's, women remain the majority of adults age 65 and older, especially among elders 85 and older and nursing home residents. The number of lesbian/gay/bisexual or transgender elders, who often face discrimination in long-term health care settings, is estimated to be 1 to 3 million, and this will grow to 2 to 6 million by 2030 (Blank, 2006; Lambert, 2005). Currently, elders of color form 19% of the age 65 and older population: 8.3% are African American, 6.4% Latino, 3.1 % Asian and Pacific Islander, and less than 1% Native American. Although the proportion of young adults to elders is currently greater in populations of color than in the Caucasian population, this pattern is also changing swiftly. By 2030 elders of color will form more than 33% of the older population, with elders age 85 and older among Asian/Pacific Islanders and Latinos being the most rapidly growing group (AOA, 2008; U.S. Census Bureau, 2006).

Women, ethnic minority elders, and the oldest members of the population face the highest rates of killer chronic illness, such as diabetes, hypertension, stroke, and heart disease. Additionally, nursing home admission rates increase with age from 1.3% for those age 65 to 74 to 15.4% for those age 85 and older (AOA, 2008; Whitfield & Hayward,

2003). The poverty rate also increases in both groups and is greatest among older women of color. To illustrate the intersections of poverty, race, gender, and health status, twice as many women than men age 65 and older are poor. Nearly three times as many older African Americans and more than twice as many Latino elders are poor compared to their Caucasian counterparts. And the rate of poverty increases with age: nearly half of those age 85 or older are either poor or nearly poor. African American and Latina women age 85 and older are the poorest groups in our society, and they face the highest rates of chronic illness (Angel & Hogan, 2004; AOA, 2008; Whitfield & Hayward, 2003). Poverty typically translates into disparities in access to health care. For example, 22% of low-income elders report that their health needs go unmet, whereas only 2.5% of middle- and upper-income elders indicate unmet needs (He, Sengupta, Velkoff, & DeBarros, 2005).

These trends toward greater heterogeneity of the older population should be viewed within the context of social work's historical commitment to social justice and working with disadvantaged populations. Because of this commitment, social workers—perhaps more than other health and social service professionals—are likely to be working daily with vulnerable elders. Yet the shortage of BSW- and MSW-level social workers with gerontological competencies to provide effective psychosocial care to the growing and increasingly diverse population of older adults and their families has been documented for nearly 30 years (Berkman, Gardner, Zodikoff, & Harooytan, 2005; Council on Social Work Education Strengthening Aging and Gerontology in Social Work Education [CSWE SAGE-SW], 2001; U.S. Bureau of Labor Statistics, 2004).

Of particular concern is that geriatric social workers are less diverse in racial and ethnic backgrounds than the current older population they serve and the U.S. civilian population (Whitaker, Weismiller, & Clark, 2006). This gap between the cultural and ethnic background of the workforce and those being served will grow with the projected increased diversity of elders by 2030. The need for a more diverse geriatric workforce occurs within the context of the overall challenges of attracting other groups with lower levels of representation among geriatric social workers who currently tend to be older and include more women than social workers serving other age groups. In addition to the imperative to increase the racial and ethnic diversity of the geriatric social work workforce, there is a need to recruit younger, male, and newly graduating BSW and MSW social workers with competencies to work effectively with elders who have been marginalized across the life course (Whitaker et al.). Strategies to address this need for a culturally diverse geriatric workforce cut across the four GSWI core programs, described on pp. 10–16 in this chapter.

Geriatric Workforce Needs

A 2008 report from the Institute of Medicine (IOM) concluded that the supply of health care providers in general is inadequate for meeting the health and psychosocial needs of future older adults (IOM, 2008). The report suggested that efforts to overcome this shortfall are complicated by the aging of the workforce itself and negative stereotypes about working with older adults. Social work was singled out as one of the health professions that needs to expand its geriatric workforce by ensuring that all social workers have geriatric competencies and by recruiting and preparing more geriatric specialists.

Similar workforce shortages were recognized as early as 1987, when it was predicted that 60,000–70,000 geriatric social workers would be required to meet the needs of older adults by 2020, a projection documented again in 2004 (National Institute on Aging, 1987; U.S. Bureau of Labor Statistics, 2004). The number of social workers in long-term care settings will also grow dramatically: from 36,000 in 2002 to 55,000 by 2012 and 109,000 by 2050 (U.S. Bureau of Labor Statistics, 2004). Employment in the field of geriatric social work is expected to increase faster than the average of all other occupations through 2014, not only because of increased life expectancy but also because of shorter hospital stays and the need for community-based care coordination at discharge (Social Work Leadership Institute, 2006). As noted above, another factor intensifying future workforce needs is that geriatric social workers are older on average (median age of 50 years) than practitioners in other fields, and thus, they are nearing retirement age. Ten percent of MSWs and 8% of BSWs reported in 2005 that they plan to retire in 2 years but other geriatric-competent social workers are not there to replace them (Whitaker et al., 2006).

Despite these multiple indicators of growing demand, a national shortage of gerontological social workers persists (Institute for Geriatric

Social Work & New York Academy of Medicine, 2005; Whitaker et al., 2006). In 2001 only 3% of the 150,000 members of the National Association of Social Workers (NASW) identified their primary area of social work practice as gerontology (Rosen & Zlotnik, 2001). This had increased by 2005 but only to 9% of a sample of licensed NASW members who identified aging as their specific field of practice; among these, less than 5% were specifically trained in gerontological social work (Whitaker et al., 2006). Yet 75% of this national sample worked in some capacity with older adults and their families, although they were generally not prepared to do so (Peterson & Wendt, 1990; Whitaker et al.). Many of these social workers may not have imagined they would ever work with "old people." But they began to see older adults in child welfare, school, and pediatric settings, partially as a result of the growth of grandparents as the primary caregivers of their grandchildren. Or they encountered elders in health and mental health settings, homeless shelters, and substance abuse or HIV/AIDS treatment centers. Despite the fact that older adults can be found in nearly every setting served by social workers, a 2004 study of the public's understanding of social work reported that 90% of respondents viewed helping children and families as the social worker's primary role (LeCroy & Stinson, 2004). With the aging of the baby boomers, nearly all social workers will interact with older adults and their families within the next 25 years, regardless of the practice setting.

Intensifying workforce needs is the decline in graduates' (2000–2004) reporting health as their primary practice area (2% of BSWs and 7% of MSWs; Whitaker et al., 2006). This is a concern because 56% of social workers in health care settings have reported caseloads consisting predominantly of older adults, but they are generally not prepared to work with older patients and may lack access to geriatric training through continuing education. Similar to gerontological social work, social workers in health care are predominantly women (89%) and are also less racially and ethnically diverse than the U.S. civilian labor force or the populations they serve (Whitaker et al.). Recruiting students from culturally and socioeconomically diverse backgrounds for health care and aging specializations or concentrations is essential to ensure that social workers are prepared to meet the needs of historically underserved elders in hospitals, community clinics, home care, and other health and long-term care settings.

Factors Underlying the Workforce Shortage

The limited amount of advanced or specialized content on aging in BSW and MSW programs contributes to the lack of a gerontologically prepared social work workforce. Fewer social work programs (49 or about 28%) offer an MSW specialization in aging now than in the early 1980s (almost 50%) or in the early 1990s (about 33%; CSWE, 2006–07; Lubben, Damron-Rodriguez, & Beck, 1992; Rosen, Zlotnick, & Singer, 2002). Of the 180 MSW programs that indicated their advanced content was organized by concentrations in 2004–05, aging was the least frequently offered advanced specialization (CSWE, 2004–05). Among 23,835 students who indicated a specific focus in their field placement, only 1,670 (7%) reported that this area of emphasis was gerontology (CSWE, 2006–07). Not surprisingly, the largest concentration/specialization remains child welfare followed by mental health and health. The extent of gerontological content has also been limited in BSW programs. For instance, nearly 30% of BSW programs in the 2006–07 CSWE's annual statistics offered no courses on aging, and most respondents indicated little (0% to 10%) gero content in foundation courses. Nevertheless, a more encouraging trend is that the rate of BSW and MSW programs that report 0% or 1%–10% gero content has decreased significantly since 2003, when the first statistics on gerontology were collected (CSWE, 2006–07). The increase in programs reporting gerontology content in foundation courses may be associated with the implementation of the CSWE Gero-Ed Center's infusion strategy in the foundation curriculum of nearly 200 social work programs (discussed in chapter 5).

The 2006–07 CSWE statistics also reflect a substantial decrease in the number of required or elective stand-alone gerontology courses offered. Even when such specialized gerontological content or course work exists, relatively few students choose to pursue it. About 25% of BSW and 20% of MSW students have taken a course in gerontology (Cummings, Alder, & DeCoster, 2005). One reason for this is that nearly 50% of MSW students state they have little or no interest in working with older adults after graduation (Cummings & Galambos, 2002). Similarly, less than 20% of MSW students cite older adults as a population they are interested in working with in the future (Cummings et al.). The reasons why students choose not to work with older adults and, conversely, factors that may contribute to students' pursuing a gerontological social work career are also extensively documented (Cummings & DeCoster, 2003; Cummings & Galambos; Gibelman & Schervish, 1997; Lubben et al., 1992; Mason & Sanders, 2004; Scharlach, Damron-Rodriguez, Robinson, & Feldman, 2000).

A significant barrier to recruitment and retention is the relatively lower salaries of geriatric social workers compared to social workers generally. Their median salaries are slightly less than the median salaries for all social workers with master's ($46,894 vs. $49,500) and bachelor's ($33,593 vs. $34,597) degrees. The reasons for considering a job change cited most frequently by social workers serving older adults included higher salary (72%), lifestyle/family concerns (53%), more interesting work (38%), and stress of the current job (35%). The relatively lower salaries are a significant barrier to students before and after graduation as they grapple with mounting student loan debt. And this potential debt load is a factor that has not been well examined for its impact among students of color in particular. Although data on loan debt specifically among geriatric social workers is not available, among NASW members surveyed in 2007, 67% incurred debt ranging from $5,000 to $100,000 while they were social work students. More than half who earned less than $19,999 a year, and 67% of those earning $20,000–$49,999 had debt greater than their annual salaries. Additionally, African Americans were more likely to have unmanageable debt than Caucasians. These findings are of concern to the profession as a whole, and particularly to the field of gerontological social work where salaries are typically lower than those in other practice areas (Ballard, 2005; Whitaker, 2008).

Factors that affect the likelihood of a student's pursuing a career in gerontological social work include early exposure to and positive interaction with older adults in classes, volunteer work, or field placements; a close personal relationship with an older adult relative; and perceived skills to work with elders (Cummings, Galambos, & DeCoster, 2003; Mason & Sanders, 2004). Additionally, the interest in working with elders apparently often emerges in a processlike fashion rather than being a sudden decision, which can make recruitment particularly challenging. Some students develop the passion for this work over years of previous contact with elders; others slowly find the dedication to it, replacing previous interests (Lawrence et al., 2002).

As a response to this critical workforce need, the GSWI has expanded the geriatric capacity of faculty, curricula, social work education programs, and the profession as a whole, and has recruited students across all three degree levels to gerontological social work practice and research.

The Hartford GSWI

As noted in the foreword, the John A. Hartford Foundation of New York City has authorized investments of more than $46 million in the GSWI since 1998, thereby accelerating the progress of a national gero-ed movement. This unparalleled investment began with a faculty development project, SAGE-SW, administered through the CSWE from 1998 to 2001. In 1999 the Hartford Geriatric Social Work Faculty Scholars (HFS) Program began with the first cohort of 10 scholars, and it enrolled its ninth cohort in 2008 for a total of 91 scholars. The Practicum Partnership Program (PPP), initiated in 1999, focused on the advanced field curriculum for MSW students and implemented a rotational model of field education and partnerships with community agencies. This program evolved in 2008 into the Hartford Partnership Program for Aging Education (HPPAE). The Hartford Doctoral Fellows (HDF) Program, first funded in 2000, provides dissertation support and professional development opportunities. In 2005 the HDF program was expanded to include a predissertation component. The CSWE Geriatric Enrichment in Social Work Education Project (GeroRich), active from 2001 to 2004, emphasized curricular and programmatic change by providing guidance and funding for 67 BSW and MSW programs nationwide to infuse geriatric competencies in foundation curricula. The latest initiative, the CSWE National Center for Gerontological Social Work Education (Gero-Ed Center), builds on the successes and lessons learned from the GeroRich project. The Gero-Ed Center, funded from 2004 through 2012, encompasses a range of programs to train faculty (the Curriculum Development Institute [CDI] Program), recruit students (the BSW Experiential Learning [BEL] Program, and the Admissions Staff Initiative), and design gero-specialized and gero-infused foundation and advanced classroom content, including the Master's Advanced Curriculum (MAC) Project and the Gero Specialized Program.

At the time of publication, the GSWI encompassed four core programs: the HFS, HDF, HPPAE, and Gero-Ed Center. Throughout this book, the HPPAE and the Gero-Ed Center are referred to as the classroom and field curriculum development programs in the GSWI, and the HFS and HDF programs are noted as promoting scholarly capacity of faculty and future faculty. A focus on leadership development, especially among historically marginalized groups, underlies the four programs. Each of these programs and the needs that motivate their distinctive but complementary approaches are briefly described on the following pages, beginning with the scholars and fellows programs that aim to expand geriatric social work research capacity.

The HFS Program

The geriatric workforce crisis is intensified by too few faculty scholars in geriatric social work available to teach the evidence-based knowledge essential to educate future social work practitioners. When the HFS program was initiated in 1999, less than 10% of faculty members in 117 graduate programs had formal training in aging. Currently, of 1,353 faculty members in the 66 social work schools that have doctoral programs, only 171 (12%) are reported to be geriatric scholars. Yet increasing geriatric leadership in social work is vital to attracting master's and doctoral students, our future leaders, to careers in aging.

Social work schools/programs continue to need new faculty who are qualified to teach empirically tested models of care that integrate knowledge of the biopsychosocial realities of older adults with expanded models of community-based practices. The HFS program offers a strategic solution to these needs, focused on developing faculty leaders in social work geriatric health care research and education. These scholars are then prepared to train social work practitioners to meet the social and health care needs of the rapidly growing population of older adults. The long-term goal is to increase programmatic and institutional capacity to educate geriatric social work practitioners. The HFS program has begun to have an impact on the context of social work education, with 23% of accredited graduate schools of social work in 27 states having Hartford scholars on faculty. To date, seven Hartford scholars working in BSW-only programs have also been funded, thereby strengthening the research capacity of undergraduate programs as well.

In addition to increasing programmatic capability, the HSF program has built the geriatric capacity of the profession as a whole and increased the visibility and desirability of geriatric social work as a professional specialty. This program has strategically aimed to build cohorts of spokespeople for geriatric social work within their own academic programs and in the professional community as a whole. The networking among the Hartford faculty scholars, Hartford national research mentors, and Hartford doctoral fellows serves as one means to create a critical mass of social workers who will be empowered to move the profession forward in gerontological scholarship. Prior to the HFS program, no mechanism existed to create this strong identification among leaders in geriatric social work.

A systematic mentoring program is central to this capacity-building strategy. Chapter 3 identifies the distinguishing characteristics of the HFS program mentoring component, which involves national research mentors and local institutional sponsors. Data regarding the effectiveness of this model are presented. The chapter concludes with a discussion of lessons learned that are salient to the design and implementation of other types of mentoring programs in other substantive areas and disciplines, even when resources are limited.

The HDF Program

The HDF program consists of two components, dissertation fellowship and a Pre-Dissertation Award. Both components share the goal with the HFS program to create a cadre of faculty with geriatric expertise who will, over time, increase the number of well-trained gerontological BSWs and MSWs. When the HDF program was initiated in 2000, of the 300 doctoral dissertations produced each year, only 7% were in geriatric social work (Lubben & Harootyan, 2002). Limited funding in gerontology in the 1990s diverted social work scholars and doctoral students to other fields, especially child welfare. Restricted funding for gerontology also reduced the prestige of geriatrics in academic institutions along with the system of faculty role models, peer networks, research assistance, and other support that universities often provide to nurture careers.

The HDF program seeks to address the next decade's projected geriatric workforce shortage by supporting future gero-focused faculty who will advance the practice of gerontological social work through research and ensure that an increased number of social work students receive appropriate educational preparation to work with older people. It does so by providing dissertation funding, extensive academic career development opportunities, and leadership training for a select group of promising doctoral students who are at the dissertation stage. In addition, the Pre-Dissertation Award component provides travel grants to the Gerontological Society of America's annual scientific meeting to encourage other doctoral students early in their studies (typically after their first year) to consider conducting dissertation research in the growing field of aging. Many of the HDF program components—promoting gerontology's stature, mentoring, peer networking and support, cohort building, career development, and leadership training—can be implemented on a small scale and do not necessarily require extensive university or external resources. They do, however, require administrative support and leadership to guide doctoral students to conduct research in areas related to improving the care of older adults and their families. And while the focus has been on gerontology, strategies of the fellows program are relevant to dean's and director's efforts to build research and scholarly capacity generally among future and current faculty.

The HPPAE

As noted above, less than 5% of MSW students currently specialize in aging, and only about 20% take specialized aging courses. Among its goals, HPPAE aims to address the fact that not enough graduate students are specializing in gerontology or receiving the field-based training needed to become skilled geriatric practitioners. To compound the situation, the systems of care for older adults are not well coordinated. This not only makes it difficult for older adults to access needed services but also means that traditional methods of preparing students may not impart adequate knowledge about the wide range of services available to elders. To meet the needs of older adults, social work students must be familiar with the matrix of aging services and the diversity of roles and functions of older people, such as the growing number of healthy and civically engaged elders. Too many students assume that field placements and career options are only available with elders with a chronic illness or disability, typically in nursing homes or hospital settings. Given this, the HPPAE adopted a rotational model of field education as a way to expose students to the matrix of community-based services, the heterogeneity of elders, and other disciplines providing care. When students witness these options firsthand, including the opportunity to work with healthy older adults, they have been found to consider a gerontological social work career (Ivry, Lawrance, Damron-Rodriguez, & Robbins, 2005).

In addition to the distinctive rotational field education model, the HPPAE is characterized by competency-driven education, strong university-community partnerships, and an expanded collaborative role for agency-based field instructors. Chapter 6 describes each of these components and derives implications for social work programs that seek to strengthen community partnerships, implement competency-based education, integrate field education across sites and populations, and recruit students to specific fields of practice other than aging.

CSWE Gero-Ed Center

The CSWE Gero-Ed Center aims to promote transformative gero capacity building in social work education programs and in the profession as a whole. It has done so through multiple tactics: a planned change approach to the infusion of gerontological competencies and content linked with the CSWE (2008) Educational Policy and Accreditation Standards; building intersections of gero social work competencies with other areas, such as with cultural competencies and with those relevant to mental health, health, and substance use; seeking to add gero competencies and content to the national licensure exam; and conducting evaluations to measure the outcomes of curricular and programmatic change on faculty, students, curricula, and the profession as a whole. More than 1,000 social work faculty members have participated in gero competency-based training (GeroRich programs and the CDIs), and 137 social work programs have infused such competencies into their curricula and programmatic structure. Faculty participants have created from the bottom up a diverse array of teaching resources, such as syllabi, case studies, and assignments, which are disseminated nationwide through the center's Web site.

Based on feedback from prior participants about the need for more diversity among CDI program participants, the Gero-Ed Center in 2007 initiated a targeted recruitment process for the CDI program, using past participants as ambassadors to reach small programs, including BSW-only programs, that have not participated in prior Hartford funding; are located in states with a higher proportion of older residents than the national average; and serve a culturally diverse student body. Center staff also recruited intensely through the CSWE Commission on Diversity and Social and Economic Justice, the CSWE Minority Doctoral Fellows Program, and the professional associations of Native American, Latina, African American, and Asian American social workers. As a result of this targeted effort, of the Cycle 2 CDI programs funded from 2008-2011, 41% are small, 81% are BSW only or joint; 13% are at historically Black colleges, 13% are at Spanish-speaking institutions, and 50% are from states with a higher percentage of older residents than the national average.

The center's overarching goal of planned change to infuse gerontological competencies within foundation curricula and programmatic structures continues but has expanded to include a number of complementary approaches for the maximum national impact on the preparation of gerontologically competent graduates. These include strategies to recruit more students to gerontological social work, such as BSW experiential learning activities and building the gero capacity of admissions and career counseling staff; expanded eLearning courses on how to bring about change in foundation and gero-specific curricula; development of specialized BSW and MSW gerontological content; and strategies to infuse gero content into foundation social work textbooks. Under the umbrella of the center, the MAC project seeks to embed gerontological competencies in specialized health, mental health, and substance use curricula, and to build gero capacity among faculty and students associated with those three specialty areas that typically attract more students than aging does. In all these initiatives, attention has been given to recruiting culturally diverse faculty and student participants and ensuring that curricular resources attend to issues of cultural competence.

Underlying the Gero-Ed Center's initiatives is the strategic planned change infusion approach developed in curriculum projects beginning with the GeroRich project in 2001. Such programmatic-level change is essential to embed gerontology in foundation curricula and organizational culture (e.g., infusing gerontology into a program's mission and goals, curriculum decision-making structure, recruitment materials, and library and media holdings). Chapter 5 describes lessons learned from the planned change model developed to infuse gero competencies in foundation courses and in specializations in the three advanced curricular areas of health, mental health, and substance use.

Building Toward Sustainability

Central to all the GSWI programs are strategies to clearly communicate their accomplishments to key constituencies, including current and potential funders and members of the social work profession and other geriatric disciplines. The principal investigators of each program as well as their participants—faculty in the HFS, CDI, GeroRich, and HPPAE programs, and doctoral students and their faculty mentors in the HDF program—have all received training in communications, marketing, and resource development strategies oriented to long-term capacity building and sustainability. Whereas externally funded projects may have positive short-term outcomes, strategies must be designed to sustain changes made through the Hartford funding to ensure that social work leaders are meeting the future need for gero-competent researchers, educators, and practitioners. Chapters 7 through 9 present lessons learned related to resource development, marketing, and institutionalization of change that are relevant not only for gerontological social work but also for other substantive areas and fields of practice.

Conclusion

The demographic changes, workforce data, and limited gerontology competencies and content in most social work programs provided the impetus for the Hartford foundation's decision to fund the GSWI. Although the GSWI has focused on geriatric social work, the kind of analysis undertaken—gathering workforce data, collecting statistics from programs nationwide, and drawing upon relevant literature—is of course transferable to other practice and research areas that seek to make the case for increased attention and resources to promote leadership capacity. In fact, some of the trends and challenges reported in this chapter are particularly relevant to specific practice areas preparing students for health and mental health settings, where social workers frequently interact with older adults and their families. This context of the well-documented need for more geriatric researchers, educators, and practitioners provides the framework for the importance of developing gerontological social work competencies and outcome measures, as described in chapter 2.

References

Administration on Aging. (2008). *A profile of older Americans: 2008.* Washington, DC: U.S. Department of Health and Human Services.

AdvantAge Initiative. (2007). *AdvantAge communities.* Retrieved March 18, 2007, from http://www.vnsny.org/advantage

Angel, J., & Hogan, D. (2004). Population aging and diversity in a new era. In K. E. Whitfield (Ed.), *Closing the gap: Improving the health of minority elders in the new millennium* (pp. 1–13). Washington, DC: Gerontological Society of America.

Ballard, A. (2005, Spring). *Understanding the next generation of nonprofit employees: The impact of educational debt.* Retrieved May 28, 2007, from http://www.buildingmovement.org/artman/uploads/educational_debt _001.pdf

Berkman, B. J., Gardner, D. S., Zodikoff, B. D., & Harootyan, L. K. (2005). Social work in health care with older adults: Future challenges. *Families in Society, 86*(3), 329–337.

Blank, T. O. (2006). Gay and lesbian aging: Research and future directions. *Educational Gerontology, 32,* 241–243.

Council on Social Work Education. (2008). *Educational policy and accreditation standards.* Retrieved November 12, 2008, from http://www.cswe.org/NR/rdonlyres/2A81732E-1776-4175-AC42- 65974E96BE66/0/2008EducationalPolicyandAccreditationStandards.pdf

Council on Social Work Education. (2004–05). *Statistics from CSWE's annual survey of accredited social work programs.* Alexandria, VA: Author

Council on Social Work Education. (2006–07). *Statistics from CSWE's annual survey of accredited social work programs.* Alexandria, VA: Author

Council on Social Work Education Strengthening Aging and Gerontology in Social Work Education. (2001). *Strengthening the impact of social work to improve the quality of life for older adults and their families: A blueprint for the new millennium.* Alexandria, VA: Author.

Cummings, S. M., Alder, G., & DeCoster, V. A. (2005). Factors influencing graduate social work students' interest in working with elders. *Educational Gerontology, 31,* 643–655.

Cummings, S. M., & DeCoster, V. A. (2003). The status of specialized gerontological training in graduate social work education. *Educational Gerontology, 29*(3), 235–250.

Cummings, S. M., & Galambos, C. (2002). Predictors of graduate social work students' interest in aging-related work. *Journal of Gerontological Social Work, 39*(3), 77–94.

Cummings, S. M., Galambos, C., & DeCoster, V. A. (2003). Predictors of MSW employment in gerontological practice. *Educational Gerontology, 29,* 295–312.

Gibelman, M., & Schervish, P. H. (1997). *Who are we: A second look.* Washington, DC: NASW Press.

He, W., Sengupta, M., Velkoff, V., & DeBarros, K. A. (2005). *65+ in the United States. U.S. Census Bureau, current population reports.* Washington, DC: U.S. Government Printing Office.

Institute for Geriatric Social Work & New York Academy of Medicine. (2005). The shortage of social workers caring for elders and their families. Retrieved January 25, 2008, from http://www.bu.edu/igsw/publications/profiles/documents/IGSW-PolicyBulletinNYAM4.04.05.pdf

Institute of Medicine (IOM). (2008). *Retooling for an aging America: Building the health care workforce.* Washington, DC: The National Academies Press.

Ivry, J., Lawrance, F. P., Damron-Rodriguez, J., & Robbins, V. C. (2005). Fieldwork rotation: A model for educating social work students for geriatric social work practice. *Journal of Social Work Education, 41*(3), 407–425.

Lambert, S. (2005). Lesbian and gay families: What we know and where to go from here. *The Family Journal: Counseling and Therapy for Couples and Families, 13*, 43–51.

Lawrence, A. R., Jarman-Rohde, L., Dunkle, R. E., Campbell, R., Bakalar, H., & Li, L. (2002). Student pioneers and educational innovations: Attracting students to gerontology. *Journal of Gerontological Social Work, 29*, 91–110.

LeCroy, C. W., & Stinson, E. L. (2004). The public's perception of social work: Is it what we think it is? *Social Work, 49*, 164–174.

Lubben, J., Damron-Rodriguez, J., & Beck, J. (1992). A national survey of aging curriculum in schools of social work. *Journal of Gerontological Social Work, 11*(3–4), 157–171.

Lubben, J., & Harootyan, L. K. (2002). Strengthening geriatric social work through a doctoral fellowship program. *Journal of Gerontological Social Work, 39*, 145–156.

Mason, S. E., & Sanders, G. R. (2004). Social work student attitudes on working with older clients. *Journal of Gerontological Social Work, 42*, 61–75.

Merck Institute & Gerontological Society of America. (2002). *The state of aging and health.* Washington, DC: Gerontological Society of America.

National Center for Health Statistics. (2006). *National vital statistics reports.* Retrieved December 2, 2008, from http://www.cdc.gov/nchs/about/otheract/aging/trendsoverview.htm

National Institute on Aging. (1987). *Personnel health needs of the elderly through the year 2020.* Washington, DC: U.S. Department of Health and Human Services, Public Health Services.

Peterson, D. A., & Wendt, P. F. (1990). Employment in the field of aging: A survey of professionals in four fields. *The Gerontologist, 30*, 679–684.

Rosen, A. L., & Zlotnik, J. L. (2001). Demographics and reality: The "disconnect" in social work education. *Journal of Gerontological Social Work, 36*(3/4), 81–97.

Rosen, A. L., Zlotnik, J. L., & Singer, T. (2002). Basic gerontological competence for all social workers: The need to "gerontologize" social work education. *Journal of Gerontological Social Work, 39*(1/2), 25–36.

Scharlach, A., Damron-Rodriguez, J., Robinson, B., & Feldman, R. (2000). Educating social workers for an aging society: A vision for the 21st century. *Journal of Social Work Education, 36,* 521–538.

Social Work Leadership Institute.(2006). *Caring for an aging America: A case for increasing the ranks of social workers who care for older adults—U.S. Department of Health and Human Services March 2006 report to Congress.* Retrieved January 25, 2008, from http://socialwork.nyam.org/nsw/cap/hhs_response.pdf

U.S. Bureau of Labor Statistics. (2004). *Occupational outlook handbook, 2008–09 edition: Social workers.* Retrieved September 15, 2008, from http://stats.bls.gov/oco/ocos060.htm

U.S. Census Bureau. (2006). *Population Division, interim statistics. Population projections by age: 2005.* Retrieved October 1, 2006, from http://www.census.gov/population/projections/52PyrmdUS1.pdf

Whitaker, T. (2008). *In the red: Social workers and educational debt.* Washington, D.C. National Association of Social Workers Retrieved January 31, 2009, from http://workforce.socialworkers.org/what's new/swanddebt.pdf

Whitaker, T., Weismiller, T., & Clark, E. (2006). *Assuring the sufficiency of a frontline workforce: A national study of licensed social workers.* Retrieved January 25, 2008, from http://workforce.socialworkers.org/studies/aging/aging.pdf

Whitfield, K. E., & Hayward, M. (2003). The landscape of health disparities among older adults. *Public Policy and Aging Report, 13,* 2–7.

CHAPTER 2

Competency-Based Education
Implications of the Hartford Geriatric Social Work Approach

**JoAnn Damron-Rodriguez, Patricia J. Volland,
M. Elizabeth Wright, and Nancy R. Hooyman**

Two major societal trends form the imperative for geriatric social work competency development. First, the growth of the older population is an environmental mandate for gerontological content in social work curricula (described in chapter 1). The 2008 Institute of Medicine (IOM) report, *Retooling for an Aging America: Building the Health Care Workforce,* identifies a series of critical geriatric workforce needs. The IOM report recommends that *all* health care professionals be prepared to work with older adults, that the recruitment and retention of geriatric specialists be accorded greater attention, and that new models of care for older adults and their families be developed, evaluated, and disseminated. This aging imperative underlies the rationale for the development of geriatric social work competencies. Foundation gerontological competencies are essential to ensure that all social work graduates are prepared to work with older adults, since most social workers interact in some capacity with this population. Similarly, advanced levels of gero competence are required for specialized geriatric practice and professional leadership in this growing field (Damron-Rodriguez, Dorfman, Lubben, & Beck, 1992; Netting & Williams, 1998; Schneider & Kropf, 1992; Whitaker, Weismiller, & Clark, 2006).

The second trend, the knowledge or information age (Haag, Cummings, McCubbrey, Pinsonneault, & Donovan, 2006), requires a more systematic approach to accountability in professional education. The exponential increase in the knowledge base required for effective social work practice has had a major impact on social work educational models. The capability of

21

Table of Acronyms	
BSW Experiential Learning	BEL
California Social Work Education Center	CalSWEC
Competency-Based Education and Evaluation	CBE
Curriculum Development Institutes	CDIs
Council on Social Work Education	CSWE
Educational Policy and Accreditation Standards (CSWE)	EPAS
CSWE National Center for Gerontological Social Work Education	Gero-Ed Center
Geriatric Enrichment in Social Work Education	GeroRich
Geriatric Social Work Education Consortium	GSWEC
Geriatric Social Work Initiative (Hartford)	GSWI
Social Work with Aging Skill Competency Scale II	GSW Scale II
Hartford Partnership Program in Aging Education	HPPAE
Institute of Medicine	IOM
Practicum Partnership Program	PPP
Strengthening Aging in Social Work Education	SAGE-SW

the social work profession to meet the needs of a growing aging population relies in part on incorporating the expanded knowledge base in the development of social work competencies. Gerontological social work is increasingly gathering evidence of the effectiveness of its interventions (Grenier & Gorey, 1998; Morrow-Howell & Burnette, 2001; Rizzo & Rowe, 2006). The process for building new knowledge exemplified in evidence-based practice, which includes clinical guidelines and best practices, is to identify a problem, apply evidence, and appraise the outcome. A similar process for targeting and assessing educational outcomes is part of competency-based education (CBE) and evaluation (Walker, Koroloff, Briggs, & Friesen, 2007).

CBE has been a major focus of the GSWI programs to increase gerontological content in the classroom and field curriculum. These programs include the Council on Social Work Education (CSWE)

Strengthening Aging in Social Work Education (SAGE-SW); the Geriatric Enrichment in Social Work Education (GeroRich) Project; and the CSWE National Center for Gerontological Social Work Education (Gero-Ed Center), specifically the Curriculum Development Institutes (CDIs), the BSW Experiential Learning (BEL) Program, and the Hartford Partnership Program in Aging Education (HPPAE). The GSWI curriculum programs have furthered the development of gerontological social work curricula, enhanced the availability and quality of teaching resources, pointed to models for preparing social workers to meet the needs of a growing aging population, and built partnerships with field supervisors and other practitioners to improve geriatric social work practice. Central to all these curriculum innovations has been the implementation of geriatric social work competencies in the classroom and the field, with an emphasis on measuring changes in competence over the course of the student's educational experience.

Specifically, the CSWE CDI and BEL programs aim to embed gerontological competencies primarily in the foundation curriculum and the overall organizational structure of social work programs where competencies are stated as educational outcomes for students completing required course work. Within these programs, *foundation competencies* are defined as the skills and knowledge expected of all students in the BSW required generalist curriculum and the MSW foundation curriculum for effective practice with older adults and their families. Complementing this focus on the foundation field and classroom curriculum, the HPPAE concentrates on tailoring CBE to prepare MSW students to become specialists in aging, using a rotational model of field education integrated with advanced classroom learning. Advanced geriatric competencies are acquired through required or elective aging-specific courses—in the classroom and field—that build on core social work and foundation gero competencies.

The competency model, now implemented for gerontological education in over a third of BSW and MSW programs across the nation, could be translated for foundation and advanced curricula in other fields of social work education and practice. Lessons learned from the geriatric social work approach to competency development, its implementation, and measurement of outcomes for generalists and specialists in the field of aging have implications for the use of CBE approaches. These innovations and lessons are particularly salient, given the Educational Policy and Accreditation Standards (EPAS; CSWE, 2008) requirement that graduates of all social work programs acquire 10 core competencies. CBE is not new to social work, with BSW-level competencies first articulated in the 1970s (Arkava & Brennan, 1976; Baer & Federico, 1979; Glick, 1971; McPheters & Ryan, 1971). Some introductory social work texts, such as the one by Morales, Shaefor, and Scott (2006), now include competencies generated by a set of tasks performed by social workers. However, the movement toward CBE is accelerating through the adoption of the EPAS (CSWE, 2008), which identifies characteristic knowledge, values, skills, and resulting practice behaviors that are operationalized in the curriculum and assessment methods, and states that programs may add to the 10 core competencies consistent with their mission and goals. The development of geriatric competencies is advanced by the EPAS (CSWE) requirement that a program's mission and goals be informed by context, including social, demographic, and global contextual factors.

The Context for CBE

Competence is defined in the literature as the demonstration of the integration of knowledge, values, and skills into practice (Bogo, Raskin, & Wayne 2002; Hackett, 2001; Vass, 1996). As an outcome performance approach to curriculum design, CBE is founded in the scientific method and is linked to the measurement and evidence of outcomes, such as students' performance in field placements and in the workplace (Koroloff & Rhyne, 1989). The definition of competencies in the EPAS (CSWE, 2008) is congruent with what is found in the literature: Competencies are clear and measurable practice behaviors with evidence-based indicators of varying levels of student performance (Bogo et al., 2002; Damron-Rodriguez, 2006).

Effective professional practice requires the capacity and judgment to use skill-based competencies differentially and critically. In other words, competencies are not to be intended as a cookbook or checklist of skills. The development of a professional identity must encompass professional judgment including ethical reasoning; critical thinking, analytical reasoning, and intellectual curiosity; self-awareness and self-reflection; and knowledge of the use of self. These professional capabilities have long been valued by social work educators as a basis for applying skills or competencies (Carraccio, Wolfsthal, Englander, Ferentz, & Martin, 2002; Damron-Rodriguez, 2006; Field, 2000; Hooyman, 2006).

The Council on Higher Education Accreditation, which oversees standards for 76 professions including nursing and social work, has adopted a competency model for accreditation, in part because of licensure requirements and standards (National Center for Higher Education Management Systems, 2000). The Hartford foundation has supported the identification of competencies for practice with older adults in medicine, nursing, and social work (American Association of Colleges of Nursing & the John A. Hartford Foundation Institute for Geriatric Nursing, 2000; American Geriatrics Society, 2000; Damron-Rodriguez, 2006). To promote CBE, the EPAS (CSWE, 2008) delineates core competencies expected for the MSW foundation and BSW generalist levels.

> Educational Policy 2.1—Core Competencies. Competency-based education is an outcome performance approach to curriculum design. Competencies are measurable practice behaviors composed of knowledge, values, and skills. The goal of the outcome approach is to demonstrate the integration and application of the competencies in practice with individuals, families, groups, organizations, and communities. (p. 3)

In addition to core competencies, MSW and BSW programs may develop further competencies that are consistent with their individual mission and goals and their larger context, including demographic changes and workforce needs. According to Educational Policy 1.2, (CSWE, 2008), programs are to make explicit what such a context includes and how their mission and goals take account of this context in the education of social work professionals.

> Educational Policy 1.2—Program Context. Context encompasses the mission of the institution in which the program is located and the needs and opportunities associated with the setting. Programs are further influenced by their historical, political, economic, social, cultural, demographic, and global contexts, and by the way they elect to engage these factors. Additional factors include new knowledge, technology, and ideas that may have a bearing on contemporary and future social work education and practice. (p. 2)

The EPAS (CSWE, 2008) states that MSW core competencies are to be augmented by knowledge and skills for advanced practice:

Educational Policy M2.2—Advanced Practice. Advanced practitioners refine and advance the quality of social work practice and that of the larger social work profession. They synthesize and apply a broad range of interdisciplinary and multidisciplinary knowledge and skills. In areas of specialization, advanced practitioners assess, intervene, and evaluate to promote human and social well-being. To do so they suit each action to the circumstances at hand, using the professional judgment learned through experience and self-improvement. Advanced practice incorporates all of the core competencies augmented by knowledge and practice behaviors specific to a concentration. (p. 8)

In sum, the development of geriatric social work competencies represents a systematic and strategic response to a major contextual shift in the practice environment: the aging of society (Damron-Rodriguez, 2007). Additionally, this focus on gerontological competencies is congruent with the EPAS 2.1 (CSWE, 2008), which states that programs may develop specialized competencies that derive from their mission, goals, and context in addition to the 10 core ones. The process by which geriatric competencies have been developed and tested is briefly described, as its primary components—comprehensive review of the evidence-based literature in the field; survey of practitioners, educators, researchers, and consumers; and consensus-building techniques—are relevant to social work educators in other areas of social work practice developing specialized competencies to meet accreditation expectations.

The Development of Foundation and Advanced Geriatric Social Work Competencies

Overview

In 1998 competencies for geriatric social work practice were developed separately through different consensus-building approaches by the CSWE SAGE-SW and the HPPAE's Geriatric Social Work Education Consortium (GSWEC), a California-based demonstration site of the HPPAE from 1999 to 2003. The primary focus of SAGE-SW was to agree upon competencies that could be used broadly in social work education. GeroRich and the Gero-Ed Center moved to relate gero competencies to generalist or foundation curricula by infusing aging into the required curricula for BSW and MSW students. The HPPAE was involved in the early stages of competency development, drawing upon the work of SAGE-SW and others, to develop competencies for advanced specialist education and to design a rating system to measure outcomes of competency-based skill improvement, largely within the field practicum. Next, the two programs agreed to work from the same set of skills but stating them differently for the foundation and specialist curricula. Thus, what varies is the application of the geriatric competencies to the learning process and the curriculum (e.g., primarily classroom or field), the depth of skills that students attain, and the nature of outcome measures. The following is a description of the stages of development of competences for one important content area, geriatric social work. These phases follow the CBE model and are relevant to competency development in other areas of social work education.

Phase 1: The Identification of Competencies

Geriatric social work competency development was initiated with the first Hartford-funded curriculum development project, CSWE SAGE-SW, through a comprehensive literature review and solicitation of expert opinions to define competencies for working with older adults and to organize them into relevant domains (Rosen, Zlotnik, Curl, & Green, 2000). The competency domain concept was adapted from *A Report of the Interdisciplinary Child Welfare Training Project: 1991–1996* (Baer, 1996). A thorough review of the gerontological social work literature produced a pool of 128 possible professional competencies across 13 professional competency domains, which after expert review was subsequently narrowed down to 65 items across three major professional domains. A more focused list of items was achieved by eliminating those that were deemed basic social work competencies and thus relevant to all areas of social work practice (e.g., case management, interviewing, and community organization skills, and principal professional ethics and values).

After additional review and pretesting, a questionnaire was mailed to 2,400 social work practitioners, educators, and researchers, Respondents were asked to classify each competency item on a 3-point scale: Level 1 competency needed by all BSWs and MSWs, Level 2 competency required by only MSWs, and Level 3 competency needed by only geriatric specialists (Greene & Galambos, 2002; Rosen et al., 2000; Rosen, Zlotnik, & Singer, 2002). The respondents judged 35 of these competencies to be Level 1, that is, indispensable to effective social work practice with older adults. The items assigned to Level 1 included 11 knowledge items (such as understanding normal physical, psychological, and social changes in later life, and assessing one's own values and biases regarding aging), 13 skill items (such as using social work case management skills to link elders and their families to resources and services), and 11 professional practice items, which identified professional ethics and values as the most fundamental of all foundation competencies. In summary, the SAGE-SW project, drawing upon a large national sample of educators, practitioners, and researchers, delineated a comprehensive list of 65 knowledge, values, and skills (competencies) as a basis for further development.

Phase 2: The Delineation of Essential Skills for Measurement: The Geriatric Social Work Competency Scale

The task of selecting a concise, measurable, and consensus-based list of skills for geriatric social work was completed by the New York Academy of Medicine's Practicum Partnership Program (now the HPPAE) through the development of the Geriatric Social Work (GSW) Competency Scale. One objective was to create measurable outcomes of aging-focused field education for social workers specializing in gerontology. This work was initiated by the GSWEC, using the SAGE-SW competencies (Rosen et al., 2000), a thorough literature review of geriatric social work education (Scharlach, Damon-Rodriguez, Robinson, & Feldman, 2000), and a focus-group process that involved asking providers, employers, graduates, and older people to identify a set of advanced geriatric social work competencies (Naito-Chan, Damon-Rodriguez, & Simmons, 2004). These competencies were then reviewed, matched, and finally synthesized with practice behaviors developed by five other HPPAE demonstration sites. All sites then worked together to establish common competencies that would form a conceptual framework for learning. The competencies were to serve as an evaluative measure of students' acquisition of aging-related skills over the course of their training. All were converted into statements of skills, which were then reviewed for clarity and validity by members of the HPPAE Evaluation Committee, composed of national experts in social work and aging.

The resulting GSW Competency Scale I is a 58-item instrument divided into five domains: (1) values and ethics, (2) assessment (individual and family, aging services, programs, and policies), (3) practice and intervention (theory and knowledge in practice, individual and family, and aging services, programs, and policies), (4) interdisciplinary collaboration, and (5) evaluation and research. The instrument was used as a pre-and posttest to measure the effect of the HPPAE's innovative demonstration programs on the skills of graduate social work students specializing in aging. As a self-rating instrument based on a scale of 1 to 10, students evaluated their aging expertise in each of these domains at the beginning of the HPPAE program (the pretest) and after they completed their aging enriched field education (the posttest at the end of the advanced year). Comparing cumulative scores for a group of students at pre- and posttest provided a measure of growth in the aging-focused skills of MSW graduates, as well as information on relative strengths and weaknesses in the five different domains of learning. The instrument was also designed as a tool for educational planning using the results of the pretest. An analysis of its use with 226 graduate social work students found the instrument to be effective in measuring field education outcomes (Damron-Rodriguez, Lawrance, Barnett, & Simmons, 2007).

In the next phase, the Social Work with Aging Skill Competency Scale II (referred to as the GSW Scale II) was constructed to eliminate double-barreled, ambiguous, and redundant items, and to lessen the time needed to administer the scale. The revised scale contains 40 items with micro and macro content now grouped into four domains: (1) values and ethics, (2) assessment, (3) intervention, and (4) aging services, programs, and policies. The revised scale measures the respondents' perceptions of their skill levels (e.g., self-efficacy) in aging practice using a 0–4 scale: from 0=*not skilled at all*, to 4=*expert skill*. Each domain can be scored by adding the responses to individual items; a total skill competency score may be calculated by adding the scores of all items. Scale II has been piloted on 41 practicing social workers whose experiences with older adults varied. The Chronbach's alpha on Scales I and II is high, and the instrument has considerable face validity and has been useful in assessing a range of skill levels (Damron-Rodriguez, 2006; Nakao, Damron-Rodriguez, Lawrance, Volland, & Bachrach, 2007).

Although the use of self-efficacy—the level of confidence felt necessary to meet specific goals—may sometimes be problematic, students' ability to self-assess is in itself an important skill (Bandura, 1997; Damron-Rodriguez, 2006; Lee & Bobko, 1994; Van Voorhis & Hostetter, 2006).

The GSW Scale II frames learning along a continuum that persists postgraduation. Thus, although students are expected to advance in competence from pre- to posttest, as in many skills areas they have room for growth after they enter the field. Further testing of norms for educational levels, including postgraduate continuing education, is needed. The GSW Scale II was implemented in Cycle 1 of the HPPAE, representing the 10 programs funded in the first cohort (1999–2003) structured as follows:

1. Values, ethics, and theoretical perspectives: Assess values and biases regarding aging and how to address the cultural, spiritual, and ethnic values of clients as well as the ethical principles involved in making decisions, including end-of-life issues.

2. Assessment: Develop interviewing skills and conduct geriatric assessments of older adults' needs, strengths, and limitations including their cognitive, physical, and social functioning; assess the needs and stress level of caregivers.

3. Intervention: Develop competency in establishing rapport and effective working relationships with older adults and family members, from helping caregivers reduce their stress level to educating families about wellness issues and disease management.

4. Aging services, programs, and practices: Outreach for older adults and their families to ensure the appropriate use of services, including budgeting, evaluating service effectiveness, and recruiting and organizing service providers, community groups, and others on behalf of older adults' needs and issues.

The GSW Scale II can be accessed through the GSWI Web site (http://www.gswi.org/). The process used by HPPAE to develop the four domains and the final self-rating scale could be a template adapted to other social work areas of specialization.

Phase 3: Review and Application of Geriatric Competencies for Foundation and Advanced Curriculum Levels

The CSWE GeroRich Project, in collaboration with the HPPAE, reviewed the 40 GSW competencies and the 65 SAGE-SW foundation competencies to ensure a fundamentally similar approach used by GeroRich and then by the Gero-Ed Center's Cycles I and 2 CDIs. These foundation competencies used by the CSWE curriculum development programs are written in terms of student outcomes for MSW foundation and BSW generalist classroom curricula. The four domains are held in common in both applications of the GSWI competencies. Thus, the resulting list of knowledge, skills, and values used by the Gero-Ed Center is intended to guide programmatic curriculum development and infusion of aging into BSW required generalist and 1st-year MSW foundation course work.

These foundation gerontological competencies were highly recommended to the 67 programs participating in the GeroRich Project and are now required by two CSWE Gero-Ed Center programs: the CDI and the BEL. Social work programs, including those participating in the new Specialized Gerontology Program, that develop specialized geriatric content building on infused curriculum are expected to use the HPPAE GSW Competency Scale. Although the HPPAE GSW scale was developed for MSW programs only, educators associated with the Gero-Ed Center suggest that this rating scale can be used along the continuum of learning for BSW, MSW, and post-MSW education. The level of anticipated skill for each item would be less for those with 1st-year MSW or BSW preparation than for those with MSW advanced-year training; however, the scale has not yet been normed for these educational levels.

Most of the faculty participants in the CDI program have used the GSW Scale II, typically at the beginning and end of a required curriculum, but they have also developed other outcome measures specific to their curriculum goals, such as different tests of gerontological knowledge. The greater attention to the acquisition of gerontological knowledge of the Gero-Ed Center's programs is consistent with the goals of the foundation level and generalist level of social work education. The use of gero competencies at the MSW foundation and BSW required generalist levels has also helped determine how much infusion is enough; in other words, how much and what type of infused geriatric content, teaching resources, and outcome measures are needed to support students' attainment of foundation gerontological competencies (Hooyman, 2006). (For further details, see chapter 5 on the planned change infusion approach of the CSWE curriculum development projects.)

Phase 4: Dissemination: Statewide Adoption for Foundation and Advanced Levels

The widespread dissemination of geriatric competencies and outcomes by the social work programs participating in the HPPAE and the Gero-Ed Center has served as a catalyst to other forms of CBE nationally. GSWI evaluation outcomes have been presented at multiple annual organization meetings including the CSWE National Gero-Ed Forum, the American Society on Aging, the Gerontological Society of America, and the Society for Social Work Research.

One state-level model is the California Social Work Education Center (CalSWEC) Aging Initiative. Drawing upon the decade of successful statewide model building in child welfare, CalSWEC in 2004 initiated labor force development in geriatric social work. Funded in part by a grant from the Archstone Foundation and building on GSWI accomplishments, the geriatric social work competencies formed the foundation for the building of a CalSWEC set of foundation and advanced social work competencies in aging that have been adopted by all 17 graduate programs of social work in California (Ranney, Goodman, Tan, & Glezakos, 2006). This CalSWEC consensus-building process is briefly described as an example of dissemination of the HPPAE competencies and a template for competency development that could be used by other statewide consortia of social work programs in other practice areas.

The CalSWEC Aging Curriculum Competencies format stipulates that competencies should address four distinct areas: (a) attention to cultural diversity, disadvantage, and culturally competent social work; (b) social work practice across the life span; (c) human behavior and social environment for older adults; and (d) social welfare policy and administration for older adults. Furthermore, each of the four sections is divided into foundation (1st-year) and advanced (2nd-year) competencies. What is exemplary about the CalSWEC Aging Curriculum is that specific course content is identified for attainment of the competencies. To ensure that the California social work programs are preparing their students for practice in their state context, the aging competencies were also distributed to about 209 community stakeholders for their comment. Additionally, staff at the CalSWEC Aging Initiative conducted a survey of all California social work programs to assess the extent of curriculum on aging and the degree to which the CALSWEC aging competencies are being adopted (Min, Ranney, Min, Takahashi, & Goodman, 2007; available at http://calswec.berkeley.edu/CalSWEC/AIComps_Foundation.pdf).

The model designed by the CalSWEC Aging Curriculum also has created a framework for writing competency-based questions by national gerontological social work leaders invited to submit questions for the licensure exams of the Association of Social Work Boards. The questions are directly linked to competencies and to the relevant evidence-based gerontological social work literature. Even if the questions are not selected for the national exam, the process of question writing has helped to refine the process of linking gero content to competencies and outcomes.

Implementation and Programmatic Experiences by HPPAE and Gero-Ed Center Sites

Implementation by HPPAE Sites

The competency-based curriculum promoted by the HPPAE is designed to be flexible, and the competencies address practice at the micro and macro levels, with the recognition that social workers who demonstrate leadership in aging need to be proficient at both levels. The HPPAE manual, created as a guide for program implementation, outlines how the GSW Competency Scale can be used in addition to demonstrating its salience as a pre- and posttests means to evaluate performance. CBE goes far beyond assessment at the beginning and end of a program. In fact, CBE, composed of six core elements, should be the organizing principle of the educational experience, not only for aging but also for other areas of advanced practice in social work. The elements as derived from the HPPAE experience are listed in following paragraphs.

Element 1: Adopt HPPAE competencies for geriatric social work education. Commitment to the HPPAE competencies must be shared by faculty, field instructors, and student advisors in aging, including those who may not be participating formally in the partnership, so that all course work and fieldwork is structured to achieve the same learning objectives. Such acceptance on the part of all partners is also essential to institutionalizing the HPPAE competencies within the program's curriculum structure.

Element 2: Identify individual student learning goals. Using the competencies as guidelines, students work with field educators to identify and tailor their learning goals, which are drawn up as a formal learning agreement. In HPPAE programs that are organized by methods competencies (e.g., interpersonal practice, administration), the geriatric social work competencies are in addition to those overall requirements in the school or department's practicum learning agreement.

Element 3: Select field sites, rotations, and assignments. Specific learning opportunities must be structured into the field site to ensure competency attainment. To provide students with the opportunities needed to develop geriatric social work expertise and leadership, field placement experiences are required where students can acquire micro and macro competencies and gain experience in more than one practice setting. The rotational model required by HPPAE is the primary strategy to ensure that students are exposed to the diversity of older adults by functional level, class, race, and/or sexual orientation, and to the varied service systems needed for effective care coordination in their future practice.

Element 4: Integrate class and fieldwork learning. Using the same set of competencies across advanced classroom and field learning is essential to designing a consistent and effective HPPAE educational program. HPPAE programs often offer specialized integrative seminars for HPPAE students, which use the competencies as an organizing principle for seminar content and assignments.

Element 5: Assess student skill level and progress. Competency-based field education entails the assessment of student progress in building skills to work with older adults. In the HPPAE model, students are evaluated before beginning their field placement and upon completion. In addition to assessing students' skill levels, the scale can also be used by classroom and field-based educators to assess the strengths and challenges in the education program itself and to help students plan their learning experiences.

Implementation by Gero-Ed Center Programs

The following steps or elements represent an ideal that faculty participants in Gero-Ed Center programs strive to reach. Over time, Gero-Ed

Center staff and faculty participants have gained a greater understanding of the complexities of the gero infusion process and the importance of a realistic incremental approach. Clearly, the process of implementation described here may require several years for social work programs to complete, evaluate, and refine.

Element 1: Select foundation gero social work competencies. All participants in the Gero-Ed Center CDI and BEL programs are expected to use the foundation gero social work competencies generated through the consensus-building process of the SAGE-SW and GSWEC and further refined by the GeroRich Project. Faculty participants in Gero-Ed programs are also instructed to delineate their course goals and objectives before selecting competencies. Understanding the distinction between course objectives and competencies has often been challenging for participants in the Gero-Ed Center curriculum development programs. As noted earlier, competencies are not simply instructional or course objectives such as: "Acquires specialized knowledge and skills for working effectively within diverse contexts." Instead, within this course objective, a performance-oriented competency or measurable practice behavior required of students is: "Use empathy and sensitive interviewing skills to assess social functioning (e.g., social skills, social activity level) and social support of your client."

Because of the time-consuming nature of competency selection and measurement, faculty participants in Gero-Ed Center programs are advised to be realistic and selective in how many competencies they attempt to infuse in each required course in any given year. Doing so tends to increase the probability of faculty support for the competency-based infusion process. This targeted, incremental approach is necessary because of the numerous other content areas that faculty seek to address in BSW required generalist or MSW foundation curriculum. When CDI programs encountered faculty resistance to such infusion, considerable time was devoted up front to garnering faculty support for the competency selection process. Without engaging foundation faculty, any gero competencies that are infused are unlikely to be sustained within the required curriculum.

Although the CSWE curriculum development projects have targeted the classroom curriculum, some participating programs have also infused gero social work competencies into the foundation field learning. This was intended to ensure that all students had at least one opportunity to work with older adults, regardless of the type of practice setting. Although this may appear to be a modest goal, such changes in the foundation field required field supervisor training to obtain their buying into gero competencies. Some CDI faculty also created integrative seminars to link foundation classroom and practicum learning.

Element 2: Identify measurable practice behaviors for each competency for gerontological practice. The EPAS (CSWE, 2008) articulates the general practice behaviors of engage, assess, intervene, and evaluate. Practice behaviors operationalize the competency and become the basis for the design of a competency-based curriculum.

Element 3: Select the knowledge, skills and values to augment each competency. This refers to the related curriculum content that needs to be taught to attain practice behaviors. In other words, faculty must spend time clarifying not only what gerontological content is taught but how it is taught to ensure that students acquire the gero competencies. In many instances, experiential activities, inside and outside the classroom, are the most effective pedagogy to attain gero competencies.

Element 4: Select foundation courses for competency attainment. Program faculty are encouraged to identify which of their current foundation courses best lend themselves to the content needed for competency attainment and start where the probability of success is greatest. For example, content for the competency "Respect and promote older adult clients' right to dignity and self-determination within the context of the law and safety concerns" could be taught in the foundation courses of Introduction to Social Work, Human Behavior and the Social Environment, Cultural Diversity and Social Justice, and Practice. For the first steps of competency infusion, faculty participants are urged to choose one of these course areas where the probability of success is greatest. They then identify supporting content on issues of aging and older adults and gero teaching resources. After completing a first phase of competency infusion and measurement, it then becomes feasible for faculty to select other foundation courses for gero infusion.

Element 5: Choose or develop teaching resources. Gero-Ed Center participating programs have access to a rich array of teaching resources on its Web site, http://www.Gero-EdCenter.org. These include gero-infused case studies, in-class exercises, discussion questions, assignments, and readings to augment and support student attainment of selected gero competencies. Exemplars of how to link content and teaching resources, particularly required evidence-based readings, to selected foundation gero competencies along with models of gero-infused foundation syllabi are also available on the Gero-Ed Center Web site. These examples could assist faculty in other fields of practice to move through a similar process of identifying content, teaching resources, and pedagogy to support students' competency attainment and link competencies to measurable student learning outcomes.

Element 6: Agree on how to assess or measure student attainment of gero competencies. Outcome measures—what students can do based on the knowledge, skills, and values acquired—are to be directly tied to the selected competencies. Because of the macro level change in curriculum and organizational culture that characterizes the Gero-Ed Center initiatives, faculty of all participating programs are required to gather data on common outcomes measures, such as the extent of student exposure to gerontological content in each foundation class. As noted above, participating faculty have also developed program-specific measures, such as reflective papers, short quizzes that measure attitudes and knowledge acquired, and before and after student ratings of competency attainment within the foundation curriculum. Many programs have used the GSW Competency Scale, typically at the point of matriculation and graduation, as a project-specific measure. The problems of validity inherent with student self-ratings or self-efficacy measures are recognized. Nevertheless, measures of students' assessment of changes in baseline skills at the beginning and end of their program are one source of useful data for determining the impact of gero infusion on students' learning. In some instances, students in the GeroRich programs rated themselves lower on the competency scale at graduation than they did at the point of matriculation in a program. This was not viewed as problematic, however. Instead, such lower ratings may reflect that as students gained professional insight, knowledge, skills, and values in the classroom and the field, they learned more about what they did not know and thus rated themselves lower than they did at matriculation (Hooyman, 2006).

HPPAE Indicators of Competency Attainment

From its inception, developing standardized methods to evaluate student achievement in progression toward learning goals has been an important aspect of the Hartford GSWI programs. The HPPAE, in particular, has focused attention on analysis of pre- and posttest outcomes measuring knowledge and competence since 2000. Each cohort of the HPPAE has been evaluated using standardized instruments including the GSW Scale II. For each cohort of HPPAE graduates, statistically significant positive learning outcomes have been achieved, including increases in geriatric knowledge and competence level. Multivariate analysis, performed in areas such as prior student experience with older people and previous course work in aging, found a positive relationship to geriatric knowledge and competency development (Birkenmaier et al., in press.; Damron-Rodriguez et al., 2007).

HPPAE evaluation has shown that demonstrable improvements occur when graduate students in social work have an aging-focused advanced curriculum and a rotational field experience that targets specific domains of competency at micro and macro levels of practice (Damron-Rodriguez, 2006; Damron-Rodriguez et al., 2007). Further evidence of competency attainment might be obtained if an analysis of students in the individual programs participating in HPPAE were compared with that of social work students in other programs that provide courses and fieldwork in aging but are not competency based.

To further evaluate HPPAE student competency outcomes and address problems inherent in self-rating scales, an adaptation of the GSW Scale II: Field Instructor Version was developed. It has been pilot tested with HPPAE students in Cohort 1. Rating their students slightly higher than students rate themselves, field instructors assessed students as significantly improving in their geriatric competence over the course of HPPAE training (Damron-Rodriguez, 2006; Nakao et al., 2007; Nakao, Damron-Rodriguez, Lawrance, Volland, & Bachrach, 2008). To further the assessment of skill attainment, future steps should include the evaluation of large numbers of students through a standardized instrument such as the GSW Scale II. This would allow for the "norming" for different levels of social work education and differences in generalist versus specialist practice.

Lessons Learned

As shown by the EPAS (CSWE, 2008), the social work profession at large is moving toward demonstration of core competencies as essential to the preparation of a qualified workforce. The HPPAE and the CSWE curriculum development projects have promoted the development, implementation, and measurement of competency-based geriatric social work. The HPPAE and the Gero-Ed Center have contributed to the national recognition of this approach. As a result, faculty members who have participated in both projects are well positioned to provide leadership on competency development for the profession as a whole and for their own programs preparing for reaccreditation after 2010. As leaders in the development of CBE, the HPPAE and Gero-Ed Center have identified lessons learned that are germane to other arenas of social work education moving toward CBE.

Curriculum for Field Education

The HPPAE and Gero-Ed Center programs seek to link classroom and field education in meaningful ways through the Gero-Ed Center foundation competencies and the GSW Competencies Scales (Damron-Rodriguez, 2006). As stated in the EPAS (CSWE, 2008), field education is the "signature pedagogy" of the social work profession, and competencies most readily become real to students in the field. By using CBE, the HPPAE designs a curriculum for the field by setting geriatric social work skill goals for the practicum experience across agency settings and formalizing these within practicum learning contracts. The GSW competency rating scale provides a guide for preceptors and field instructors to structure learning experiences for students. Several HPPAE sites have developed checklists and evaluation forms to fit the GSW Scale II in addition to the field instructor version of this instrument. As noted above, although the CSWE Gero-Ed Center programs target classroom curriculum, many faculty participants also sought to infuse foundation competencies in the BSW senior year and MSW 1st-year field experience. Although unexpected, this attention to the field is conceptually solid, because learning in the required classroom curriculum should be integrated with generalist or foundation practice in the field.

Faculty and Field Instructor CBE Training

To ensure the success of a competency-based model, social work education programs must educate faculty and agency-based field instructors who are teaching foundation and advanced practice classroom and field courses on the importance of using the competency-based instrument in setting educational goals and priorities for students and on how the competencies are to be used. CBE will not become part of the program's explicit and implicit curriculum unless faculty and field instructors are fully engaged in the dynamic process that drives competency-based learning. A multipronged, selective, feasible, and tiered approach for the infusion of geriatric competencies in required curriculum is essential (Hooyman, 2006).

Put quite simply, obtaining agreement on competencies and outcome measures among faculty and field supervisors is hard and sometimes messy work. It is difficult to negotiate agreement regarding outcome measures that can reasonably be achieved in the field and the classroom, given the multiple demands upon faculty time and constrained curricular space. One reason that a competency-based approach is such difficult work is that most faculty members are accustomed to teaching in terms of content organized by traditional curriculum structures, not competencies. This pattern will change with the 2010 implementation of the EPAS (CSWE, 2008).

Linkage Between Classroom and Field Education

The HPPAE evaluation provides evidence of the importance of linkage of classroom and field in skill outcomes. Specification of the complementary roles in the educational process for reaching particular competency goals is needed in order to advance CBE. Competencies developed and measured as part of students' field experiences will influence the classroom curriculum over time. Similarly, the infusion of geriatric social work competencies in the required classroom curriculum has often resulted in foundation field sites offering more gerontological learning opportunities. Given the dynamic interplay between classroom and field learning, it is imperative that students in the future are evaluated on the same set of competencies in the classroom and the field settings.

Effective linkage of field and classroom learning also requires that foundation textbooks used in the required curriculum include content on aging processes and geriatric social work competencies. To parallel curriculum infusion, CBE necessitates that changes occur in the readings required of students. Toward that end, the CSWE curriculum development projects staff have assessed existing textbook content suitable to the attainment of geriatric social work competencies and are working with foundation textbook editors and authors to increase such content (Tompkins, Rosen, & Larkin, 2006). Similarly, new texts that employ a competency-based approach are pivotal to linking the gero competencies to social work curricula (Greene, Cohen, Galambos, & Kropf, 2007).

Measurement and Evaluation of Competence

Objective measurements of performance have traditionally been one of the weakest aspects of social work education and practice and need to be more widely incorporated in all areas of social work. Assignments in the classroom that are competence based and complement those in the field are imperative but frequently lacking. The specification of a learning goal in terms of a skill is only a first step in a CBE approach. The syllabi or learning contract must also delineate the content and teaching resources needed to gain the competency, the measurement techniques that will be used, and the expected outcome level. Using tools such as the GSW Scale II and the field instructor version is one means of measurement of outcome.

Strategies to Sustain CBE

The HPPAE and Gero-Ed Center have the advantage of external funding for programs to implement and evaluate competency attainment. Similarly, both have faced the challenge of institutionalizing and sustaining CBE to evaluate student performance and tailor learning experiences once funding ends. Fortunately, sustainability is enhanced by objective measures of performance that demonstrate student preparation and achievement to program decision makers, such as curriculum committees, other governance structures, practicum advisory groups, and academic administrators. Most important, the 2010 implementation of the CSWE EPAS will help to institutionalize gero competencies within professional social work education.

Future Directions

The national leaders of the HPPAE and the Gero-Ed Center have identified future priorities in three areas: competency development, implementation, and measurement. The following are highlighted areas of competency development.

Feedback from faculty and student participants has pointed to the need for more macro research, community practice, and policy competencies. In addition, further delineation of competencies or practice behaviors related to leadership capability in the field of aging was deemed necessary. An HPPAE committee of social work educators and practitioners drafted a set of 10 competencies for a fifth domain of the GSW Scale II—Leadership in the Field of Aging Practice. These are being reviewed by faculty participants from the HPPAE and Gero-Ed programs. Given social work's commitment to social justice and social change, the development and refinement of these additional community change and policy competencies is critical.

The HPPAE rotational model provides opportunities for students to acquire micro and macro skills. However, students in macro field placements typically have fewer opportunities to obtain the clinical practice skills that form the majority of the GSW competencies. Additionally, for competency development, the profession as a whole needs to focus on the promotion of cultural competence in working with historically disadvantaged populations and its intersection with foundation and specialized geriatric competencies. Gero competencies must reflect the growing diversity of the older population in terms of race/ethnicity, gender, sexual orientation, social class, spirituality, and functional ability.

In preparation for the 2010 enactment of EPAS, the GSWI programs are providing leadership to a national competency work group charged with relating the gero competencies to the 10 EPAS competency domains. This will be a step toward embedding the gero competencies in the structure of social work education, further drawing on lessons learned from the Hartford GSWI experiences with competency development and measurement.

The second direction in future CBE activities relates to educational implementation. An effective competency-based process helps (a) identify the pedagogical approaches and resources necessary to (b) teach the content on aging and older adults, which is (c) required to support students in attaining gero competencies. However, relatively few social work programs have effectively identified the specific course content in the form of relevant evidence-based literature in geriatric social work and of teaching resources (case studies, discussion questions, assignments, and readings) needed for competency attainment. Particularly in terms of foundation competencies for the classroom, faculty need to move beyond thinking of competencies as multiple-choice questions to be completed by students to the broader areas of study that a class lecture, discussion questions, role plays, assignments, or case studies can be built around that will engage students with each competency area. Similarly, faculty must consider the most effective pedagogy for teaching competencies—the *how* of teaching geriatric content, not just *what* they teach (Hooyman, 2006).

Additionally, advanced gero competencies need to be designed and implemented in a manner that strengthens the role of the field instructor in specialist education. The agency-based field educator is key to ensuring that students have the real-world experiences that build on the knowledge acquired in the classroom. CBE provides a curriculum for field education by directing the learning experience toward obtaining a specified set of skills under the direction of skilled field supervisors.

The third direction for enhancing a CBE approach is improved measurement tools. Measures of professional competence that are more objective than rating scales are required (Damron-Rodriguez, 2006). A few social work programs are moving toward the gold standard of objective measurement, as defined by medicine and now used in nursing: the Objective Structured Clinical Examination. Originally an in-person assessment with patients performed by actors, it can also be developed in a video format (Baez, 2004).

Last, embedding of geriatric competencies in licensing exams remains a necessary long-term strategy. As social work programs engage CBE to meet future accreditation standards, many could benefit from technical assistance, especially in relation to how to measure graduates' performance of such skills in the workplace. Faculty participants in the Gero-Ed Center and HPPAE initiatives are well poised to assist their colleagues.

Conclusion

The strength of the GSWI development of geriatric social work competencies is its thorough and iterative consensus-building process. In retrospect, even more frequent and formalized communication among the HPPAE and the Gero-Ed Center programs might have led to a more coordinated and systematic process of competency development and implementation in the foundation and advanced curriculum. That said, the GSWI has implemented CBE in aging in a wide range of social work programs in the classroom and field curriculum for generalist and specialist social work education. The continued building of a CBE approach must include agreeing on outcome measures (in addition to the student and field instructor self-assessment), linking evidence-based content to the competencies, and identifying the most effective pedagogical approaches and teaching resources for each competency. Limited national staff resources for ongoing measurement and evaluation of competency implementation and attainment are further challenges. Accomplishments and challenges of CBE lie ahead for other social work fields of practice. As noted previously, a 2008–09 national work group is addressing issues identified in the "Future Directions" section on pp. 41–43, and relating the geriatric competencies to the EPAS and to cultural competencies developed by the National Association of Social Work.

Because of HPPAE and CSWE curriculum development projects, more than 250 social work schools and departments have engaged in the process of geriatric CBE, positioning them well for future competency work and serving as a model for how other programs might engage in similar processes. Our hope is that the innovation of a comprehensive approach to CBE in one field of practice–aging—and the lessons learned from the hard work of these programs nationwide will be of value to institutions implementing the competency-based approach of the EPAS (CSWE, 2008) as a basis for accreditation for professional education.

References

American Association of Colleges of Nursing & the John A. Hartford Foundation Institute for Geriatric Nursing. (2000). *Older adults: Recommended baccalaureate competencies and curricular guidelines for geriatric nursing care.* Washington, DC: American Association of Colleges of Nursing.

American Geriatrics Society. (2000). Core competencies for the care of older patients: Recommendations of the American Geriatrics Society. *Academic Medicine, 75*(3), 252–255.

Arkava, M. L., & Brennan, E. C. (Eds.). (1976). *Competency-based education for social work: Evaluation and curriculum issues.* New York: Council on Social Work Education.

Baer, B. L. (1996). *A report of the interdisciplinary child welfare training project: 1991–1996.* Green Bay: University of Wisconsin-Green Bay, Social Work Program.

Baer, B. L., & Federico, R. C. (Eds.). (1979). *Educating the baccalaureate social worker: A curriculum development resource* (Vols. 1–2). Cambridge, MA: Ballinger.

Baez A. (2004). Development of an objective structured clinical examination (OSCE) for practicing substance abuse intervention competencies. An application in social work education. *Journal of Social Work Practice in the Addictions, 5*(3), 3–20.

Bandura, A. (1997). *Self-efficacy: The exercise of control.* New York: Freeman Press.

Birkenmaier, J., Rowan, N., Damron-Rodriguez, J. A., Lawrance, F. P., & Volland, P. (in press). Social work knowledge of facts on aging: Outcome evidence from a national field education initiative. *Journal of Gerontology and Geriatric Education.*

Bogo, M., Raskin, M., & Wayne, J. (2002). *Thinking out of the box: Developing new approaches for field education.* New York: Field Consortium.

Carraccio, C., Wolfsthal, S. D., Englander, R. Ferentz, K., & Martin, C. (2002). Shifting paradigms: From Flexner to competencies. *Academic Medicine, 77*(5), 361–367.

Council on Social Work Education. (2008). *Educational policy and accreditation standards.* Retrieved November 12, 2008, from http://www.cswe.org/NR/rdonlyres/2A81732E-1776-4175-AC42-65974E96BE66/0/2008EducationalPolicyandAccreditationStandards.pdf

Damron-Rodriguez, J. (2006). Moving ahead: Developing geriatric social work competencies. In B. Berkman (Ed.), *Handbook of social work in health and aging* (pp. 1051–1068). Oxford, UK: Oxford University Press.

Damron-Rodriguez, J. (2007). Social work practice in aging: A competency-based approach for the 21st century. In R. Greene, H. Cohen, C. Galambos, & N. Kropf (Eds.), *Foundation of social work practice in the aging field: A competency-based approach* (pp. 1–16). Washington, DC: NASW Press.

Damron-Rodriguez, J. A., Dorfman, R., Lubben, J. E., & Beck, J. C. (1992). A Geriatric Education Center faculty development program dedicated to social work. *Journal of Gerontological Social Work, 18*(3/4), 187–201.

Damron-Rodriguez, J., Lawrance, F. P., Barnett, D., & Simmons, J. (2007). Developing geriatric social work competencies for field education. *Journal of Gerontological Social Work, 48*(1), 139–160.

Field, L. (2000). Organizational learning: Basic concepts. In G. Foley (Ed.), *Understanding adult education training* (pp. 159–173). Sydney, Australia: Allen & Unwin.

Glick, L. J. (Ed.). (1971). *Undergraduate social work education for practice: A report on curriculum content and issues.* Syracuse, NY: Syracuse University School of Social Work.

Greene, R., Cohen, H., Galambos, C. & Kropf, N. (2007). *Foundations of social work practice in the field of aging: A competency-based approach.* Washington, DC: NASW Press.

Greene, R., & Galambos, C. (2002). *Social work's pursuit of a common professional framework: Have we reached a milestone? Advancing gerontological social work education.* New York: Haworth Press.

Grenier, A., & Gorey, K. (1998). The effectiveness of social work with older people: A meta-analysis of conference proceedings. *Social Work Research, 2,* 60–64.

Haag, S., Cummings, M., McCubbrey, D., Pinsonneault, A., & Donovan, R. (2006). *Management information systems for the information age* (3rd Ed.). Toronto, Canada: McGraw-Hill Ryerson.

Hackett, S. (2001). Educating for competency and reflective practice: Fostering a conjoint approach in education and training. *Journal of Workplace Learning, 13*(3), 103–112.

Hooyman, N. (2006). *Achieving curricular and organizational change: Impact of the CSWE Geriatric Enrichment in Social Work Education Project.* Alexandria, VA: Council on Social Work Education.

Institute of Medicine. (2008). *Retooling for an aging America: Building the health care workforce committee on the future health care workforce for older Americans,* Washington, DC: The National Academies Press.

Koroloff, N. M., & Rhyne, C. (1989). Assessing student performance in field instruction. *Journal of Teaching in Social Work, 3*(2), 3–16.

Lee, C., & Bobko, P. (1994). Self-efficacy beliefs: Comparison of five measures. *Journal of Applied Psychology, 79,* 364–369.

McPheters, H. L., & Ryan, R. M. (1971). *A core of competence for baccalaureate social welfare and curriculum implications.* Atlanta, GA: Southern Regional Education Board.

Min, L., Ranney, M., Min, J. W., Takahashi, N., & Goodman, C. (2007, October). *Statewide adoption of geriatric social work competencies.* Paper resented at the 53rd annual meeting of the Council on Social Work Education, San Francisco.

Morales A., Shaefor, B., & Scott, M. (2006). *Social work: A profession of many faces* (11th ed.). Boston: Allyn & Bacon.

Morrow-Howell, N., & Burnette, D. (2001). Gerontological social work research: Current status and future directions. *Journal of Gerontological Social Work, 36,* 63–81.

Naito-Chan, E., Damron-Rodriguez, J., & Simmons, W. J. (2004). Identifying competencies for geriatric social work practice. *Journal of Gerontological Social Work, 43*(4), 59–78.

Nakao, K. C., Damron-Rodriguez, J. A., Lawrance, F. P., Volland, P. & Bachrach, P. S. (2007, November). *Examination of the psychometric properties of the Knowledge of Aging for Social Work Quiz (KASW).* Paper presented at the 60th annual meeting of the Gerontology Society of America, San Francisco.

Nakao, K. C., Damron-Rodriguez, J. A., Lawrance, F., Volland, P., & Bachrach, P. (2008, January). *Validation of the Practicum Partnership Program geriatric social work competency scale II.* Paper presented at the annual meeting of the Society for Social Work Research, Washington, DC.

National Center for Higher Education Management Systems. (2000). *Competency standards model: Another approach to accreditation review.* Washington, DC: Council on Higher Education Accreditation.

Netting, F. E., & Williams, F. G. (1998). Can we prepare geriatric social workers to collaborate in primary care practices? *Journal of Social Work Education, 34*(2), 195–210.

Ranney, M., Goodman, C. C., Tan, P., & Glezakos, A. (2006). Building on the life-span perspective: A model for infusing geriatric social work. *Journal of Gerontological Social Work, 48*(1), 83–96.

Rizzo, V. M., & Rowe, J. (2006). Studies of the cost-effectiveness of social work services in aging: A review of the literature. *Research on Social Work Practice, 16*(1), 67–78.

Rosen, A. L., Zlotnik, J. L., Curl, A. L., & Green, R. G. (2000). *The CSWE/SAGE-SW national aging competencies survey report.* Alexandria, VA: Council on Social Work Education.

Rosen, A. L., Zlotnik, J. L., & Singer, T. (2002). Basic gerontological competence for all social workers: The need to "gerontologize" social work education. *Journal of Social Work Education, 36,* 521–538.

Scharlach, A., Damron-Rodriguez, J., Robinson, B., & Feldman, R. (2000). Educating social workers for an aging society: A vision for the 21st century. *Journal of Social Work Education, 36,* 521–538.

Schneider, E. L., & Kropf, N. P. (1992). *Gerontological social work: Knowledge, service settings, and special populations.* Chicago: Nelson-Hall.

Tompkins, C. J., Rosen, A. L., & Larkin, H. (2006). An analysis of social work textbooks for aging content: How well do social work foundation texts prepare students for our aging society? *Journal of Social work Education, 42,* 3–24.

Van Voorhis, R. M., & Hostetter, C. (2006). The impact of MSW education on social worker empowerment and commitment to client empowerment through social justice advocacy. *Journal of Social Work Education*, 42, 105–121.

Vass, A. A. (Ed.). (1996). *Social work competencies: Core knowledge, values and skills.* London: Sage.

Walker, J. S., Koroloff, N., Briggs, H. E., & Friesen, B. J. (2007). Implementing and sustaining evidence-based practice in social work. *Journal of Social Work Education, 43,* 361–375.

Whitaker, T., Weismiller, T., & Clark, E. (2006). *Assuring the sufficiency of a frontline workforce: A national study of licensed social workers.* Retrieved January 25, 2008, from http://workforce.socialworkers.org/studies/aging/aging.pdf

PART II

Activating Stakeholders in Gerontology Across Social Work Education

CHAPTER 3

Building Faculty Capacity in Gerontology Through Mentoring

The Hartford Faculty Scholars Program

Barbara Berkman, Peter Maramaldi,
Daniel B. Kaplan, and Lydia Ogden

Overview

The proliferation of faculty mentoring in the United States since the 1990s (Danielson, 1999) has resulted from the proven effectiveness of mentoring programs in furthering professional success and career satisfaction outside academia (Collins, 1994; Hildebrand, 1998; Walsh, Borkowski, & Reuben, 1999). Currently, in the academic world, mentorship is seen as a significant means to improve teaching and research (Wilson, Perreira, & Valentine, 2002) and to develop extramural and intramural networks (Goodwin, Stevens, & Bellamy, 1998). Furthermore, through building research and professional practice capacity (Maramaldi et al., 2004) a mentoring program focused on a specific substantive area of scholarship, such as aging, can help build a critical mass of faculty capable of redirecting the scholarship focus in a professional field (Schuster, 1993). The Hartford Geriatric Social Work Faculty Scholars (HFS) Program uses a mentoring model that has contributed to such a shift in academic social work over the past 10 years. Its success in increasing the number and cultural diversity of faculty focused on aging offers lessons for the creation, sustainability, and ongoing growth of effective faculty mentoring programs in other substantive arenas in social work and in other disciplines.

The first part of this chapter presents the purpose and functioning of mentoring programs in general, as well as describes frequently used mentoring models, aims, and issues. The second part elucidates the theoretical framework for the HFS program and the structure of its mentoring model and specifies some of the lessons learned about mentoring that derive from a decade of HFS program experience and growth.

Purpose of Mentorship in Professional Education

In general, mentoring is intended to optimize the scope of professional learning (McBain, 1998) and career mobility (Walsh et al., 1999), and it creates a helping relationship between two professionals, at different stages in their careers, who work together to support the junior professional's development (Schapira, Kalet, Schwartz, & Gerrity, 1992). Mentors guide and nurture growth in their assigned or chosen mentees (Kaye & Hogan, 1999) and while acting as advisors, provide information, knowledge, and the benefits of their experience (Starcevich & Friend, 1999).

In professional education, such as social work, informal mentoring can occur among faculty sharing common values about life and work (Watson, 1999) and has the potential to inspire lifelong teaching and research trajectories (Danielson, 1999). Whether informal or part of a formal program, academic mentoring tends to focus on assistance with research and scholarship, teaching, and grant writing (Goodwin et al., 1998; Fisher, 1998). The academic mentoring relationship in professional schools also helps in the development of important self- concepts such as competence and confidence, as well as other leadership skills (Mahayosnand & Stigler, 1999; Walsh et al., 1999). Mentors are presumed to provide valuable psychological functions, such as affirmation, encouragement, and acceptance. These functions are believed to contribute to the mentee's professional identity and socialization (Pincus, 2007; Walsh et al.), creating a mechanism to affirm professional behavior and values (Goodwin et al.).

Ideally, the mentoring relationship provides an academic environment where it is safe for mentor and mentee to take risks and experience personal and professional discovery and growth. Junior faculty may make mistakes or embark on unsuccessful ventures in new areas. Candid discussions of these efforts are not likely to occur among faculty members where pressures for tenure and promotion might inhibit them from revealing anything that could be perceived as a failure or weakness. However, in the academic mentoring relationship, such discussions are expected and maximized as opportunities for learning.

Mentorship Models

Four phases in the mentoring relationship, which occur in most mentoring models, are initiation, cultivation, separation, and redefinition (Beech & Brockbank, 1999; Hill & Bahniuk, 1998). During initiation, the mentee admires, respects, and trusts the mentor. The mentor feels this respect and thinks that he or she has something to offer the mentee. In the cultivation phase, which can last up to several years, the mentee develops competence, confidence, and professional identity as a result of career support. The mentor feels proud of the help he or she has been able to give the mentee's career development. The separation phase is characterized by a change in the relationship between mentor and mentee. The mentee becomes more independent and empowered, and the nature of the relationship, therefore, alters. Sometimes, negative feelings and hostility mark this phase because the mentee may feel he or she needs continued support, or the mentor struggles with letting go. However, if the mentor and protégé work together, they can move to the redefinition phase in which the relationship is reshaped to meet new and more collegial needs.

Traditional mentoring models have a tendency to be hierarchical, occurring through gravitational force. In these relationships, professionals seeking career advancement are pulled toward more experienced and accomplished professionals who provide advice, support, encouragement, guidance, knowledge, and other opportunities for desired advancement (Bauer, 1999; Beech & Brockbank, 1999). These hierarchical models can exacerbate existing disparities in power between mentor and mentee (Beech & Brockbank) and may limit opportunities for people who historically have been marginalized from established networks, such as women and people of color (Bauer; Richey, Gambrill, & Blythe, 1988). Such restrictions may result from informal norms of inclusion or exclusion in the culture of a given group, which can unwittingly create exclusive networks that are difficult for outsiders to penetrate.

By contrast, although contemporary mentoring models feature a similar gravitational pull, the focus is on exchange of knowledge in *partnerships*, de-emphasizing hierarchical arrangements (Hill & Bahniuk, 1998). Such models are inclusive in nature and are based on the notion that people and ideas can flourish in reciprocal mentoring relationships that are mutually beneficial to mentee and mentor, and where there is a supportive learning situation in which the mentor takes a sincere interest in the mentee's career (Hill & Bahniuk; Pincus, 2007; Rowley, 1999; Starcevich & Friend, 1999). Within this reciprocal model, mentoring may be constructed as a helping relationship between professionals at differing stages of career development who come together so that the senior professional can cultivate the junior professional's advancement (Schapira et al., 1992). Some think this is best accomplished through an adult-learning model characterized by a low-pressure, power-free, self-discovery approach that allows the mentor and mentee to freely share their own experiences and to value one another's distinctive skills and contributions to the mentoring relationship (Starcevich & Friend, 1999).

When the interplay between mentor and mentee is supportive and nonjudgmental, each has the opportunity for an interactive and collaborative learning process of discovery and growth (Chase, 1998; Isaacs, 1998). Mentors frequently report receiving more than they give, because by sharing knowledge accumulated over many years they feel valued and reinvigorated (Antonucci, Edelstein, & Johnson, 2003; Maramaldi et al., 2004). Notably, mentors may sharpen their own professional growth as the result of the mentoring relationship (Mahayosnand & Stigler, 1999). By providing new insights and a fresh perspective on shared professional interests in a rewarding environment (Messmer, 1998; Peyton, Morton, Perkins, & Dougherty, 2001; Suggs, 1986), mentees can fuel the mentors' enthusiasm for invigorating their own research (Lee, Dennis, & Campbell, 2007) by exposing them to new ideas, emerging technology, and shifts in the culture of their own profession (Collins, 1994; Hill & Bahniuk, 1998). As a result, mentees have an impact on the thinking and behavior of their mentors (Hardy, 1998) in a two-way exchange of knowledge with the potential for synergistic effects.

Empathy is a key element of a balanced rapport (Bower, Diehr, Morzinski, & Simpson, 1998), which together with mutual support and a shared vision of the mentee's future career allows mentoring to advance one's professional development (Morton & Kennedy, 1999; Rowley, 1999). The successful mentee thrives in a relationship that flows naturally from the resolute belief that a mentor is capable of making a significant and positive impact on the life of another through a substantial investment of time and energy (Rowley, 1999), and the mentor receives satisfaction from supporting a future leader.

Theoretical Framework for the HSF Program

The *diffusion of innovation* theory (Rogers, 1962/1995, 2002), which the HFS program is based on, proposes that new ideas, termed *innovations*, are adopted based on the relative value of the innovation—the innovation is better than what it supersedes. To be adopted, innovations must be compatible with existing values, experiences, and needs, and must not be difficult to understand or use. The ability of an innovation to be observed and taught is another element that plays into the diffusion and adoption of innovations. Early theorists of innovation diffusion focused on the stages of innovation adoption and qualities of innovation adopters (Dearing, 2008). However, in the last decade research on the process of diffusion of innovation has supported the importance of opinion leaders, including those within peer networks and those who are champions of specific causes (Dearing; Rogers, 2002). Research has demonstrated that individuals with expertise and leadership in substantive areas are the best promoters of innovation and knowledge (Dearing; Gira, Kessler, & Poertner, 2004).

This conceptual framework, widely used in health and educational contexts (see Dearing, 2008, for an overview; Goldman, 1994; Lapinski & Witte, 1998), is a good match for a social work initiative that aims to develop specialized professional capacities in a specific substantive area, such as health and aging. Programs intending to contribute to capacity building of a substantive area in a profession depend on well-respected, socially integrated innovators to spread new practices or knowledge throughout the professional field.

In the HFS program, the National Research Mentors fill the role of socially integrated innovators while simultaneously preparing mentee-scholars to eventually assume that same role. Respected mentors encourage new scholars to generate and disseminate knowledge in health and aging. The mentee-scholars have begun to train the next generation of professionals through the courses they teach and to prepare their students to provide competent services in their area of specialized practice, in this context, health and aging. Thus, mentors and mentees collaborate to build a large cadre of professionals who share common values and goals, furthering progress toward strengthening social work professional capacity in health and aging. The HFS program recruits well-established, nationally respected gerontologists as mentors, creates new mentors, and grooms innovators who influence the field of social work by enhancing gerontological social work's research, teaching, and practice capacity.

The HFS Program Mentoring Model

Five interacting components of the HFS program promote the success of the scholars as leaders in the field of gerontological social work: research mentoring, institutional sponsorship, a professional development plan, a funded research project, and institutes and workshops focused on building skills in research, teaching, and policy. Similar components, either individually or in combination, are transferrable to other areas within social work that aim to build faculty scholar capacity.

The conceptual model for the HFS mentoring program capitalizes on the recruitment and nurturing of emerging faculty leaders to produce an upsurge of gerontology-focused academic activity in social work. The faculty scholars are selected through a highly competitive process, based on prior accomplishments, commitment to gerontology, leadership potential, and the strengths of a formal research proposal to be completed during the 2-year program. By providing opportunities for funding, mentorship, and professional development, the HFS program has attracted social work scholars from culturally diverse backgrounds and with varied foci—such as oncology, substance use, interpersonal violence or mental health—bridging these specific interests to the common link of gerontology. Each scholar proposes and implements a significant research project focused on advancing social work knowledge in health and aging. As the core element, this program employs a formal, semistructured, long-distance research mentoring model to develop the skills of new faculty scholars focused on gerontological research and gerontology-infused teaching and professional activities. The mentor is assigned by the program's director of mentoring, drawing from a national roster of highly skilled gerontological researchers. Mentors are from social work programs other than that of the scholar's and matched on the basis of methodological and substantive expertise. The mentor's primary responsibility is the provision of ongoing consultation to the scholar regarding the research project. Mentors are particularly active in the early stages of research project development and implementation, when years of experience can offer creative solutions and indispensable support to new researchers. To enable the fulfillment of their responsibilities, the mentors are provided an honorarium and receive funds to attend two institutes with their scholar and to visit the scholar's school and/or research site.

Another important element of the HFS program is the relationship established between the scholar and an institutional sponsor. Institutional sponsors are chosen by the scholars at the time of application and are based at the academic institution where the scholar is employed. Institutional sponsors are responsible for serving as a role model who will provide support, guidance, and political sponsorship germane to the scholar's home institution. These duties are designed to help the scholar navigate the academic work environment, particularly the expectations related to promotion and tenure, and facilitate her or his entry into university-based and other professional and organizational networks. Working with their institutional sponsor, scholars establish a professional development plan with specific target goals and competencies. The plan is used to guide and inform the scholar's development and effectiveness as a professional and leader in the field.

The triadic relationship between scholar, mentor, and institutional sponsor is the foundation of the mentoring model, mobilizing intra-mural and extramural resources to help advance the scholars' professional development. The formal assignment of two types of supportive mentorship is a critical facet, with each mentor and sponsor focusing on separate but interacting areas of professional development and learning objectives. The triadic nature of the mentoring relationship provides a nonhierarchical exchange of knowledge, as well as a balance that helps to prevent any potential power struggles that might dampen the benefits of mentorship.

To further the goal of professional development, scholars also participate in a number of skill-based educational institutes and workshops focused on research, teaching, and leadership. These institutes provide opportunities for scholars to engage in formal and informal events where they find peer support, build networks and cohort relationships, and share their progress with one another. Throughout the program, the scholars are prepared and encouraged to publish and to infuse gerontological content into the courses they teach.

Over time, this growing network of faculty scholars, having received effective mentoring through the HFS program, has emerged among a new generation of leaders in the gerontological social work field. Former Hartford Scholars now serve as mentors to current scholars, recruiting applicants to the HFS program and Hartford Doctoral Fellows (HDF) Program, and providing leadership in the Hartford Partnership

Program for Aging Education (HPPAE) and the National Center for Gerontological Social Work Education (Gero-Ed Center) programs. The success of the mentorship model of the HFS program can be measured, in part, by the willingness and ability of former scholars to serve as the next wave of mentors. Of the 26 Hartford doctoral fellows recruited as of April 2008, 24 were brought in by Hartford faculty scholars; of the 60 recipients of the Pre-Dissertation Awards (described in chapter 1), all but 7 were from programs where Hartford scholars participated in recruitment (Berkman, Kaplan, & Harootyan, 2008). Of the 67 sites of the HPPAE, 48% have Hartford faculty scholars involved in the operations of the programs (Berkman et al.). In addition, the scholars are assuming significant roles in the Gero-Ed Center's Curriculum Development Institutes (CDIs) and other Gero-Ed programs. Similarly, the Geriatric Enrichment in Social Work Education (GeroRich) Project and CDI programs have served to recruit faculty into gerontological social work and provide them with the support to apply for leadership opportunities; among GeroRich and CDI faculty participants, 29 are Hartford scholars, 2 are Hartford doctoral fellows, and 23 serve as national mentors through Gero-Ed and Hartford scholar programs. As leaders in the field of aging, the Hartford faculty scholars have had a direct impact on faculty in other GSWI programs, and faculty from other GSWI projects have benefited from being scholars.

Lessons Learned From the HFS Program

During the first 10 years of the HFS program, 91 accomplished scholars have participated in a mentorship process that has benefited multiple parties: the Hartford Scholars, their mentors, and their students. And most important, the research and training of new social work practitioners in aging undertaken by these scholars contribute to improved services and care coordination for older adults and their families. As the HFS program staff have worked to develop and enhance the mentorship component of the program, they have learned many lessons about mentoring and the program as a whole, and have used these lessons to improve program functioning. Faculty mentoring programs in other social work practice fields or other disciplines may benefit from this discussion of the elements of effective mentoring, as summarized in Table 3.1.

Table 3.1

ELEMENTS OF EFFECTIVE MENTORING

◆ The most effective partnerships develop when both parties give and take, and both derive benefits in professional and personal satisfaction from the relationship (Hill & Bahniuk, 1998).

◆ The process may involve a formal, planned exchange of information or more spontaneous coaching—being in the right place and the right time— to give immediate advice, support, or feedback (Kaye & Hogan, 1999).

◆ Mentoring requires a commitment of time, energy, and readiness to help. However, finding a balance is the key to avoiding burnout and the key to ensuring satisfaction (Kaye & Hogan, 1999).

◆ Good mentors know how to share their own stories and experiences so that they illustrate lessons they want their partners to learn (Kaye & Hogan, 1999).

◆ Clear communication and expectations set the stage for a strong learning partnership (Kaye & Hogan, 1999).

◆ In some cases, mentors have found it useful to actually set up a working agenda to guide the process (Messmer, 1998).

◆ The mentor, although busy in her or his senior-level responsibilities, is available when needed, is someone whose opinions and judgments are respected, is genuinely interested in the mentee's work, encourages rather than criticizes, and communicates the belief that a person is capable of transcending present challenges and of accomplishing great things in the future (Lasley, as cited in Rowley, 1999).

◆ In a two-way process, the mentee must plan in order to use her/his time with the mentor effectively (Krechowicka, 1998).

◆ Mutual expectations of mentors and mentees are crucial in the effectiveness of the relationship. Issues may be overlooked or ignored if no guidelines are established at the beginning (Morton & Kennedy, 1999).

◆ Tight structure, accountability, mutual respect, and a working rapport are keys to successful mentoring programs (Hayes, 1998).

◆ Consistent with research findings, *teacher* and *partner* are chosen as the best descriptive words for one's most effective mentor (Starcevich & Friend, 1999).

Note: From "Mentoring New Faculty Across Borders: The Conceptual Base for the John A. Hartford Geriatric Social Work Faculty Scholars Program," by P. Maramaldi and B. Berkman, 2007, in *Alliance of Universities for Democracy: Vol. 12. Perspectives in Higher Education*, pp. 168–174. Blagoevgrad, Bulgaria: American University in Bulgaria. Copyright 2007 by American University in Bulgaria. Adapted with permission.

Matching Mentors and Mentees

An important and potentially problematic feature of mentoring in general is the pairing of mentor and mentee. Mentors are usually selected for their individual areas of expertise (Messmer, 1998) and often provide a unique blend of professional, academic, and emotional support (Mahayosnand & Stigler, 1999). By thinking beyond institutional and social-work-specific walls in selecting the national research mentor, the mentee and mentor have the opportunity to be paired with a person who clearly fits their individual strengths and needs, and to work together toward developing a synergistic relationship that enhances the impact of the mentorship.

To repeat, the HFS program pairs each junior scholar with a seasoned national mentor, along with a local institutional sponsor. The national and local focus of this type of mentoring initiative—the national focus is on research skills and the local focus is on professional development—provides diversified intellectual stimulation and creates a mutually supportive and highly connected network of colleagues who are committed to furthering knowledge and practice capacity in an underdeveloped substantive area (Maramaldi et al., 2004).

The objectives of the mentoring relationship must be mutually agreeable to both parties, with ample time allotted to achieve goals (Walsh et al., 1999). The mentor's sincere commitment to help the mentee is instrumental to the success of the process (Van Collie, 1998). The mentee, too, must not be passive. Rather, she or he must be committed to work on the relationship, often taking the lead in maintaining it (Antonucci et al., 2003; Starcevich & Friend, 1999) by sharing what she or he needs so the mentor can respond to those needs and build on the mentee's strengths. In the HFS program, the specific 2-year, time-limited research program offers a structured focus and time frame to the mentoring relationship. These elements are designed to decrease the power struggles and challenges that might be otherwise faced in mentorship, especially during the separation phase, described earlier in this chapter. However, in many cases the mentor and scholar continue to work together and even collaborate on new projects after the junior scholar completes the HFS program.

In designing such a program, it is important not to ignore the potential conflict in a triadic mentoring model. In the early years of the

HFS program, relatively few of the institutional sponsors in the scholars' schools or departments were gerontologists. These sponsors were senior faculty committed to the scholars' professional development. Thus, at the inception of the program, the national research mentor and the institutional sponsor were clearly differentiated, with the national research mentor focused on aging research, which was usually not the expertise of the institutional sponsor. As the HFS program has grown and the number of gerontological faculty at institutions has increased, in part because of the program itself, more institutional sponsors are gerontologists and sometimes former Hartford scholars. Thus, there is the potential for conflicting input regarding the scholars' research. When conflict has arisen, the director of research mentoring has worked with the scholars and the mentors to resolve the differing opinions. In addition, conflict can be avoided if the national research mentor is careful not to become overly involved in the scholar's professional development, particularly as it relates to programmatic issues such as guidelines for tenure, which vary across institutions.

Developing Mentoring Skills

The sophisticated process of high-quality mentorship may come naturally to some, but most new mentors also need education and skill building, guidance, and ongoing support to provide optimal tutelage and encouragement to junior scholars. Although the role of the mentor is to give direct advice, mentors cannot force mentees to accept it. How advice is presented may determine whether it is well received, especially when mentors need to offer critiques of mentee writing and/or other such skills. For example, to reduce the considerable anxiety that may arise as a mentee receives criticism, or perceives such feedback as a failure to meet high expectations for performance, mentors can phrase critiques in terms of "common academic expectations" instead of "here is what I think you should do differently." New mentors should be given published papers on effective mentoring as well as tips and suggestions from seasoned mentors to help prepare them for the job.

Identifying seasoned mentors who will be available to support and guide new mentors as they encounter various challenges and uncertainties is important. Written examples of potential areas of mentor involvement will also help to clarify if certain activities are actually within the purview of the mentor. A wide array of activities exist that allow new scholars to benefit from their mentors' wisdom and support, and mentors may assume many roles during their tenure with a mentee. A mentoring program must clarify these multiple roles and responsibilities for all involved and help prepare mentors to meet the challenge. Activities of mentorship may relate to research projects and skills, scholarship, and career development. The specific areas of guidance given by the mentors and the institutional sponsors identified through the HFS program are listed in Table 3.2. As noted earlier in this chapter, mentors and sponsors may offer conflicting advice in some areas, and consultation with the director of mentoring may be valuable in resolving such differences.

One of the most effective means of mentor training in the HFS program is through in-person peer consultation. Mentors meet with other mentors to share the mentoring experience and solicit advice. To facilitate the free exchange of knowledge and mentoring techniques among HFS mentors, the program conducts annual meetings where mentors, scholars, and program staff routinely gather in one site. During these mentor-to-mentor meetings, the director of mentoring solicits feedback, gathers suggestions for educational topics for future mentor meetings and content for print materials, offers praise and recognition of mentor accomplishments, and provides immediate consultation for current challenges and concerns. In the HFS formal mentoring program, the director of mentoring and the program's national director are available to discuss any scholar-mentor issues that may arise throughout the 2-year program. Many schools or departments now have directors of research, or senior faculty, who could take on such responsibilities in a school-based mentoring program.

Long-Distance Mentoring Works

A mentorship program should establish structures and expectations of professional conduct that encourage open communication between mentor and mentee (Maramaldi et al., 2004), and promote flexibility regarding frequency of contact and the mentor's level of involvement with the mentee's research and career development. Because each mentoring relationship must be uniquely constructed to meet the mentee's needs, different approaches to mentoring are to be expected. The mentorship program can work to ensure that mentees know they have access to their assigned mentors and possibly to other mentors in the network as well.

Table 3.2
AREAS OF MENTOR AND INSTITUTIONAL SPONSOR GUIDANCE IN THE HFS PROGRAM

Research design and research project implementation issues (e.g., feasibility)

Hiring, training, and supervision of staff

Resource management

Institutional review board processes and requirements

Fiscal management

Grant writing and identification of research opportunities or future funding sources

Data analysis

Manuscript writing and publication issues

Editorial board participation

Preparation for conference presentations

Promotion and tenure issues

Obtaining career development awards

Collaborating across faculty disciplines

Outreach efforts and building community networks

Time management and stress management

Self-promotion and visibility

Consultation on teaching

Socialization to the profession or discipline

Changing universities and other career changes

Strategies of community and professional service

Note. Adapted from the minutes of the Mentor to Mentor meeting of the Hartford faculty scholars, led by David Biegel, October 20, 2007.

Long-distance mentoring relationships can help extend the mentee's professional reach beyond the borders of his or her institution and local community, and can build an ever-growing network of collaboration around the specific field of practice being advanced by the program. Because of the benefits of face-to-face interactions, the HSF program encourages all scholars and mentors to arrange for meetings at national conferences and institutes they both attend. In fact, such a meeting is scheduled during the early weeks of each program cycle at an institute where the new scholars present their research and have consultation time with their new mentors.

The rapid and free exchange of ideas through e-mail and telephone communications allows long-distance mentoring relationships to develop and to transcend distance and institutional or state borders. Although e-mail may seem impersonal, it is the most appropriate communication form for long-distance mentoring because it eliminates the need to schedule as many face-to-face meetings throughout the year, and mentors and mentees can reply at any hour of the night or day (Haworth, 1998). Although e-mail lacks some advantages of face-to-face conversations, studies indicate that it can help mentees feel less intimidated when approaching someone who is likely to be more established and experienced (Kaiser, 1998). However, those few Hartford scholars who are innately shy, or culturally unaccustomed to relating through electronic and telephone exchanges, have felt intimidated by such communication with the mentors. In those situations, the careful planning of communication schedules, as well as candid discussions between mentor and scholar about what types of content are acceptable in each communication forum have been useful, especially when the scholar and mentor are first getting to know one another.

Mentoring Relationships Evolve Over Time

As the relationships progress and the scholars' skills develop, many of the mentors have reported that their relationships with scholars have become collegial in nature, surpassing the initial role of mentor/mentee. Several such pairs have embarked on collaborative research projects. Similarly, institutional sponsors have developed effective relationships with scholars beyond the expectations of the program, serving as advocates for the scholars, generously offering time and support, assisting with institutional review board protocols, securing time dedicated to research projects, and making connections within the local community for research partnerships (Maramaldi et al., 2004). This appears to be a common pattern found in mentoring programs, where strong mentoring relationships develop into new types of associations even after the formal mentoring has ended (Lee et al., 2007).

Cultural Sensitivity Enhances Mentoring Relationships

Culture plays an important role in any relationship, and the experiences of mentors and mentees with one another are no exception (Evans & Cokley, 2008). With a powerful influence over expectations related to authority, respect, and seniority, cultural norms often guide interpersonal styles of relating, long-distance communication patterns, and collaborative behaviors. The scholars of the HFS program are diverse in many aspects, including a substantial variation in gender, age, sexual orientation, race, and ethnicity. In addition, the scholars come from different regions of the country, represent various ideological beliefs, and belong to many religious groups. In the Hartford program's nine cohorts, only 65% of the scholars are Caucasian. Similar diversity is characteristic of the HFS National Research Mentor roster as well. Tuning in to the many strengths of this diversity has promoted the benefits of the mentor/scholar relationships as well as the HFS program overall.

Although a formalized forum for addressing cultural sensitivity for mentors and scholars is being developed at the time of publication, case-by-case discussions of diversity-related challenges have been invaluable to date and have served as lessons to be passed down through the ranks of mentors and scholars over time. The essential component of these lessons is flexibility. Rigid adherence to specific expectations regarding communications, collaborative relationships, or interpersonal dynamics can diminish the effectiveness of mentoring. Some issues were commonly reported, whereas others were unique to particular individuals. Although differences within groups are to be expected, themes of concern from mentoring relationships have helped to inform efforts toward greater cultural sensitivity within the program. For example, several Asian American female scholars have experienced difficulty in voicing their needs for additional support to male Caucasian senior mentors. It is challenging to isolate which cultural memberships interact to create this dynamic. However, in such instances, simple solutions can focus on the clarification of mentor and scholar availability, preferred communication methods, and objectives for the mentorship.

Similar challenges and responses are described in detail in the University of Michigan Rackham School of Graduate Studies (2006) guide-book, *How to Mentor Graduate Students: A Guide for Faculty at a Diverse University*. This comprehensive review of mentoring strategies includes rich examples of how to sensitize those in the mentoring process to the "issues faced by students from historically underrepresented or marginalized populations" (p. 21). Mentoring programs would benefit from careful planning to respond to the relational concerns common across groups and specific to certain groups by gender, race/ethnicity, sexual orientation, nationality, class, and more. Consideration of these many themes, as listed in Table 3.3, provides a powerful illustration of the magnitude and importance of such a planning effort.

Throughout the HFS program's 10-year history, once a challenge or obstacle was identified by a scholar or mentor, culturally sensitive interventions were employed to transform the mentoring relationship into a more productive and positive experience for all involved. Anticipation of such obstacles is preferable; however, the HFS program strongly encourages each new cohort of mentors and scholars to maintain sensitivity to cultural factors, as well as an attitude of flexibility and a considerable investment of time and effort at the beginning of the relationship in addressing these critical issues.

Mentoring Relationships Build Community

Mentors may assist the mentee in establishing important networks for professional career growth by facilitating connections with other academics, researchers, and potential collaborators. As mentees confront different challenges or discover new intellectual interests, accomplished mentors may tap into their cadre of professional connections and link the mentees with the appropriate circles of topical or methodological expertise. In this way, communities of intellectuals continually expand and reorient, welcoming each new generation of academics and opinion leaders and ensuring the evolution of knowledge in the content area. Effective mentors participate in this role because they realize there is a need to build positive and sustaining communities to create an environment where all can flourish and be nurtured (Lee et al., 2007).

In the HFS program, the nine cohorts of scholars, mentors, and institutional sponsors who have participated in the program thus far, as well as the staff, have created a community of relationships and networks over time that spans multiple disciplines, generations, levels of career achievement, and geographic localities. Year after year these committed individuals locate each other at meetings and conferences and through

Table 3.3
CONCERNS RELATED TO RELATIONSHIPS WITH MENTORS

- Need for role models
- Questioning the canons
- Fear of being categorized as a "single-issue" scholar
- Feelings of isolation
- Burden of being a spokesperson
- Seeking balance

Women
- Assertiveness
- Competitiveness
- Importance of positive feedback

Lesbian, Gay, Bisexual, Transgendered Individuals
- Homophobia
- Heterosexism
- Disclosing

Race and Ethnic Minority Individuals
- Stereotyping

International Individuals
- Issues of culture and language
- Social stresses

Individuals from Working-Class Backgrounds
- Economic concerns
- Summer professional opportunities
- Difference in background experiences

Note. From *How to Mentor Graduate Students: A Guide for Faculty at a Diverse University*, by the University of Michigan Rackham School of Graduate Studies, 2006, Ann Arbor: Regents of the University of Michigan. Copyright 2006 by The Regents of the University of Michigan. Adapted with permission.

journal publications. The community is readily available to each new entrant and appears to take genuine interest in the teaching, research, and general well-being of its members. This interest is neither surprising nor accidental. The mentors and scholars are encouraged to offer support, encouragement, and assistance to one another. This is the nature of a mentorship network. In addition, the substantive orientation of each member of the community creates a kind of cohesion that unites the community around the theme of gerontological social work. The buzz of intellectual curiosity experienced at large HFS program events attests to this effect. The benefits of such a community are many. In each biannual evaluation survey, Hartford scholars speak of a sense of belonging and of kindred minds and hearts. Some scholars may be the only gerontologist in their university program, and they are thrilled to interact with peers from the HFS network at each opportunity. They enjoy speaking comfortably in the language of gerontological jargon and acronyms, and saying the familiar names of programs and research pioneers in aging. They relish the common knowledge of biopsychosocial phenomena of older individuals, societal trends, demographic changes, and the politics of global aging. Participation in the HFS community can instill confidence, accelerate careers, and generate positive feelings for each member. Most importantly, it helps to keep the scholars committed to the goal of teaching and researching in gerontological social work.

The Importance of Evaluation

Evaluation should be incorporated in the design and implementation of a mentoring program model. In the HFS program, every current scholar, mentor, and institutional sponsor is surveyed twice each year with regard to the accomplishments of the scholar's research and professional development goals. Suggestions are also collected to ensure programmatic improvements. Most importantly, these surveys gather information on the quality of the mentoring relationships and allow program staff to think critically about specific matches of mentors to scholars, as well as structural elements of the program and types of programmatic support. Evaluation surveys also reinforce the scholars' sense of accountability to professional development goals set at the beginning of the program. They provide an excellent opportunity to capture data that document the explicit impact of the mentoring program through various outcome measures, such as scholarly publications and presentations, participation in curriculum development and community leadership activities, and grants, awards, and honors received. Evaluations are also conducted on each of the program institutes, meetings, and workshops to capture participant feedback essential to guiding future activities. Evaluations provide feedback that informs programmatic changes as well as communication with program funders.

The Creation of Social Capital

An unexpected lesson learned from the HFS program is the impact of the creation of social capital. Although this program was not designed to demonstrate the value of increased social capital in an academic discipline, it appears that it has nonetheless manifested the most positive aspects of the concept. Social capital is roughly defined as the norms and networks that enable people to act collectively (Woolcock & Narayan, 2000) and that have positive consequences for the individual and the community. In short, social capital refers to the advantages created through relationships and group memberships (Portes, 1998). Although it does not appear that the concept has been applied to functioning within academia, a diverse array of sociological studies have demonstrated that communities with varied stocks of networks and associations are in a stronger position to achieve their goals and overcome obstacles than those without these (Portes, 1998; Wolcok & Narayan, 2000).

In the simplest view, more social capital is better than less. Although the complexities of institutional and other environmental contexts sometimes disprove this hypothesis, in many cases increased social capital does in fact provide advantages to those who hold it. "Individuals draw on the benefits of close community membership that enables the members to acquire skills and resources in networks that transcend their community, thereby progressively joining the mainstream" (Woolcock & Narayan, 2000, p. 232). Social capital in any network can be leveraged to maximize the efficiency of its use.

Social capital can be measured in several ways. One measure is how relationships among group memberships affect economies (Woolcock & Narayan, 2000). Funding and mentoring from the HFS program adds monetary value to participation in gerontology-focused research. The appeal of focusing one's substantive work in gerontology moves beyond the intellectual and practical concerns of the field to the financial. That gerontology has become a well-funded research area gives power to faculty who choose it as their focus. Since the program's inception in 1999, Hartford scholars have attained $54.6 million in leveraged funding from federal and foundation sources. This is 4.1 times the Hartford foundation investment to date of $13.3 million. Faculty gerontologists have become essential to university social work schools or departments, not only because of the importance of their chosen substantive area but also because of the financial boost their research funding can give their program. As such, the HFS program has helped increase the social capital of those in the field of gerontology.

Another measure of social capital is membership in formal and informal associations and networks (Woolcock & Narayan, 2000). The number of group memberships is tied to the potential for opportunities. Through the formal and informal networking embedded in the HFS program, associations and networks are gained. Evaluation of the program thus far points to such added opportunities, including collaborations and opportunities for research projects and published articles beyond those related to the HFS projects. In the first 10 years of the HFS program, the first eight cohorts of Hartford scholars have been extraordinarily productive since receiving program funding and support. (Cohort 9 has just begun its program and no data have been collected at this time.) Their professional outcomes include 761 articles in peer-reviewed journals, 346 books and/or book chapters, 132 curricula developed with gerontological content, 2,814 research grants, 1,825 presentations, and 194 awards or honors. These staggering numbers speak to the multiple levels of value added to the faculty of universities and colleges where the scholars are employed. The lesson learned from the HFS program regarding social capital in academic settings is that it can be deliberately created for the benefit of not only the members of the immediate social network but also their departments, universities and, at least within the field of social work, their clients and their families receiving services.

Conclusion

The HFS program successes support the use of a reciprocal mentoring model that involves an interwoven exchange among scholars, mentors, and institutional sponsors, as well as broader professional networking opportunities. The model also verifies the value of the time-limited approach to the mentoring relationship and the focus on a research project and/or a professional development plan, because such boundaries allow for a smoother transition into a collegial relationship after participation in the program. Mentors should be provided with training and guidance that will enhance their performance in this critical role. Long-distance mentoring is not only possible but is also a desirable counterpart to local mentoring because it cuts through common barriers such as professional competition and fear of professional compromise. Although face-to-face meetings are valuable, and nuances of e-mail communication need to be negotiated, the free exchange of ideas can be more easily facilitated through e-mail than through trying to organize meetings or arrange telephone calls. Furthermore, the ability to find appropriate mentor matches is greatly enhanced when using a national roster of qualified mentors. Mentors and mentees gain from such mentoring relationships, especially when sensitivity to cultural diversity is incorporated in the mentorship process. Evaluation is an integral part of any such mentoring program, as it allows mentors and mentees to voice their concerns as well as their successes, and allows the program to monitor outcomes and impact. Finally, mentoring programs focused on funded research projects have the potential to create social capital, further propelling any desired capacity building in a substantive area, and to provide the capability of shifting a profession's focus to address emerging societal needs.

References

Antonucci, T., Edelstein, B., & Johnson, J. C. (2003, Spring). Master mentoring. *Adult Development and Aging News*, 6–10.

Bauer, T. (1999). Perceived mentoring fairness: Relationships with gender, mentoring type, mentoring experience, and mentoring needs. *Sex Roles, 40*(3/4), 211–225.

Beech, N., & Brockbank, A. (1999). Power/knowledge and psychosocial dynamics in mentoring. *Management Learning, 30*(1), 7–24.

Berkman, B., Kaplan, D., & Harootyan, L. (2008). *Hartford Faculty Scholars Program site visit pre-evaluation update: Activities and results, January–April 2008.* New York: Hartford Faculty Scholars Program.

Bower, D., Diehr, S., Morzinski, J., & Simpson, D. (1998). Support-challenge-vision: A model for faculty mentoring. *Medical Teacher, 20*(6), 595–597.

Chase, N. (1998). Every manager is a mentor. *Quality, 37*(10), 88.

Collins, P. (1994). Does mentorship among social workers make a difference? An empirical investigation of career outcomes. *Social Work, 39*, 413–419.

Danielson, C. (1999). Mentoring beginning teachers: The case for mentoring. *Teaching and Change, 6*(3), 251–257.

Dearing, J. W. (2008). Evolution of diffusion and dissemination theory. *Public Health Management and Practice, 14*(2), 99–108.

Evans, G. L., & Cokley, K. O. (2008). African American women and the academy: Using career mentoring to increase research productivity. *Training and Education in Professional Psychology, 2*(1), 50–57.

Fisher, J. Jr. (1998). Mentoring your way to greatness. *Executive Excellence, 15*(5), 19.

Gira, E. C., Kessler, M. L., & Poertner, J. (2004). Influencing social workers to use research evidence in practice: Lessons from medicine and the allied health professions. *Research on Social Work Practice, 14*(2), 68–79.

Goldman, K. D. (1994). Perceptions of innovations as predictors of implementation levels: The diffusion of a nationwide health education campaign. *Health Education Quarterly, 21*, 433–445.

Goodwin, L., Stevens, E., & Bellamy, G. (1998). Mentoring among faculty in schools, colleges and departments of education. *Journal of Teacher Education, 49*(5), 334–343.

Hardy, L. (1998). Mentoring: A long-term approach to diversity. *HR Focus, 75*(7), S11.

Haworth, K. (1998). Mentor programs provide support via e-mail to women studying science. *The Chronicle of Higher Education, 44*(32), A29–A30.

Hayes, K. (1998). What it takes to be a mentor. *Chartered Accountants Journal of New Zealand, 77*(6), 62–63.

Hildebrand, K. (1998). Mentoring programs. *Colorado Business Magazine, 25*(6), 66–67.

Hill, S., & Bahniuk, M. (1998). Promoting career success through mentoring. *Review of Business, 19*(3), 4–7.

Isaacs, N. (1998). Mentors gain ground. *Infoworld, 20*(40), 113–114.

Kaiser, J. (1998). Mentoring by e-mail. *Science, 281*(5385), 1919.

Kaye, B., & Hogan, J. (1999). Improve teamwork. *Executive Excellence, 16*(6), 17–18.

Krechowiecka, I. (1998). Moving on up: An ABC guide to…mentoring. *The Guardian,* Dec. 4.

Lapinski, M., & Witte, K. (1998). Health communication campaigns. In L. Jackson & B. Duffy (Eds.), *Health communication research: A guide to developments and directions* (pp. 139–161). Westport, CT: Greenwood Press.

Lee, A., Dennis, C., & Campbell, P. (2007). Nature's guide for mentors. *Nature, 447,* 791–797.

Mahayosnand, P., & Stigler, M. (1999). The need for mentoring in public health. *American Journal of Public Health, 89*(8), 1262–1263.

Maramaldi, P., & Berkman, B. (2007). Mentoring new faculty across borders: The conceptual base for the John A. Hartford Geriatric Social Work Faculty Scholars Program. *Alliance of Universities for Democracy: Vol. 12. Perspectives in Higher Education* (pp. 168–174. Blagoevgrad, Bulgaria: American University in Bulgaria.

Maramaldi, P., Gardner, D., Berkman, B., Ireland, K., D'Ambruoso, S., & Howe, J. L. (2004). Mentoring new social work faculty: A gerontological perspective. *Gerontology & Geriatrics Education, 25*(1), 89–106.

McBain, R. (1998). Human resources management—New perspectives on mentoring. *Manager Update, 9*(3), 23–32.

Messmer, M. (1998). Participating in a mentoring program. *Management Accounting, 80*(6), 12.

Morton, R., & Kennedy, M. (1999). Advice from the experts. *Healthcare Executive, 14*(2), 44–45.

Peyton, A., Morton, M., Perkins, M., & Dougherty, L. (2001). Mentoring in gerontology education: New graduate student perspectives. *Educational Gerontology, 27,* 347–359.

Pincus, H. A. (2007, November). *Advancing interdisciplinary mentoring in research.* Paper presented at the 60th Annual Scientific Meeting Preconference Workshop of the Gerontological Society of America, Washington, DC.

Portes, A. (1998). Social capital: Its origins and applications in modern sociology. *Annual Review of Sociology, 24*(1), 1–24.

Richey, C., Gambrill, E., & Blythe, B. (1988). Mentor relationships among women in academe. *Affilia, 3*(1), 34–47.

Rogers, E. (1995). *Diffusion of innovations.* New York: The Free Press. (Original work published 1962)

Rogers, E. M. (2002). Diffusion of preventative innovations. *Addictive Behaviors, 27*(6), 989–993.

Rowley, J. (1999). The good mentor. *Educational Leadership, 56*(8), 20–22.

Schapira, M., Kalet, A., Schwartz, M., & Gerrity, M. (1992). Mentorship in general internal medicine: Investment in our future. *Journal of General Internal Medicine, 7,* 248–251.

Schuster, J. H. (1993). Preparing the next generation of faculty: The graduate school's opportunity. In L. Richlin (Ed.), *Preparing faculty for the new conceptions of scholarship* (pp. 27–38). New Directions for Teaching and Learning, No. 54. San Francisco: Jossey-Bass.

Starcevich, M., & Friend, F. (1999, July). Effective mentoring relationships from the mentee's perspective. *Workforce,* Workforce Extra, 2–3.

Suggs, P. (1986). The mentoring relationship: A professional asset. *The Gerontologist, 26,* 449.

University of Michigan, Rackham School of Graduate Studies. (2006). *How to mentor graduate students: A guide for faculty at a diverse university.* Ann Arbor: Regents of the University of Michigan.

Van Collie, S. (1998). Moving up through mentoring. *Workforce,* *77*(3), 36–42.

Walsh, A., Borkowski, S., & Reuben, E. (1999). Mentoring in health administration: The critical link in executive development/practitioner application. *Journal of Healthcare Management, 44*(4), 269–280.

Watson, S. (1999). A guiding hand. *Computerworld, 33*(26), CW26–CW27.

Wilson, P., Pereira, A., & Valentine, D. (2002). Perceptions of new social work faculty about mentoring experiences. *Journal of Social Work Education, 38,* 317–333.

Woolcock, M., & Narayan, D. (2000). Social capital: Implications for development theory, research, and policy. *World Bank Research Observer, 15*(2), 225–249.

CHAPTER 4

Cultivating a New Generation of Scholars

The Hartford Doctoral Fellows Program

James Lubben, Linda Harootyan, and Carmen Morano

The need for financial support, mentoring, and professional development opportunities for social work doctoral students crosses all substantive areas of research and teaching. The Hartford Doctoral Fellows (HDF) Program is the largest private source of support for social work doctoral students in the United States. The John A. Hartford Foundation of New York City has awarded $12.5 million over 8 years to the HDF program. The initial grant established the dissertation fellowship component of the HDF program in 2000. The HDF Pre-Dissertation Award component was added to the program in 2004. Although the HDF program has focused on the preparation of doctoral graduates with gerontological research and teaching expertise, the program could serve as a useful model for other substantive areas of social work that also seek to promote doctoral education. Key components of the HDF program addressed in this chapter, which could be translated to other areas in social work, include financial support, professional development, cohort building, and academic career guidance. Underlying each of these components is a commitment to recruiting highly qualified students from diverse backgrounds. Factors associated with the success of this program are germane to other initiatives to promote doctoral students' scholarly success and professional development.

The Need for Programmatic Support for Doctoral Students

The shortage of people with a doctorate and a professional degree in social work capable of teaching in programs accredited by the Council on

Social Work Education (CSWE) is widely recognized (Anastas, 2006; Lubben, 2008; Zastrow & Bremner, 2004). The situation is particularly acute with respect to social work faculty with expertise in aging. The basic premise undergirding the HDF program is that tomorrow's social work faculty will be the most efficiently located and effectively cultivated among today's social work doctoral students. Thus, the dearth of properly trained social workers for an aging society cannot be corrected unless the shortage of geriatric social work doctoral students can be overcome.

One of the first steps in making the case for the funding and development of the HDF program was to gather data documenting the shortage of doctoral graduates with expertise in aging. Such an assessment and documentation of the need is the logical initial step in any area seeking to increase doctoral student support. In the years prior to the establishment of the HDF program very few social work doctoral graduates were interested in aging and in pursuing an academic career in gerontological social work. For example, in 1999 only 20 of the more than 250 social work doctoral dissertations throughout the United States focused on older adults. Even more remarkable, in 2007 only 5 of the 1999 gerontological social work graduates held full-time tenure-track appointments in a CSWE-accredited program. The HDF program has offered a significant solution to this crisis through a systematic nationwide effort to recruit, train, and sustain an expanding cadre of talented doctoral students in geriatric social work.

Barriers to Doctoral Study in Geriatric Social Work

A number of barriers hinder doctoral study in social work generally and in geriatric social work in particular. These include inadequate financial support for doctoral education in social work, a limited number of faculty with expertise in geriatrics and gerontology, insufficient mentorship regarding careers in geriatric social work, and constrained opportunities for peer support and learning. The HDF program has been able to develop strategies to address each of these barriers that are also relevant to overcoming obstacles in doctoral student support in other areas.

Limited financial support is most critical. Compared to many other disciplines, doctoral students in social work, regardless of field of study, receive only a modest amount of financial assistance. This deficiency is particularly acute at the dissertation stage. The CSWE (2005) reported that less than one half of social work doctoral students received any financial aid in 2003. Among those who had completed their formal course work, the situation was even worse. Less than one fourth of these more advanced doctoral students received any financial assistance. Given the paucity of support to social work doctoral students generally, it is understandable that the prospect of financial assistance is extremely powerful in reinforcing students' interest in a given area or deflecting them into new areas.

Faculty mentoring for doctoral students is critical to their success. The limited number of faculty mentors for doctoral students interested in conducting research on and teaching about aging has been a problem. Fortunately, the number of doctoral faculty identified with aging in social work programs appears to be increasing, according to data gathered by the Hartford Faculty Scholars (HFS) program staff (see chapter 3). These data, collected from the Group for the Advancement of Doctoral Education (GADE) schools, suggest that over the last 5 years there has been a more than 25% increase in the number of tenure-track faculty with aging expertise, as demonstrated by publications, grants, or other scholarly products. This increase may, in part, result from the success of the HFS program (described in chapter 3). However, these data also demonstrate considerable variability among universities and colleges in this regard. Whereas some GADE programs have made a strong commitment to aging, others are lagging far behind. For example, 26% of GADE doctoral programs have at least five faculty members with expertise in aging. However, 20% of the 71 GADE programs have only one or no faculty member with expertise in aging.

Without strong doctoral faculty mentorship, students are severely at a disadvantage in locating faculty research projects or other appropriate repositories of research on aging that could provide data for their dissertations. Further, the absence of a faculty mentor may impede a student's gaining access to other important campus resources on aging, such as lectures and colloquia, and often inhibits entry to a community of geriatric scholars and the growing number of gerontological social work professional organizations.

Inadequate faculty mentorship presents another significant barrier for doctoral students' making the transition to an academic career. Although some faculty members in doctoral programs offer academic career guidance on an individual basis to students whose research interests coincide with their own, most doctoral programs offer only limited mentoring related to professional development arenas other than research. For example, relatively few doctoral programs provide formal training in teaching, curriculum building, or the development of basic professional skills (e.g., résumé writing, "job talks," and interviewing) for a successful academic career. Doctoral students interested in aging have thus faced the barrier of a limited number of geriatric researchers as mentors in addition to constraints on other types of professional development. Until enough geriatric social work faculty members are based in schools and departments offering doctoral degrees, doctoral students with an interest in aging remain at a competitive disadvantage compared to students in other specialized areas.

Peer support and cohort building are important to career trajectories. For example, much of doctoral education involves learning how to share one's work in progress, as well as how to learn from others working on related topics. The collegiality fostered by such shared learning at the doctoral level can enhance the development of skills essential for successful faculty careers. However, the small number of geriatric social work students in most doctoral programs can limit cohort building and peer support.

The HDF program aims to overcome these barriers and intervene at a critical juncture in a social work doctoral student's career. Support for doctoral students at the dissertation stage is essential because the selection of a dissertation topic tends to delineate career trajectories. For example, a junior professor's first publications are often drawn from his or her dissertation research. These publications, in turn, often open up additional research grant opportunities, generally exploring similar topics and populations.

When the HDF program started, it only offered a dissertation grant component along with professional development opportunities at national conferences (Lubben & Harootyan, 2002). In 2005, a Pre-Dissertation Award (PDA) component was added. The PDA was designed to identify students interested in aging at an early stage of their doctoral studies and assist in nurturing their interest. The primary purpose for the PDA is to expand the size and quality of the applicant pool for the HDF dissertation fellowship component. Additionally, an expanded applicant pool can promote expanded networks of peer support

The HDF Program

The organizing principles undergirding the HDF program are captured by the fundamentals of social capital theory (Halpern, 2005; Kawachi & Berkman, 2000; Lin, 2001). Halpern provides a framework that identifies three basic components of social capital: *network, norms,* and *sanctions.* Halpern also delineates the three key functions of networks as *bonding, bridging,* and *linking.* Accordingly, the HDF program aims to expand membership in the network of geriatric social work scholars through a careful selection process that seeks to identify talent and commitment. The HDF program promulgates norms such as expecting that all Hartford doctoral fellows will pursue an academic career and secure a tenure-track appointment in a CSWE-accredited program. Sanctions come in the form of expression of disappointment or outright disapproval when a Hartford doctoral fellow appears to stray from desired norms, such as not completing his or her dissertation in the 2-year time period. The preconference workshops and various activities at the professional meetings attended by the fellows are designed to increase bonding among the fellows, as well as bridge or link the fellows with other key constituents in the community of gerontology and social work education.

These components of social capital theory are promoted by the Hartford fellows package that includes a dissertation grant, preconference professional development workshops, supplemental academic counseling, cohort building and network development, and marketing and career services.

Dissertation Grants

Doctoral students at the dissertation stage are selected each year through a national request for proposals and a rigorous selection process. Doctoral fellows must conduct a high-quality dissertation research project focused on enhancing the health and well-being of older adults and their caregivers. To date, 78 doctoral students have received the Hartford doctoral fellowship, which consists of a 2-year package of financial support.

The dissertation grant protects 50% of a fellow's time to focus on timely completion of a high-quality doctoral dissertation. The dissertation research must substantively analyze a set of questions dealing with the health and well-being of older adults, their families, and/or their caregivers. Using Halpern's (2005) framework, the dissertation grants facilitate the HDF program's ability to promote and reinforce (sanction) desired norms. The dissertation grant can be used for expenses directly related to the fellow's dissertation research project, including travel to professional conferences to present preliminary findings and a monthly stipend.

The size ($50,000 over 2 years), competitiveness, and prestige of the HDF dissertation grant have increased the status and visibility of geriatric social work doctoral training. The student's university must provide a $10,000 match each year of the dissertation grant. This match requirement is intended to increase the likelihood of the Hartford fellow's being selected as a teaching or research assistant in his or her program. Experience and skills acquired by being a teaching or research assistant are often essential when the fellow applies for a tenure-track faculty position. The match also provides evidence of institutional commitment to the preparation of doctoral students with geriatric expertise.

Professional Development Workshops

Professional development opportunities are a critical component of the HDF program. The fellow's professional growth is strengthened through membership in a select group of social work and gerontological professional organizations and funding to attend the associated national conferences and preconference meetings. Four preconference workshops over the 2-year period focus on enhancing the fellow's scholarly and teaching skills development. Congruent with social capital theory, these workshops facilitate peer support and identification with the field of geriatric social work. Professional organizations in other social work specializations could promote similar types of mentoring and networking at their conferences, even without major funding.

These preconference workshops emphasize strategic academic career planning and refinement of scholarly expertise. The Gerontological Society of America (GSA) and the American Geriatrics Society (AGS) preconference workshops focus primarily on the interdisciplinary nature of gerontology and geriatrics, along with issues around scholarship and teaching in such an environment. More specific skill development topics offered in workshop format include the use of technology in scholarship, sources of research funding, public speaking, research methodologies, and writing for publication. Topics covered at the Society for Social Work and Research (SSWR) preconference workshops encompass teaching techniques, curriculum building, academic leadership, and understanding the academic job market. For fellows attending the CSWE Annual Program Meeting (APM), staff of the CSWE National Center for Gerontological Social Work Education (Gero-Ed Center) offer workshops on strategies for teaching gerontological competencies and extensive gero curricular resources.

Supplemental Academic Career Advising

Addressing the shortage of geriatric social work faculty mentors in many doctoral programs, the HDF program provides counsel and guidance regarding strategic career planning and decision making. As suggested by Halpern's (2005) roster of key functions of social capital, fellows are helped in taking full advantage of the extensive network of gerontologists and social work scholars. This component of the program augments the institutionally based mentoring in gerontology and geriatrics and also facilitates extended professional networking. This programmatic component generally takes place during the professional meetings where preconference institutes are offered. Additional consultation is readily available by e-mail and telephone in between the various preconference institutes. This supplemental advising model is relevant to many social work specialties and other gerontological disciplines, and is particularly germane to initiatives to recruit students from historically disadvantaged populations who may have limited access to specialized mentors in their home institutions.

The primary mentor for fellows is their dissertation chair whose authority in that role is fully respected by HDF staff and supplemental academic career advisors. Supplemental academic career advisors are distinguished geriatric social work faculty members who have also been chairs of doctoral programs at their universities. There is a sense of partnership, with the HDF program director and supplemental academic career advisors' maintaining regular communication with the fellow's dissertation chair, and for cases in which the chair is not an expert in aging, communicating with the doctoral committee member with gerontological expertise. The fellow's dissertation chair and aging/social work expert are invited to attend receptions and similar social gatherings for Hartford fellows at the GSA, AGS, CSWE, and SSWR annual meetings. In these informal settings, these key members of a fellow's dissertation committee meet the HDF faculty and staff and gain an increased appreciation for the HDF program.

Cohort Building and Network Development

Congruent with social capital theory, the program supports cohort building and peer networking among the Hartford fellows, Hartford faculty scholars, and a select group of leading gerontologist and social work educators through in-person meetings, skill building, social events at workshops at annual meetings of major professional organizations, and long-distance communications (e.g., electronic mail lists, e-mail, and conference calls). The doctoral fellows form strong bonds with one another that continue to provide peer support and counseling beyond the 2-year period of their fellowship. Further, the doctoral fellows gain increased self-confidence to mingle with the national leaders in gerontology and social work. Contacts generated by networking activities with faculty scholars and other leaders have directly led to academic career opportunities. The centrality of peer support networks to the HDF model is salient in other areas of doctoral specialization and does not necessarily require external funding. Designing opportunities for doctoral students to meet, share their research, and learn from one another at professional conferences is a professional development strategy transferrable to a wide range of social work research areas as well as other geriatric disciplines.

Marketing and Placement Services

To enhance the fellow's placement in the best possible faculty position, a number of strategies are employed. Hartford doctoral fellows benefit from special training at preconference institutes and from the Hartford academic career advisors regarding the nuances of the academic job market. Fellows also receive training on how to promote their candidacy for a faculty appointment and successfully compete in the academic job market and launch their careers. For example, they participate in workshops on how to develop a high-quality curriculum vitae and hone academic job-interviewing and contract negotiation skills.

To promote hiring Hartford doctoral fellows, a compact disc packet containing the curriculum vitae of fellows in the job market is distributed annually to all deans and directors of all schools and departments of social work in the United States. In addition, the packet is sent to all members of GADE. Fellows are sponsored to attend the CSWE APM in the year they choose to enter the academic job market. Because the CSWE APM is the primary venue for preliminary interviews for open faculty positions, it is essential that fellows seeking faculty appointments attend the APM to make the first cut of applicants deserving further consideration.

The HDF Program Selection Process

Eligibility for the Hartford Doctoral Fellowship

The eligibility criteria for a Hartford doctoral fellowship reflect traits deemed most likely to facilitate expanding the number of social work faculty dedicated to aging. These criteria are briefly reviewed here because of their relevance to providing doctoral student support in other substantive areas in social work and other geriatric disciplines. The HDF program targets students enrolled in full-time doctoral programs in the United States who are committed to seeking full-time faculty positions in programs accredited by the CSWE. The HDF applicant's campus dissertation committee must have approved the dissertation proposal prior to the application receipt date. One member of the applicant's doctoral committee, preferably the chair, must have expertise in gerontological research relevant to the proposed dissertation research project. The expert in aging monitors the doctoral fellow's progress through the dissertation and ensures appropriate development of gerontological research knowledge and skills.

Recruitment

As noted in chapter 1, geriatric social workers are less diverse in racial and ethnic backgrounds than the current older population they serve and the U.S. civilian population (Whitaker, Weismiller, & Clark, 2006). This gap between the cultural and ethnic background of the workforce and those being served will grow with the projected increased diversity of elders by 2030. Similarly, there is a need to attract other groups with lower levels of representation among geriatric social workers who currently tend to be older and include more women than social workers serving other age groups.

Given these demographic patterns, the HDF program is committed to reaching doctoral applicants from underserved populations as well as those from a wide range of states and types of institutions. Of the cohorts to date, the fellows have come from 22 states, and 34 universities are represented. More than one fourth of them are members of underrepresented racial and ethnic groups. More specifically, 18% are from Asian-Pacific Islander, 4% from African American, 3% from Latino/Latina, and 1% from Native American backgrounds. Approximately one fifth of the fellows are male.

Selection Procedures

Hartford doctoral fellows are selected through a nationally competitive process that places priority on such criteria as an applicant's commitment to a career in academics and in geriatrics, scholarly merits of the application, and evidence of the institution's support of the applicant. All applicants receive extensive comments from expert reviewers and are encouraged to reapply if their proposal does not meet the program's high standards.

When the HDF program was initiated, applicants did not have to have an approved dissertation proposal but merely had to be within 8 months of approval at the time of their application. These broad eligibility criteria resulted in an extremely diverse pool of applicants at various stages of their dissertation research, complicating the selection process as well as the completion trajectories. Accordingly, this policy was changed so that now all applicants must have their dissertation proposals approved prior to the application receipt date.

Another early lesson learned was that a single, annual application deadline did not work well for the doctoral students we were trying to attract. Some students were not quite far enough along with their dissertation proposal to meet the deadline, but by the following year they were too far along. This problem was quickly addressed by adopting two deadlines a year, February and August, for each cohort selected. The National Program Advisory Committee also welcomed the prospect of providing promising applicants with extensive feedback on their proposals and encouraging them to revise and resubmit in the next selection cycle. This was not possible with only one selection cycle a year.

Accomplishments of the HDF Program

The success of the HDF program is particularly apparent when the academic career status of Harford doctoral fellows in Cohort 1(selected in 2001) is contrasted with those individuals who were not selected. Among the 17 applicants in Cohort 1, 7 were chosen to become Hartford doctoral fellows. One applicant not selected for Cohort 1 reapplied and was subsequently selected for Cohort 2 in 2002. Only 3 of the 9 applicants in 2001 who were not selected for a fellowship presently hold tenure-track faculty appointments. By contrast, all 7 Cohort 1 fellows hold tenure-track appointments in highly ranked social work programs.

Table 4.1 lists the accomplishments of Hartford doctoral fellows who were selected from 2001 to 2005 and compares their early-career accomplishments with those of HDF program applicants during that period who were not chosen for a fellowship. Overall both groups have been highly successful in completing their dissertations. However, the Hartford doctoral fellows are much more likely to hold a tenure-track faculty appointment (65% vs. 39%). Hartford fellows are almost twice

Table 4.1

CAREER ACCOMPLISHMENTS OF DOCTORAL FELLOWS FROM COHORTS 1–5

Cohorts 1–5	HDF[a] (%)	Non-HDF[b] (%)
Completed dissertation	95	86
Hold tenure-track appointment	65	39
Hold faculty appointment in a CSWE-accredited program	62	36
Hold faculty appointment in GADE doctoral program	59	11
Hold SW faculty appointment in a research university (Carnegie Classification)	51	14
Selected as a Hartford Faculty Scholar	38	0

Note. [a]HDF: Hartford doctoral fellows; N=37.
[b]Non-HDF: Applicants not accepted into the HDF program; N=28.

as likely to have a full-time faculty appointment in a CSWE-accredited program as their non-HDF counterparts (62% vs. 36%). Even more dramatic, the Hartford doctoral fellows are more apt to hold a faculty appointment in a research university in the Carnegie Foundation for the Advancement of Teaching (2008) classification schema (51% vs. 14%). Similarly, Hartford doctoral fellows are more than five times more likely than their nonfellow counterparts to have an appointment in a university offering a doctoral program in social work. Fourteen Hartford fellows have been selected as Hartford faculty scholars from highly competitive applicant pools, whereas none of those who were not selected for a Hartford doctoral fellowship from 2001 to 2005 have become scholars.

Hartford fellows have demonstrated exceptional leadership skills, suggesting that this approach to doctoral support promotes capacity building. Some fellows have received awards for their dissertation research and teaching from their home universities and professional associations. The momentum established in the first 7 years of the HDF program continues to grow, along with increased competition for the funding.

Lessons Learned from the HDF Program

One lesson learned, which is transferrable to other social work research areas and other disciplines, is the centrality of faculty mentorship for recruiting and cultivating a doctoral student's interest in aging. Yet, most faculty and universities do not have the resources required to cover all the bases for successfully launching students' academic careers in geriatric social work. Thus, much of the HDF program is designed to augment what students receive from their home institution but not to take over the central mentoring role of their dissertation chair. For example, many of the workshops dealing with demystifying the academic job market and improving one's communication skills are in response to previous cohorts suggesting that their institutions had not adequately provided such training for them.

Another early lesson involved marketing the HDF program to recruit applicants. Initially the communications strategy for promoting the program was largely directed toward social work education administrators, notably deans and directors, as well as chairs of social work doctoral programs. It quickly became apparent that this audience was not the most effective vehicle for reaching doctoral students. The communication strategy was revamped to focus on reaching students more directly. The strongest example of this recruitment approach is the PDA, described on p. 92 in this chapter. Another example is scheduling recruitment breakfasts at key conferences to directly reach doctoral students and secure their contact information. Similarly, the program made increased use of faculty members of the Association for Gerontology in Education in Social Work (AGESW), a national organization of individuals committed to gerontological social work, to identify potential students with an interest in aging and to provide a means for the HDF program staff to contact those students. The program has also exploited the growing number of computer electronic mailing lists reaching doctoral students and has monitored Web pages at GADE universities to make sure they link to the HDF Web site. The HDF program director and members of the HDF's National Program Advisory Committee have made strategic campus visits speaking directly to gatherings of students about the HDF program. Congruous with social capital theory, Hartford faculty scholars and doctoral fellows from earlier cohorts have also been mobilized to assist in recruiting new cohorts of doctoral fellows. In all these recruitment efforts, attention is given to increasing the diversity of the pool of applicants to the HDF program.

Of relevance to all social work doctoral initiatives is the lesson learned regarding the great heterogeneity of doctoral programs in social work (Lubben, 2008). Although all are committed to the preparation of social work scholars, the approach to acquiring such skills varies considerably. Given the strong emphasis on a high-quality dissertation research proposal, applicants from research-intensive universities appear to have a distinct advantage in the application process for a Hartford doctoral fellowship. However, this may merely reflect some self-deselection, as one of the selection criteria is a commitment to seeking a full-time faculty appointment, which favors those who entered doctoral programs with a strong research emphasis.

Perhaps the greatest unanticipated lesson learned over the years has been the extent of student interest in aging. Clearly the interest has proven to be greater than was first thought because of the growing number of applications for the fellowship and the strong interest in the PDA. This suggests that many students entering doctoral programs in the past may have been interested in aging but found themselves shifting to other research areas because of lack of funding and academic mentoring support at their institutions. Accordingly, the necessity to continue investing in outreach is paramount. Each doctoral student in a new cohort who expresses an interest in aging must be identified and provided with a nurturing place to cultivate that interest.

The Hartford PDA

The PDA is for students enrolled in a doctoral program in the United States who have not yet completed their dissertation proposal. As noted earlier, this is a primary means to expand the applicant pool for the fellowship. Activities that are a key part of the PDA build upon Halpern's (2005) framework for social capital theory. The objectives of the program are to

1. expose more doctoral students to gerontological social work research,
2. expand the number of dissertations that seek to improve the health and well-being of older people and their families,
3. enhance the grant-writing skills of participants, and
4. increase the number of qualified applicants to the HDF program.

To achieve these goals, the PDA provides funding for 2 years, enabling awardees to attend preconference workshops at the GSA's Annual Scientific Meeting where activities are designed to facilitate bonding among the award winners as well as with HDF faculty and staff. The PDA also includes membership in the GSA and the AGESW, which illustrates bridging and linking activities suggested by Halpern's (2005) framework. In addition to the full-day preconference workshop at GSA, award winners are required to attend daily breakfast meetings that address a substantive topic each day, as well as other GSWI-related events throughout the GSA conference. During the various networking events, the PDA recipients are introduced to participants in the GSWI, particularly the HDF and HFS programs.

Each year 20 students at an early stage of their doctoral program are selected for a PDA. In between the face-to-face meetings at GSA, HDF program staff maintains contact with award winners through e-mails and other forms of communication. The following are the major components of the HDF PDA.

Travel Grants

PDA recipients are brought to the GSA meeting to foster their interest in aging and thereby ultimately enhance the pool of applicants for the HDF program. Under the current grant arrangements, these same 20 students meet again the following year at GSA to further reinforce their interest in conducting dissertation research on aging. At both meetings, the PDA winners have an opportunity to meet current and past Hartford doctoral fellows and Hartford faculty scholars, as well as other gerontological social work leaders, and to learn more about social work research on aging.

Grant Writing and Dissertation Proposal Seminars

PDA recipients attend a full day of seminars conducted in collaboration with AGESW to help them develop grant-writing skills and research proposals so they will be highly competitive for a Hartford doctoral fellowship. For example, workshop sessions include such topics as "Using National Data Sets for a Dissertation," "The Role of Theory and Conceptual Frameworks," and "What Reviewers Look for in Hartford Doctoral Fellows' Applications."

Cohort Building and Network Development

Similar to the HDF dissertation program, the preconference PDA workshops focus on building a sense of community and support and on nurturing PDA recipients' interest in gerontology and geriatrics. Accordingly, it has proven important to foster mentoring relationships between PDA winners and doctoral fellows, faculty scholars, and members of AGESW. Congruous with social capital theory, these opportunities for formal and informal networking help students develop personal connections to scholars who share common research and teaching interests and they reinforce new norms and expectations regarding dissertation topics and career aspirations.

Accomplishments of the Hartford PDA Component

From the standpoint of identifying potential talent and fostering interest in geriatric social work, the PDA has been very successful and is a recruitment approach transferrable to other research areas of doctoral education. This new component of the HDF program partially accounts for the increase in the number and quality of applications for the Hartford doctoral fellowship. The 80 students who have received PDAs represent 24 states and 43 universities, demonstrating additional evidence of the program's ability to recruit doctoral students throughout the United States. As with the Hartford doctoral fellows, more than one fourth of the PDAs are members of underrepresented racial and ethnic groups. More specifically, 11% are from Asian-Pacific Islander, 10% from African American, 6% from Latino/Latina, and 1% from Native American backgrounds. Approximately one fifth of the PDAs are male.

The PDA component of the HDF program received an impressive 56 applications in its 1st year. In subsequent years the number of applicants for the PDA has averaged 34. Although only 20 applicants can be funded, the HDF program staff encourages the other applicants to continue to nurture their interest in aging and perhaps to reapply for the PDA or even apply directly for a Hartford doctoral fellowship if they are close to having an approved dissertation proposal. It is also noteworthy that many of the sponsors of PDA applicants are Hartford faculty scholars. In some cases, even former doctoral fellows have sponsored successful applicants.

The PDA component has already succeeded in exposing more students to geriatric and gerontological social work research and in increasing interest in the HDF program. In 2006, the first full year after the PDA component was initiated, 27 people applied for the Hartford doctoral fellowship, representing a 75% increase in applications over the previous year. Two thirds of the applicants for the HDF dissertation fellowship in 2007 had been PDA recipients. Already 13 recipients from Cohort 1 have successfully competed to become Hartford doctoral fellows, and 6 are expected to apply in the near future. Only 1 student in the first PDA cohort has decided not to pursue a dissertation in aging.

Lessons Learned from the PDA Program

Among the lessons learned from the first 3 years of the PDA component is the importance of institutional support to the success of the PDA recipients. Although all PDA applications include a letter of support from an institutional sponsor, the amount of institutional support and the presence of current or former Hartford doctoral fellows or Hartford faculty scholars in the home institution are critical to nurturing the student/participant's interest in a career as a gerontological social work researcher/educator. The review committee for the PDA gives considerable weight to the sponsor's commitment to the student and to the field of aging.

Summary

It is widely recognized that social workers play a critical role in health care for older people. Unfortunately, there is also a well-documented critical shortage of trained geriatric social work practitioners and the faculty needed to prepare future generations of them. Doctoral training is a critical juncture for addressing this problem. Today's doctoral students are tomorrow's social work faculty who will undertake research necessary to define best practice models and who will train the next generation of social work practitioners. The number of doctoral graduates with expertise in aging remains inadequate for the anticipated demand for new geriatric social work faculty. The dearth of properly trained social workers, including those from historically underserved populations, for an aging society cannot be corrected unless this shortage of geriatric social work doctoral students can be overcome.

The HDF program offers a significant solution to this crisis through a systematic, nationwide effort that recruits, trains, and sustains a cadre of talented doctoral students in geriatric social work who also represent culturally diverse backgrounds. The PDA component has enabled the HDF program to identify doctoral students early in their doctoral programs so their budding interest in aging can be nurtured and reinforced. The fellows program has fostered an intellectually stimulating, mutually supportive network of faculty and students involved in geriatric social work doctoral research and training. Partially because of the HDF program, the number of social work dissertations in gerontology has risen, as has the number of recent graduates seeking full-time social work faculty appointments.

The HDF program has begun the important task of cultivating the next generation of geriatric social work faculty who will become teachers, role models, and mentors for future generations of social workers caring for older people and their families. These future faculty leaders will add gerontological strength to social work programs, a strength needed to attract even more students at undergraduate and graduate levels to careers in geriatric research and practice. Early signs of success in the HDF program offer promise that social work now has expanded its capacity to contribute to improved health and well-being among older adults and their families in our rapidly aging society.

The HDF also illustrates how the fundamentals of social capital theory can be employed to promote doctoral education and train the next generation of social work faculty. For example, both the HDF and PDA programs fostered the development of strategic networks of gerontological scholars to empower doctoral students to *bond, bridge, and link* with leaders in the field of gerontological social work. Furthermore, the two programs fostered the *norm* among the select group of doctoral students that securing a full-time faculty appointment in a CSWE accredited program is most highly desired. This norm was reinforced through an array of program components. Furthermore, the HDF and PDA programs also sought to keep students on track with this career objective and employed various means to *sanction* those who strayed. The HDF program is a social capital investment in the profession through doctoral education. Clearly, this commitment along with the key components of the HDF program can be readily adapted to promote doctoral education in other facets of social work.

References

Anastas, J. W. (2006). Employment opportunities in social work education: A study of jobs for doctoral graduates. *Journal of Social Work Education, 42,* 195–209.

Carnegie Foundation for the Advancement of Teaching. (2008). *The Carnegie classification of institutions of higher education.* Retrieved December 1, 2008, from http://www.carnegiefoundation.org/classifications/index.asp

Council on Social Work Education. (2005). *Statistics on social work education in the United States: 2003.* Alexandria, VA: Author.

Halpern, D. (2005). *Social capital.* Cambridge, UK: Polity Press.

Kawachi, I., & Berkman, L. (2000). Social cohesion, social capital, and health. In L. Berkman & I. Kawachi (Eds.), *Social epidemiology* (pp. 174–190). New York: Oxford University Press.

Lin, N, (2001). Building a network theory of social capital. In N. Lin, K. Cook, & R. S. Burt (Eds.), *Social capital* (pp. 3–29). Hawthorne, NY: Aldine de Gruyter.

Lubben, J. E. (2008). Social work education: Doctoral. In T. Mizrahi & L. E. Davis (Eds.), *Encyclopedia of social work* (20th ed., pp. 114–117). New York: Oxford University Press.

Lubben, J. E., & Harootyan, L. K. (2002). Strengthening geriatric social work through a doctoral fellowship program. *Journal of Gerontological Social Work, 39*, 145–156.

Whitaker, T., Weismiller, T., & Clark, E. (2006). *Assuring the sufficiency of a frontline workforce: A national study of licensed social workers.* Retrieved January 25, 2008, from http://workforce.socialworkers.org/studies/aging/aging.pdf

Zastrow, C., & Bremner, J. (2004). Social work education responds to the shortage of persons with both a doctorate and a professional social work degree. *Journal of Social Work Education, 40*, 351–358.

CHAPTER 5

A Planned Change Model

Council of Social Work Education's Curricular and Programmatic Development Programs

Nancy R. Hooyman and Sadhna Diwan

Understanding the challenges and rewards of a successful, innovative transformation of a classroom curriculum has enormous importance for any specialty area in social work or any discipline. The practice-driven imperative focused on client service that has always been at the heart of social work compels social work educators toward periodic curricular renewal and advancements. Vital lessons have been learned related to curricular and programmatic change through the three Council on Social Work Education (CSWE) curricular development initiatives funded by the John A. Hartford Foundation of New York City that have concentrated on classroom curriculum. These three programs share the goal to promote the gerontological competence of all graduates from BSW and MSW social work programs nationwide.

First, the CSWE Strengthening Aging and Gerontology in Social Work Education (SAGE-SW; CSWE SAGE-SW, 2001) emphasized faculty development, providing individual faculty with extensive gero teaching resources to infuse in their classes. But all too often the participating faculty members were not able to obtain the support of their colleagues to implement such resources in their courses, leaving the gero faculty members carrying the bulk of the responsibility for teaching gero competencies.

Subsequently, the CSWE Geriatric Enrichment in Social Work Education Project (GeroRich) emphasized programmatic development as central to curricular change and faculty preparation by supporting participating schools and departments through the process of planning, implementing, and evaluating the infusion of gero content in foundation curriculum. The GeroRich initiative recognized the importance of acquiring key stakeholders' support and changing the organizational culture (e.g., a program's mission and goals, curriculum decision-making structure, recruitment materials, and library and media holdings) to build programmatic gero capacity beyond individual faculty members (Hooyman, 2006; Hooyman & St. Peter, 2006).

Most recently, the CSWE National Center for Gerontological Social Work Education (Gero-Ed Center) has built upon what has been learned through the foundation infusion strategy of GeroRich. Through the two cycles of the center's Curriculum Development Institute (CDI) program, a greater emphasis has been placed on working with social work schools and departments to set outcome-based goals and select and measure gero competencies and content for each area of foundation curriculum. Based on feedback from participants in the two other curricular development initiatives, greater attention has also been given to strategic outreach to students and faculty from historically underserved populations. The success of targeted recruitment is described in chapter 1.

In addition to the CDI program, the Gero-Ed Center encompasses a range of initiatives to recruit students to gerontological social work: It works with foundation textbook authors to infuse gero content; designs gero-specific curricular structures such as concentrations, minors, or certificates; and creates gero-infused specialized classroom content, particularly by embedding gero competencies in the areas of health, mental health, and substance use through the Master's Advanced Curriculum (MAC) project. All these curricular development programs have, to varying degrees, used a planned change approach built upon a model for diffusion of innovations and have intensely recruited among programs nationwide to ensure the participation of faculty from culturally diverse backgrounds.

This chapter begins with the rationale for and an overview of the planned change theory used for the infusion of gerontological competencies in the curriculum and the organizational culture. Within the framework of the planned change model, strategies and guidelines related to the infusion of gero competencies in the foundation curriculum are first presented, followed by the approach of embedding aging in the advanced practice areas of mental health, health, and substance use. The lessons learned related to curricular and programmatic change that are identified in this chapter are germane to faculty and academic administrators seeking to embed content on populations other than older adults and in fields of practice other than aging, and are salient in other geriatric disciplines. Similarly, the ways in which key stakeholders (faculty, academic administrators, students, practitioners, and, to some extent, older adults) became engaged in the Hartford-funded curriculum development initiatives are relevant to all social work areas of specialization that seek to strengthen programmatic capacity and leadership capability. Last, the competency approach of the CSWE foundation and advanced curriculum development initiatives is particularly germane to all programs, given the CSWE (2008) Educational Policy and Accreditation Standards (EPAS) competency-based approach to education.

An Infusion Approach Within the Curriculum

The curricular change initiatives of CSWE SAGE-SW, GeroRich, and the Gero-Ed Center programs emphasized an infusion approach rather than gero specialization to ensure that all social work graduates have foundation gerontological competencies (Damron-Rodriguez & Lubben, 1997; Hooyman, 2006; Hooyman & St. Peter, 2006; Hooyman & Tompkins, 2005; Kropf, 1996; Meredith & Watt, 1994; Watt & Meredith, 1995). More recently, the MAC Project has aimed to infuse gerontological competencies in three areas of advanced specialization—health, mental health, and substance use—which reach substantially more students than age-specific curricular structures, such as gerontology concentrations or specializations. The impetus for the goal of reaching all students is derived from workforce data, described in chapter 1, which consistently document that the majority of social workers work in some capacity with older adults and their families, regardless of the practice setting (Berkman, Silverstone, Simmons, Volland, & Howe, 2001; Damron-Rodriguez & Lubben; Peterson & Wendt, 1990; Whitaker, Weismiller, & Clark, 2006). Congruous with the CSWE (2008) EPAS, programs are to reflect their context in their curriculum, with the potential to identify demographic and workforce needs as critical components of the larger external environment and where students need more training.

The CSWE curriculum development programs have emphasized a foundation rather than a gero-specialized approach for the following reasons. A gero-specialized curricular development approach, while providing advanced competencies and expanded depth and specificity of learning, typically reaches only those students who self-select gerontology as their particular specialized area. Indeed, even if more programs had the fiscal and teaching resources and student demand to offer specialized content in aging, this would not meet the growing need for social workers with basic gerontological competencies who interact with older adults in nonaging-focused settings (Damron-Rodriguez & Lubben, 1997; Rosen & Zlotnik, 2001). Thus, the additional infusion of advanced competencies in specializations other than gerontology is needed, especially in advanced areas such as health and mental health that serve large numbers of older adults and attract more students than do aging specializations (Scharlach, Damron-Rodriguez, Robinson, & Feldman, 2000). On the other hand, programs that successfully infuse competencies in their required foundation curriculum and nonaging advanced curriculum will presumably be well positioned to develop some level of specialization in gerontology through such endeavors as stand-alone courses, minors, certificates, and concentrations.

An infusion approach operationally means that gerontological competencies, content, and teaching resources are embedded in (i.e., woven into) every aspect of required courses at the foundation or nongero advanced level: goals and objectives, readings, lectures, class discussions and exercises, assignments, audiovisual resources, and criteria for evaluating student outcomes (Bogolub, 1998; Cummings & Kropf, 2000; Rosen, Zlotnik, & Singer, 2002). Faculty participants are also expected to include content related to the growing diversity of older adults in terms of race/ethnicity, gender, social class, functional ability, and sexual orientation. When gerontological competencies are inextricable from the course structure and requirements, such content is more likely to be sustained and institutionalized across time and to reach the broad student population than are age-specific offerings that depend on student demand and extra teaching and fiscal resources (Hooyman, 2006; Hooyman & St. Peter, 2006).

Implementing an infusion approach requires overcoming the resisting forces that often characterize curricular change efforts (Lewin, 1947, 1957). Regardless of the field of practice or population served, faculty may oppose an infusion approach if they perceive it as "adding one more thing" and requiring giving up content they already teach (Damron-Rodriguez, Villa,

Tseng, & Lubben, 1997; Lubben, Damron-Rodriguez, & Beck, 1992; Olson, 2002). Although social work faculty members often contend that the curriculum "bucket" is already full, an infusion approach can "stir the bucket in new ways" as a way to promote faculty motivation to change. It can creatively reconfigure required course content by building intersections with aging and other substantive areas. For example, Human Behavior and Social Environment courses, which typically include aging in the last class sessions, can begin with old age rather than infancy by tracing the older adult across the life span and examining how earlier life experiences affect well-being in old age (Joyner & DeHope, 2007). Child welfare curricula can make explicit the needs of the growing number of grandparents who are the primary caregivers for their grandchildren (Johnson-Dalzine, 2007). Courses on cultural diversity can articulate the intersections of age, race, gender, functional ability, spirituality, and sexual orientation with health and economic disparities across the life course as an organizing course construct (Owens-Kane, 2007). This approach to identifying intersections with existing course content helps ensure that gerontological content is not just added on with a reading or two, mentioned once in the course description, or taught in the last class session or by a guest lecturer (Kropf, 1996, 2002). With an infused curriculum, issues of aging and older adults become normative or business as usual for the required curriculum (Hooyman, 2006). This strategy of finding ways to enrich and strengthen curricula by building intersections across fields of practice or populations served and by attending to diversity issues is also germane to curricular change in other substantive areas.

The Planned Change Model of Curricular and Organizational Change

As noted in chapter 3, several of the GSWI programs have drawn upon the diffusion of innovation theory (Rogers, 1962, 1995, 2002). In terms of the CSWE curricular development programs, it was assumed that faculty, academic administrators, and other key stakeholders would be more receptive and motivated to infuse gerontological competencies in their curriculum—in foundation and advanced nongero courses—if the gero-enriched curriculum can be shown to be better than what exists (Dorfman & Murty, 2005). As noted above, the primary value of a gero-infused curriculum is to ensure that social work graduates are prepared for demographic and workforce needs. To be adopted, innovations must be compatible with values, experiences, and needs of key stakeholders, and they must not be difficult to understand or to use (Dearing, 2008; Gira, Kessler, & Poertner, 2004). To increase the probability that key stakeholders would be receptive to and adopt the innovation of a gero competency-based infusion approach to curriculum change, GeroRich and the Gero-Ed Center systematically used a planned change model.

The planned change model developed by the GeroRich program encompasses diffusion of innovation theories but also builds on the force-field analysis and three-step change theory of Lewin (1947, 1957) and the process of change theory of Lippitt, Watson, and Westley (1958). These early theorists of organizational change emphasized the benefits of changing individuals who are formed into a group rather than modifying individuals separately, and thus they emphasized the importance of group decision making. In other words, drawing upon systems theory, they viewed people as the hub of all organizational changes; curriculum and programmatic changes require individuals to change.

According to Lewin (1947, 1957), planned change is a process that occurs by adding forces in the desired direction or by diminishing opposing forces. Change within organizations will occur when the combined strength of one force is greater than the combined strength of an opposing set of forces (Robbins, 2003). The change process involves disequilibrium—learning something new as well as discontinuing current attitudes, behaviors, or organizational practices—through which driving forces overcome restraining ones. Resistance to change is found even when the goals of change are highly desirable. To overcome resistance to change, strategies are needed to

1. *Unfreeze* the status quo.
2. *Move* to a new level.
3. *Refreeze* at the new level.

Central to the third phase—the refreezing level—are strategies, including policies and procedures, to reinforce new behaviors, attitudes, and organizational practices and to ensure sustainability (Burnes, 2004; Cummings & Worley, 2001; Kritsonis, 2004–05; Lewin, 1947, 1957).

Lippitt et al. (1958) extended Lewin's three-step change approach by developing a seven-step theory that focuses more on the change agent's role and responsibility than on the evolution of the change itself. The seven phases are as follows:

1. Diagnose the need.
2. Assess the motivation and capacity for change.
3. Assess the resources and motivation of the change agent.
4. Choose progressive change objects and develop appropriate action steps and strategies.
5. Clarify the role of the change agent for all parties involved.
6. Maintain the change.
7. Withdraw gradually from the change agent role as the change becomes part of the organizational culture.

Throughout the seven phases, the change agent's self-efficacy (e.g., having the confidence in the ability to take action and persist in the action) is central to the success of the change. Similar to Rogers' (1962, 1995) diffusion of innovations, Lewin (1947, 1957) and Lippitt et al. (1958) emphasized that changes are more likely to be sustained if they are adopted by subparts of the system immediately affected. Both of these theories of planned change have been critiqued as too rational and goal oriented and as failing to recognize the importance of personal factors such as stakeholders' feelings and experiences (Kritsonis, 2004–05; Robbins, 2003). Nevertheless, they remain useful models for educational and organizational change.

The planned change model to modify curriculum and programmatic structure developed by the GeroRich Program and Gero-Ed Center draws upon Lewin's (1947, 1957) concepts of unfreezing, moving/changing, and refreezing, and recognizes the centrality of the change agent's vision and role. However, it modifies Lippitt and colleagues' (1958) seven phases of planned change and takes account of personal factors that can affect change (Kritsonis, 2004–05; Robbins, 2003). The Gero-Ed Center model encompasses the following phases:

1. Planning, which includes conducting a curricular and organizational analysis and environmental scan, and selecting competencies and outcome measures of competency attainment (e.g., Lewin's unfreezing and Lippitt and colleagues' phases of diagnosis, assessing the motivation and capacity for change and identifying sources of support and resistance to change).
2. Implementation or action steps, beginning with strategies to gain the support of key stakeholders for the change—academic administrators, faculty, students, and community

partners (e.g., Lewin's moving and Lippitt and colleagues' choosing action steps and strategies; acquiring support for the change agent).

3. Evaluation or measurement of outcomes, which is not made explicit in Lewin or Lippitt and colleagues' theories of change.

4. Sustainability or institutionalization of curricular and programmatic changes (e.g., Lewin's third phase of refreezing and Lippitt and colleagues' stage of maintaining the change and the withdrawal of the change agent as the desired change becomes institutionalized as part of the organizational culture).

The process of planned change in the CSWE curricular development projects was found to be similar regardless of program size (small/large), rural or urban location, and degree level (undergraduate/graduate), although specific strategies to engage key stakeholders, overcome resistance, and institutionalize the change did vary by the program's organizational culture and structure (Hooyman, 2006; Reinardy & Zoff, 2006). This chapter derives lessons learned from phases 1–3—planning, implementation, and evaluation—that are transferrable to curricular and organizational change in other areas, whereas chapter 9 focuses on phase 4, strategies for sustainability.

Foundation Curriculum

The application of the planned change model to the foundation curriculum and programmatic structure is first described, followed by a discussion of its relevance to embedding gerontological competencies in the advanced or specialized areas of health, mental health, and substance use. In both CSWE change initiatives, the change agent, who had applied for the funding, almost certainly had the motivation and self-efficacy to change, but the extent of resources to plan, implement, and sustain the change varied with the degree of support from academic administrators and other key stakeholders in the change agent's institution.

The Planning Phase

A strategic and carefully planned curricular and organizational change process is the framework for ensuring the sustainability of changes made. The planning phase begins with documenting the need for change through analyses of the curriculum and the social work program's organizational structure—the *implicit curriculum* or larger educational environment as defined by the EPAS (CSWE, 2008). A careful curricular analysis or diagnosis forms the basis for unfreezing the existing curriculum and deciding which foundation classroom and field courses to target first. Course audits and content analyses are ways to review the competencies, content, and teaching resources in each course specific to a particular curricular area, point to substantive gaps, and assess stakeholders' motivation and capacity for change.

Although analyses of course syllabi is the first step, what is stated on a syllabus or course outline may not reflect what is actually taught in the classroom, which points to the need for a multifaceted curricular analysis. Input from students, faculty, practitioners, and other community stakeholders through advisory boards, focus groups, written or online surveys, one-on-one interviews, or small-group meetings can supplement course syllabi review (Kolomer, Lewinson, Kropf, & Wilks, 2007; Lee & Waites, 2006). The effectiveness of different strategies to obtain key constituencies' input varies by program size and whether ongoing mechanisms for such feedback already exist (e.g., meetings of lead instructors for foundation courses, annual exit surveys of students). However, input and feedback from these constituencies are likely to enhance their ownership of the process of infusion, which appears to be essential to the maintenance or sustainability of the changes made (Kritsonis, 2004–05; Lippitt et al., 1958; Robbins, 2003).

The diagnostic phase also includes an organizational analysis of the implicit curriculum that can be conducted simultaneously with a curricular analysis; this programmatic level diagnosis aims to determine the extent to which substantive issues are institutionalized or absent in social work programs and to identify structural factors that affect a program's readiness to change by acting as supports or obstacles (e.g., capacity to unfreeze from what exists) to the infusion of new course content. The EPAS (CSWE, 2008) defines the implicit curriculum as the educational environment in which the explicit formal curriculum is offered, including policies and procedures and governance structures to provide a "culture of human interchange, the spirit of inquiry, and the support for difference and diversity" (CSWE, p. 10). This curriculum is considered as important as the explicit curriculum in shaping the professional character and competence of the program's graduates.

Programmatic areas analyzed include mission statements, department policies, and governance documents; print and electronic materials that describe the mission and goals (e.g., course catalogs, recruitment brochures, orientation handouts, Web sites, and articles in program newsletters or alumni magazines); library and audiovisual holdings; artwork and other representations in the building (e.g., bulletin boards, posters, book displays); formal events (e.g., student recruitment sessions, orientations, annual lectures); student clubs; and faculty recruitment priorities and fund-raising initiatives (e.g., position descriptions to recruit faculty, development brochures, case statements, proposals to potential donors). Embedding gerontology in the overall organizational structure—refreezing the change through organizational practices and policies—is central to institutionalizing the changes made, thus ensuring their continuation (Meredith & Watt, 1994; Reinardy & Zoff, 2006; Watt, 1996; Watt & Meredith, 1995).

An organizational analysis also identifies structural factors that are barriers to or supports for programmatic change, similar to Lewin's (1947; 1957) approach of reducing disequilibrium by adding forces in the desired direction or diminishing restraining forces. These structural variables include(a) key stakeholders (faculty, academic administrators, community practitioners, students, and others) who may support or resist curricular change and (b) programmatic factors, such as how curriculum decisions are made and institutionalized in a program. Both sets of structural supports or barriers must be addressed to sustain the infusion of gerontology in the curriculum and in the social work program as a whole. Failure to engage in an organizational change process may explain, in part, why prior gerontological curriculum development initiatives in the 1970s and 1980s were not sustained, despite the quality and potential usefulness of the teaching resources developed by such projects. Simply providing faculty with curricular materials fails to address numerous resistant forces, such as faculty's negative attitudes about aging, competing teaching interests, lack of expertise on how to use gero teaching resources, and limited incentives for changing one's teaching (Hooyman & St. Peter, 2006; Richardson, 1999; Rosen et al., 2002; Schneider, 1984; Schneider, Decker, Freeman, & Syran, 1984).

As noted above, diagnosing key stakeholders' extent of support for and resistance to change is congruous with the identification of the implicit curriculum. The concept of implicit curriculum also gives more weight to environmental influences and personal factors than is the case with Lewin or Lippitt's theories of change (Kritsonis, 2004–05; Robbins, 2003). Obtaining faculty support is the highest priority. Because curriculum is the domain of the faculty, curricular change will not succeed without faculty ownership (Hooyman & St. Peter, 2006; Lewin, 1947, 1957; Reinardy & Zoff, 2006). Sources of resistance among faculty typically include the tenure and university reward systems; competing demands on faculty time and priorities among research, teaching, and service; constrained curricular space; and norms of academic freedom. In addition, personal factors such as an individual's predisposition toward change, mistrust and fear of the unknown, self-interest, habit, personality conflicts, and fear of failure may intensify opposition to change (Burnes, 2004; Kristsonis; Robbins). The intensity of these opposing forces may vary by faculty rank, length of tenure (e.g., newly appointed faculty may be more open to curricular change), and nature of the appointment (tenure, adjunct, or joint).

The structure of many social work programs often presents barriers to the infusion of gero content (Green, Dezendorf, Lyman, & Lyman, 2005; Reinardy & Zoff, 2006). Structural arrangements in the internal and external environment encompass governance and decision-making polices and procedures, which can act as reinforcement and opposition to change. These include how decisions about course content are made, implemented, and monitored; program autonomy in the university or college; the extent to which academic administrators are involved in curricular decisions; fiscal and in-kind resources (time, supplies, space); location of programs (such as branch or satellite campuses); types of faculty appointments (including adjuncts and part-time faculty); and other programmatic demands (e.g., promotion and tenure reviews, a reaffirmation self-study, or central administration expectations). Organizational analyses can make explicit the extent to which structural arrangements already attend to particular curricular areas and where such arrangements might actually impede change.

An underlying assumption of the GeroRich and Gero-Ed Center programs is that translating curriculum and organizational analysis data into curriculum change goals requires the development of competencies and outcome measures (Damron-Rodriguez, 2007). According to the EPAS (CSWE, 2008), competency-based education is an outcome performance approach to curriculum design. The foundation gero competencies used in this planned change model, some of which explicitly address cultural competence, offer an example of how social work programs might develop competencies in addition to those identified as core by the EPAS (CSWE).

In the CSWE gero curricular development projects, social work programs select from existing lists of foundation and advanced competencies, as described fully in chapter 2. In other curricular areas in social work education, faculty will need to develop competencies specific to a population or area of specialization that fit within the EPAS (CSWE, 2008) and are in addition to the 10 core competencies required for BSW and MSW programs. This new policy states that programs may develop additional competencies as long as they address needs identified in programs' assessment of their larger context, including demographic and workforce needs. Programs are then to make explicit how their mission and goals take account of this context (see Educational Policy 1.2 and Educational Policy 2.1 in CSWE, 2008).

As elaborated on in chapter 2, an assessment system is central to competency-based education to measure the extent to which competencies have been met (Greene, Cohen, Galambos, & Kropf, 2007). Agreeing on outcome measures may be the most difficult part of competency development. The process of doing so, however, can generate faculty's buying into the competency-based approach. Although the *ideal* measure of social work competencies would be graduates' performance in the workplace, the Gero-Ed Center's emphasis is on measuring students' competencies—what they can do—at the completion of their BSW or MSW program. Pre- and posttest surveys of knowledge and skills (such as the Geriatric Social Work Competency Scale, developed by the Hartford Partnership Program for Aging Education, described in chapter 2) have been used by the majority of participating programs.

The Implementation Phase

Assessments of structural arrangements and key stakeholder support provide the underpinning for implementing strategies to engage stakeholders' buying into the action phase of the planned change model. The implementation stage of moving to a new level of curriculum and programmatic structure encompasses Lippitt's (Lippitt et al., 1958) phase of choosing progressive change objects, including developing action steps and strategies. Congruous with the diffusion of innovations theory, effective action strategies are typically those that are aligned with a program's mission and goals, feasible to implement, able to be tested incrementally or in stages, and relatively more advantageous to the stakeholders than what already exists in the curriculum and programmatic structures (Dearing, 2008; Dorfman & Murty, 2005; Gira et al., 2004; Rogers, 2002).

A primary lesson learned through the GSWE curriculum development programs, which is relevant to other curricular change efforts, is the importance of being selective about what can be accomplished within specific time frames. Few programs are able to infuse gero competencies and content in all their foundation courses in a short time period, especially in large programs with multiple sections of foundation courses. Instead, success has been greatest when faculty change agents target the specific foundation courses and sections in consultation with faculty who are already receptive opinion leaders in their social work program. To illustrate, several programs developed a tiered approach to change, starting with foundation courses, such as Human Behavior and Social Environment or Cultural Diversity, with the greatest probability of success as a way to unfreeze what exists (Fredriksen-Goldsen, Bonifas, & Hooyman, 2006; Lee & Waites, 2006). This selective approach is congruous with Lippitt et al.'s (1958) phase of choosing progressive change objects with a high probability of success.

Obtaining support from key stakeholders is typically the most time-consuming phase of the planned change process and must take account of personal factors that often do not lend themselves to a rational, goal-oriented planned change approach (Burnes, 2004; Kritsonis, 2004–05). Administrative support is also critical because it affects acceptance by faculty, practitioners, and students. Although the support of academic administrators (deans, directors, or chairs) is essential, it is not sufficient for sustainable curricular and organizational change. Since curricular change is the faculty's domain, faculty across ranks, including adjunct faculty, need to have a sense of ownership of the curricular change process and outcome, perceive how the change benefits them, and be willing to modify what they teach. In accordance with the diffusion of innovations theory, faculty members are more likely to own the process when their curriculum decision-making roles are respected, for example, when they are presented early with opportunities to be involved, such as helping to review data from curricular analyses, set outcomes-based goals, and select gero competencies for their foundation area, rather than perceiving the infusion of gero competencies as a top-down approach (Dorfman & Murty, 2005; Fredriksen-Goldsen et al., 2006; Green et al., 2005).

The timing and mechanisms to engage faculty should fit with a program's organizational norms related to decision making and collegiality. For example, e-mail updates may be effective in a large program where faculty meet infrequently but less so in a small program where faculty often interact informally. In these instances, stopping by colleagues' offices or talking with them during lunch, or even in the hallways, can be effective because of the frequent face-to-face interaction that is normal for small programs. Faculty and curriculum committee meetings can be a way to secure faculty support in small programs but may be less successful in programs where such meetings are too large to generate discussion (Hooyman, 2006; Schank & Hermann, 2007).

The most effective but most time-consuming strategies to obtain faculty support are one-on-one or small-group interviews to learn about colleagues' teaching and research interests, expertise, and passions (Ranney, Goodman, Tan, & Glezakos, 2007). Because this individualized approach is resource intensive, it may be more realistic, especially in large programs, to use existing structures—curriculum committee or foundation faculty meetings, e-mail updates, and Web-based teaching resources—to engage faculty (Hooyman, 2006; Hooyman & St. Peter, 2006).

Faculty participants in the three CSWE curriculum change programs (CSWE SAGE-SW, GeroRich, and Gero-Ed Center) identified several elements that were useful for them in obtaining colleagues' support in the change process. These would translate well to other efforts to generate faculty collaboration (see Table 5.1).

A successful curricular and organizational change strategy also engages community stakeholders: field supervisors, alumni/alumnae, agency directors, and clients (older adults and their families). Bringing practitioners' multiple and diverse perspectives to the change process typically results in an enriched practice-relevant curriculum that takes account of the larger context of the social work program, including workforce and demographic needs. Administrators of the CSWE curriculum development programs found that the creation of advisory structures (such as councils, committees, or task groups) involving practitioners, faculty,

Table 5.1
BUILDING FACULTY AND ORGANIZATIONAL COLLABORATION FOR CHANGE

Start →	Reach out to those who are already receptive, then leverage their support to influence others.
Ask faculty →	What would you like to see occur as a result of the change process? Listen openly to the expertise they can contribute.
→	What is your interpretation of the data gathered on curricular needs?
→	What assistance do you need with infusing more gero content? Approach this process as collaboration.
Listen →	Solicit colleagues' feedback and concerns related to gero curricular change. By understanding the sources of resistance, realistic targeted strategies can be developed.
Mobilize →	Discover, free up, and activate colleagues' passion in teaching, research, and service—and then connect aging with what they really care about.
→	Tap into what is already on their plate and help them manage this by "rearranging the curriculum bucket." For example, build intersections with the content areas important to them, and then find ways to further their scholarly goals, such as copresenting or coauthoring papers on how to build intersections for curricular infusion.
Follow up →	Consistently follow up, encourage, and model how to infuse curricular resources or competencies.
→	Finally, always find ways to thank and publicly recognize colleagues who make changes.

and students helps build an effective community partnership for infusing gero competencies in classroom and field curricula. An advisory structure that builds on practitioners' current knowledge of practice trends can also help ensure communication, accountability, and continuity in the curriculum change process. Additionally, such structures have spin-off benefits, such as designing more field placements, service learning, and employment options for students to work with older adults and their families. Focus groups to gather data on policy and practice trends are less resource intensive than advisory structures but are also effective ways to learn about the community context and obtain community support. Another way to engage practitioners in the curricular infusion process is to ask them to provide case studies for classroom pedagogy based upon their practice experience (Ernst & Sowbel, 2007; Hooyman, 2006; Singleton, 2007).

Students, too, are stakeholders to be engaged, and not just through recruiting them for specialized courses, field placements, and gero-focused careers. The foundation infusion approach assumes that embedding gerontology in the required curriculum is the most effective long-term strategy for recruitment to gerontology and that students in other specializations such as health care can develop a commitment to gain basic knowledge and skills for working with older adults. Acquiring such competencies in nonaging courses will have an impact on their future careers, whatever form they take (Kolomer et al., 2007; Waites & Lee, 2007).

Addressing pedagogical issues—the *how* of teaching gerontology, not only the *what*—increases the likelihood of recruiting students to gerontological social work. For example, delivering a brief curriculum module on healthy aging can increase knowledge about the resilience of older adults but typically has less impact on attitudes (Olson, 2002). Experiential opportunities to interact with older adults, such as interviews on issues facing elders, oral life histories, service learning, and other volunteer opportunities, are often the most effective strategies to address students' limited experience with elders; change attitudes, anxieties, and behaviors; and recruit students for gerontological placements and careers. For example, students who participate in service learning involving elders tend to show a more positive attitude toward the members of the group they interact with, and in some instances, increased interest in a gerontological social work career (Cummings, Adler, & DeCoster, 2005; Cummings & Galambos, 2002; Curl, Simons, & Larkin, 2005; Gorelik, Damron-Rodriguez, Funderburk, & Solomon, 2000; Hamon & Way, 2001; Jarrott, 2001; Kropf, 2002; Mason & Sanders, 2004; Paton, Sar, Barber, & Holland, 2001; Tan, Hawkins, & Ryan, 2001; Weinreich, 2003). Additionally, the opportunity to reflect on one's experiential learning, for example through a reflective practice assignment, appears to increase the likelihood of attitudinal change (Cohen, Hatchett, & Eastridge, 2007).

Although numerous GeroRich and CDI programs created opportunities for their students to interact directly with elders, only a small number sought older adults' input into the curriculum change process, largely because of the extensive time and effort needed for obtaining faculty agreement to engage in dialogue (Hooyman, 2006). In instances where older adults were invited to discuss their experiences with social workers, this provided a valued perspective on gero curriculum content (Kolomer et al., 2007). Ideally, all curriculum change initiatives would take account of the client or consumer perspective, but the pressures of limited time and resources may preclude their voices from being heard.

Across all strategies, certain principles apply regardless of the particular stakeholder group:

- Personal contact tends to be most effective in overcoming resistance to the planned change.
- Multifaceted, multitiered contacts across time are needed.
- Win-win situations arise from building intersections with other substantive areas, looking for common interests, creating partnerships and developing overarching curricular themes that are broad enough to secure widespread support (e.g., life span, intergenerational, multigenerational, and multicultural or diversity themes; Corley, Davis, Jackson, & Bach, 2007; Fredriksen-Goldsen et al., 2006; Joyner & DeHope, 2007; Ranney, Min, Takahasi, & Goodman, 2007).

Evaluation

Planning for evaluation must take place at the beginning of any curriculum change project. Time should be devoted up front to choosing curricular and organizational change goals, selecting competencies, and developing outcome measures specific to those goals and competencies. Obviously these goals and measures will evolve somewhat over the years, but it is critical to start out a project by thinking through how evaluation will be conducted (Damron-Rodriguez, 2007; Galambos & Greene, 2007; Hooyman, 2006).

Gathering baseline or starting-point data provides a framework for assessing a program's progress and accomplishments. For example, an effective way to evaluate students' attainment of gero competencies is to have them complete the Geriatric Social Work Competency Scale at the beginning and end of their foundation year, as described in chapter 2 (Damron-Rodriguez, 2007; Damron-Rodriguez, Lawrance, Barnett, & Simmons, 2007). GeroRich and Gero-Ed Center participants gathered data on common outcomes measures at pre- and postinfusion of gero competencies, such as the number of foundation courses that included gerontological content and the number of students exposed to gero content in the foundation curriculum. Other measures, developed by participating programs to be congruous with their goals and organizational culture, were the number of students in aging-focused placements, the number of students interested in a gerontological social work career, and the analysis of gero content in student admissions and recruitment materials.

In addition to quantitative outcome measures, qualitative data from an ongoing process evaluation—what worked, what did not work, and why—can help shape future curricular and organizational change strategies. Students, rather than the syllabus itself, are typically the best source of data on the extent to which competencies and content are actually infused in the classroom and field. Implementing a data feedback loop with faculty and students about what the project leaders are learning will increase the overall community sense of ownership of the change process. Such an approach is in keeping with Lippitt and colleagues' (1958) assertion that communication, feedback, and group coordination are essential to the maintenance of the change.

Sustainability

Lewin (1947) and Lippitt et al. (1958) emphasize the importance of maintaining or freezing the changes made in curriculum and organizational structure. As mentioned earlier, chapter 9 focuses on sustainability of the overall efforts of the GSWI. Embedding gerontological competencies in the existing curriculum and programmatic structure was the primary sustainability approach used in the three curricular change initiatives. In addition, sustainability requires a range of dissemination mechanisms, marketing techniques, and, most important, continual communication and collaboration among gero and nongero faculty and administrators (Hooyman, 2006). Despite intensive efforts by participating programs to sustain changes made, faculty turnover— the loss of the lead change agent or primary gero advocate—remains problematic to maintaining gero changes.

Advanced Curriculum: Areas of Specialization

Whereas GeroRich and the CDI Programs emphasized infusion of gero competencies in the foundation or required generalist curriculum, the MAC Project, funded from 2007 to 2009, designed a complementary strategy. As stated previously, the MAC Project focuses on the development of strategies and resources to infuse gerontology in three areas of advanced practice specialization: health, mental health, and substance use. Of the strategies described under the section "Foundation Curriculum" on p. 106, the greatest similarities occur in strategies for planning (documenting the need for change, and the possible focal points for initiating the change process) and for implementation (engaging key stakeholders and obtaining their support for infusing gero competencies in the three advanced areas). Examples of the use of the planned change model for gero infusion in the advanced curriculum are described under "Planning" on p. 118 and under "Implementation" on p. 119.

Although infusion of content in the BSW required generalist courses and the MSW foundation courses prepares all social work students with beginning-level gerontological competencies, such foundation knowledge is not specific enough for practice in the specialty areas students select in the advanced year of the MSW curriculum. As noted in chapter 1, a large percentage of licensed social workers reported encountering older adults in a variety of mental health and health settings that are not aging specific, but the vast majority of such professionals had little, if any, specific knowledge of the aging process and how such knowledge might be relevant to addressing health and behavioral health issues in these settings (Whitaker et al., 2006). Another impetus for the advanced specialization MAC Project approach derives from the 2003–2004 CSWE statistics: Among 180 accredited MSW programs, 64% offered specialized courses in mental health, 39% in health, and 24% in substance use, whereas only 18% provided courses in aging (Diwan & Hooyman, 2006).

Thus, the specialty courses in these three advanced areas seemed to be the logical place in the curriculum to strategically increase practice-specific gerontological competencies. At present few MSW programs include knowledge or practice experience specific to aging populations in these advanced fields of practice (Berkman, Gardner, Zodikoff, & Harootyan, 2007; Diwan & Hooyman, 2006). Therefore, increasing gerontological content in these three specialty areas presumably will have a significant impact on improving the care provided to older adults and their families by social workers in health, mental health, and substance abuse settings. The focus is on the graduate-level curriculum because undergraduate programs do not offer advanced practice content; however, they may offer specialized course work in minors, certificates, or stand-alone courses. Accordingly, the model used by the MAC Project could be applied to other nonaging specialized or advanced course work in social work and other disciplines.

The MAC Project drew upon the four phases of the planned change model used for the CSWE foundation curriculum. However, the phases became less linear because they were applied to two different strategic directions:

1. Developing resource reviews of the state of evidence-based knowledge and available curricular resources relevant to social work practice with older people in health, mental health, and substance use.

2. Funding 14 MSW programs through Gero Innovation Grants (GIG) to develop, implement, and evaluate different methods to infuse gerontological competencies in classroom courses for the three specialty areas and related field opportunities.

In fact, Lewin and Lippitt's models of planned change have been critiqued for being too linear, with some organizational theorists advocating a more cyclical approach, where the individuals and organizations move back and forth through the phases of planned change (Kritsonis, 2004–05; Prochaska & DiClemente, 1992). The Gero-Ed planned change model takes account of individual and organizational characteristics that affect the change process.

Building on the lessons learned from the GeroRich and the CDI programs, the following strategies or approaches from the planned change model were used to design and implement the MAC Project. Each of these strategies is also germane to other substantive areas in social work or other disciplines.

Planning

Similar to the diagnosis needed for unfreezing what exists, it was critical to gain an in-depth, qualitative understanding of the structure and content of the advanced curricula as well as the current state of social work education related to the specialty areas. To do so, two advisory panel meetings were held, composed of faculty from a range of social work programs nationally whose primary areas of scholarship were in at least one of the three specialty areas. The purpose of these planning meetings was to obtain additional input on the need to increase gerontological competencies in the specialty areas, on sources of potential resistance among faculty in these specialized areas, and on strategies to design a project that significantly contributes to the field and generates interest among MSW programs nationally. Issues of cultural diversity in each of the three specialty areas were also identified. These planning meetings focused on understanding the structure and content of advanced curricula across the spectrum of social work programs and locating possible avenues or focal points for unfreezing or initiating change. The principle of the necessity of stakeholder support from the inception of planning is reflected by the amount of time and resources devoted to these advisory groups. Group members suggested that a synthesis and integration of recent research and teaching in the three specialty areas was critical to overcoming potential faculty resistance to infusing evidence-based gero content in the advanced curriculum. This recommendation formed the basis for the Resource Reviews Project. Another key area of need that was identified was the lack of easy-to-use curricular materials that faculty could draw upon to promote the gerontological competencies of students in advanced courses. This recommendation was the platform for developing the GIG.

Implementation

Engaging key stakeholders, that is, faculty with primary expertise in the specialty areas, was one of the main strategies for implementation of the MAC Project initiatives. Time devoted to engagement was essential because the MAC Project was seeking to involve faculty whose research and teaching were not in gerontological social work. Faculty from a variety of social work programs whose scholarly interests were in one or more of the three specialty areas were included in all stages of the project as advisory board members engaged in planning, expert panelists for the resource reviews, and reviewers and project directors of the GIG. Acceptance from such a diverse group of faculty from a range of MSW programs provided valuable information, resources, and direction to the overall MAC Project, and strengthened the reach and the sustainability of the innovations in social work programs. In effect, it served to increase a buzz about the MAC Project's specialized approach and receptivity to this infusion approach among social work educators nationwide.

Another significant implementation strategy has been to encourage innovation across a spectrum of social work programs by focusing on designing specific new teaching methods that could be disseminated nationwide. Similar to the Gero-Ed Center's work with foundation curricula, the approach to developing GIG teaching innovations draws on Rogers' (2002) work on perceived attributes of innovations that increase the likelihood of their adoption: That is, they are easy to use, can be tried on a limited basis before adoption, offer observable results (increase in gero competencies), and are compatible with the existing practices and values of schools and departments.

Data gathered at the inception of the planning phase through the survey of specialized content in MSW programs (Diwan & Hooyman, 2006) and the advisory meetings showed that programs deliver their advanced content in the specialty areas through an array of curriculum structures—specializations, concentrations, and advanced generalist and specialized elective courses. Given this, a broad and varied approach to developing teaching innovations and infusing gero content in the specialty areas was necessary to ensure their relevance to the wide range of social work programs offering courses in the three areas of advanced curriculum. Accordingly, the innovations, which include the development of DVDs, modules on specific topics, and clinical case studies, have been designed not only for infusion in specialized practice courses but also for more general advanced clinical practice and advanced generalist curricula. Programs have also been expected to include content on diversity as it applies to the populations served.

For example, in the substance use area one social work program is designing and implementing a module on assessment of alcohol use among older adults for infusion in a required practice course, Clinical Assessment and Differential Diagnosis, which is part of a clinical concentration in the advanced curriculum. By designing case studies that portray alcohol misuse in Mexican American families, the innovation helps address diversity issues relevant to the older adult population served by the program's graduates. All students in the concentration will be exposed to this innovation. Another program created a video demonstrating a substance use intervention with older adults that focuses on the application of motivational enhancement strategies and brief intervention therapy, both of which are recommended as evidence-supported treatment strategies (Agency for

Health Care Research and Quality, 2007). The innovation is located in two substance use courses required for all students who specialize in substance use treatment at that school. The implementation of a cutting-edge, evidence-supported treatment strategy with older adults has also generated enormous interest among field supervisors who seek to develop these practice skills as well as learn about specific applications to an older population. The appeal and relevance of the innovation to field instructors will serve to reinforce the gero content with student interns and graduates.

In terms of health and mental health curricula, one program has embedded gerontological content in the required courses in its health and mental health concentration and created a new course on mental health and aging. A second program is placing its innovation (e.g., modules on topics such as cognitive function, assessment of pain, and interdisciplinary teamwork) in all courses required in the health and mental health practice track within an advanced generalist concentration.

The resource reviews themselves are designed to synthesize the current evidence related to practice with older adults, including elders from underserved populations, in the specialty areas. This is a significant innovation in terms of reviewing a large body of research and developing it into user-friendly, culturally relevant materials that faculty can draw on to update their teaching resources and gerontological content. Promoting these resources and demonstrating their applicability across a wide range of curriculum structures has helped programs overcome some of the barriers to adopting specialized gero innovations.

Finally, communication strategies such as the use of an electronic mailing list for the GIG, periodic meetings of the resource review team cochairs and the GIG project directors, and dissemination of products at professional meetings has helped to coordinate collaboration among different MAC Project groups and reiterate a common vision and purpose. Such communication has maintained the focus of the funded programs, increasing visibility of the innovations and ensuring accountability on the part of grantees.

Evaluation

The evaluation strategies used for the programs funded by the GIG focus on two areas: the production of specific deliverables (teaching innovations to increase advanced gerontological competencies) and the assessment of advanced competencies. Some social work programs are creating their own competency assessments in addition to using the Geriatric Social Work Competency Scale. Further, given the advanced level of the curriculum, programs are also using the advanced competencies developed by the California Social Work Education Center (Ranney, et al., 2007). Programs have tailored their lectures, case studies, and interactive materials toward achieving these competencies, and have selected measures to assess competency attainment. The evaluation of the resource reviews has concentrated on obtaining peer assessments of the materials produced; criteria for assessment include the extent to which the materials cover key and relevant topics and are user friendly (e.g., readily adoptable) for faculty without gerontological expertise. Presentations of the resource reviews at national conferences have attracted gerontologists and those with primary interests in the specialty areas and in field education.

Sustainability

The challenges for sustainability of the educational innovations in the advanced curriculum parallels the issues found in the foundation curricular change approach. Sustainability has been emphasized with the GIG from the point of application and throughout the first year of funding. Ongoing communication among the staff of the GIG, feedback from the MAC Project staff related to progress made, and the potential institutionalization of changes are also intended to build the sustainability of the changes. Since the GIG programs are, at this point, in the implementation phase, evaluating the extent to which the innovations will be continued after funding is premature.

Conclusion

The models of diffusion of curricular innovations and planned change characterizing the CSWE curriculum development programs point to strategies that could be used by faculty seeking to bring about change in other curricular areas in social work and other disciplines. As we reflect on the planned change process, the primary lesson learned relates to the absolute importance of obtaining faculty support to ensure sustainable curricular and organizational changes. An area endemic to curricular and programmatic change is overcoming the resistance to change among faculty and other key stakeholders. The amount of time, resources, and attention devoted to obtaining faculty support is a defining characteristic of all program participants in the GeroRich and the CDI programs In most instances, the time needed for obtaining colleagues' acceptance far surpassed what participating faculty had anticipated as necessary. Buying into something is not merely giving lip service to the desired change or making incremental changes in a syllabus; such surface changes will not be sustained if at the same time the stakeholder faculty fail to select gero competencies, to link gero content and teaching resources to competencies, or to change the what and the how of teaching. And the change leader must follow up on the stakeholders' expressions of support for the change by engaging in individual consultation, seeking feedback, and providing ongoing assessment of the curriculum and organizational structure.

Another essential strategy with the MAC Project has been to involve faculty who represent the perspective of the adopters of the innovation in the development, implementation, and dissemination of innovations. Engaging faculty who are not gerontologists but instead teach the advanced courses in the three specialty practice areas has helped to ensure that innovations are tailored to the needs of and likely to be adopted by nongero faculty.

For programs that do not have the benefit of external funding to implement curriculum and programmatic change, careful planning, diagnosis, and an assessment process that involves faculty from the inception of the changed process may be challenging to implement; nonetheless these are essential. It is incumbent on academic administrators to provide the release time or other resources for the designated change agents to be able to devote the necessary time to engage key stakeholders and secure their support toward changing what and how they teach.

References

Agency for Health Care Research and Quality. (2007). *Practice guideline for the treatment of patients with substance use disorders.* Retrieved December 3, 2008, from http://www.guideline.gov/summary/summary.aspx?doc_id=9316&nbr=4985&ss=6&xl=999

Berkman, B., Gardner, D., Zodikoff, B., & Harootyan, L. (2007). Social work and aging in the emerging health care world. In C. Tompkins & A. Rosen (Eds.), *Fostering social work gerontology competence* (pp. 203–217). New York: Haworth Press.

Berkman, B., Silverstone, B., Simmons, W. J., Volland, P. J., & Howe, J. L. (2001). Social work gerontological practice: The need for faculty development in the new millennium. *Journal of Gerontological Social Work, 34*(1), 5–23.

Bogolub, E. B. (1998). Infusing content about discharging legal responsibilities into social work practice classes. The example of mandated maltreatment reporting. *Journal of Teaching in Social Work, 17*(1/2), 185–199.

Burnes, B. (2004). Kurt Lewin and the planned change approach to change: A re-appraisal. *Journal of Management Studies, 41*(6), 977–1002.

Cohen, H., Hatchett, B., & Eastridge, D. (2007). Intergenerational service learning: An innovative teaching strategy to infuse gerontology content into foundation courses. In C. Tompkins & A. Rosen (Eds.), *Fostering social work gerontology competence* (pp. 161–178). New York: Haworth Press.

Corley, C., Davis, P., Jackson, L, & Bach, M. (2007). Spirit of aging rising: Cross-cutting thematic modules to enrich foundation graduate social work courses. In C. Tompkins & A. Rosen (Eds.), *Fostering social work gerontology competence* (pp. 299–310). New York: Haworth Press.

Council on Social Work Education. (2008). *Educational policy and accreditation standards.* Retrieved December 4, 2008, from http://www.cswe.org/NR/rdonlyres/2A81732E-1776-4175-AC42-65974E96BE66/0/2008EducationalPolicyandAccreditationStandards.pdf

Council on Social Work Education Strengthening Aging and Gerontology in Social Work Education. (2001). *Strengthening the impact of social work to improve the quality of life for older adults and their families: A blueprint for the new millennium.* Alexandria, VA: Council on Social Work Education.

Cummings, S., & Kropf, N. (2000). An infusion model for including content on elders with chronic illness in the curriculum. *Advances in Social Work, 1*(1), 93–105.

Cummings, S. M., Adler, G., & DeCoster, V. A. (2005). Factors influencing graduate social work students' interest in working with elders. *Educational Gerontology, 31,* 643–655.

Cummings, S. M., & Galambos, C. (2002). Predictors of graduate social work students' interest in aging-related work. *Journal of Gerontological Social Work, 39,* 77–94.

Cummings, T., & Worley, C. (2001). *Organization development and change* (7th ed.). St. Paul, MN: West Publishing.

Curl, A. L., Simons, K., & Larkin, H. (2005). Factors affecting willingness of social work students to accept jobs in aging. *Journal of Social Work Education, 41*(3), 393–406.

Damron-Rodriguez, J. (2007). Social work practice in aging: A competency-based approach for the 21st century. In R. Greene, H. Cohen, C. Galambos, & N. Kropf (Eds.), *Foundations of social work practice in the field of aging: A competency-based approach* (pp. 1–16). Washington, DC: NASW Press.

Damron-Rodriguez, J., Lawrance, F. P., Barnett, D. & Simmons, J. (2007). Developing geriatric social work competencies for field education. In C. Tompkins & A. Rosen (Eds.), *Fostering social work gerontology competence* (pp. 139–160). New York: Haworth Press.

Damon-Rodriguez, J., & Lubben, J. (1997). The 1995 White House Conference on Aging: An agenda for social work education and training. *Journal of Gerontological Social Work, 27*(3), 65–77.

Damon-Rodriguez, J., Villa, V., Tseng, F., & Lubben, J. (1997). Demographic and organizational influences on the development of gerontological social work curriculum. *Gerontology and Geriatrics Education, 17*(3), 3–18.

Dearing, J. W. (2008). Evolution of diffusion and dissemination theory. *Public Health Management and Practice, 14*(2), 99–108.

Diwan, S., & Hooyman, N. (2006). *Need for increasing gerontological competencies in MSW advanced curriculum areas: Mental health, substance use and health.* Retrieved December 4, 2008, from http://www.gero-edcenter.org/mac/MACConceptPaper.pdf

Dorfman, L. T., & Murty, S. A. (2005). A diffusion of innovations approach to gerontological curriculum enrichment: Institutionalizing and sustaining curricular change. *Gerontology and Geriatrics Education, 26,* 35–50.

Ernst, J., & Sowbel, L. (2007). Bringing the community in: Partnerships for aging enrichment. In C. Tompkins & A. Rosen (Eds.), *Fostering social work gerontology competence* (pp. 387–404). New York: Haworth Press.

Fredriksen-Goldsen, K, Bonifas, R., & Hooyman, N. (2006). Multigenerational practice: An innovative infusion approach. *Journal of Social Work Education, 42*(1), 25–36.

Galambos, C., & Greene, R. (2007). A competency approach to curriculum building. In C. Tompkins & A. Rosen (Eds.), *Fostering social work gerontology competence* (pp. 111–126). New York: Haworth Press.

Gira, E. C., Kessler, M. L., & Poertner, J. (2004). Influencing social workers to use research evidence in practice: Lessons from medicine and the allied health professions. *Research on Social Work Practice, 14*(2), 68–79.

Gorelik, Y., Damron-Rodriguez, J., Funderburk, B., & Solomon, D. H. (2000). Undergraduate interest in aging: Is it affected by contact with older adults? *Educational Gerontology, 26,* 623–638.

Green, R. K., Dezendorf, P. K., Lyman, S. B., & Lyman, S. R. (2005). Infusing gerontological content into curricula: Effective change strategies. *Educational Gerontology, 31,* 103–121.

Greene, R., Cohen, H., Galambos, C., & Kropf, N. P. (2007). *Foundations of social work practice in the field of aging: A competency-based approach.* Silver Spring, MD: NASW Press.

Hamon, R. R., & Way, C. E. (2001). Integrating intergenerational service-learning into the family-science curriculum. *Journal of Teaching in Marriage and Family, 1*(3), 65–83.

Hooyman, N. (2006). *Achieving curricular and organizational change: Impact of the CSWE Geriatric Enrichment in Social Work Education Project.* Alexandria, VA: Council on Social Work Education.

Hooyman, N., & St. Peter, S. (2006). Creating aging-enriched social work education: Process of curricular and organizational change. *Journal of Gerontological Social Work, 41*(3), 9–29.

Hooyman, N., & Tompkins, C. (Eds.). (2005). Gerontological Social Work [Special issue]. *Journal of Social Work Education, 41*(3).

Jarrott, S. E. (2001). Service learning at dementia care programs: A social history project. *Journal of Teaching in Marriage and Family, 1*(4), 1–12.

Johnson-Dalzine, P. (2007). Preparing social work students to work with grandparents in kinship care: An approach to infusion of content materials into selected core social work courses. In C. Tompkins & A. Rosen (Eds.), *Fostering social work gerontology competence* (pp. 405–420). New York: Haworth Press.

Joyner, M., & DeHope, E. (2007). Transforming the curriculum through the intergenerational lens. In C. Tompkins & A. Rosen (Eds.), *Fostering social work gerontology competence* (pp. 127–138). New York: Haworth Press.

Kolomer, S. Lewinson, T., Kropf, N., & Wilks, S. (2007). Increasing aging content in social work curriculum: Perceptions of key constituents. In C. Tompkins & A. Rosen (Eds.), *Fostering social work gerontology competence* (pp. 97–110). New York: Haworth Press.

Kritsonis, A. (2004–05). Comparison of change theories. *International Journal of Scholarly Academic Intellectual Diversity, 8*(1), 1–7.

Kropf, N. (1996). Infusing content on older people with developmental disabilities into the curriculum. *Journal of Social Work Education, 32*(2), 215–226.

Kropf, N. P. (2002). Strategies to increase student interest in social work. *Journal of Gerontological Social Work, 39,* 57–67.

Lee, E. O., & Waites, C. E. (2006). Infusing aging content across the curriculum: Innovations in baccalaureate social work education. *Journal of Social Work Education, 42,* 49–66.

Lewin, K. (1947). Group decision and social change. In T. Newcomb & E. Hartley (Eds.), *Readings in social psychology.*(pp. 183–214). New York: Henry Holt.

Lewin, K. (1957). *Field theory in social sciences.* New York: Harper & Row.

Lippitt, R., Watson, J., & Westley, B. (1958). *The dynamics of planned change.* New York: Harcourt, Brace.

Lubben, J. E., Damron-Rodriguez, J., & Beck, J. C. (1992). A national survey of aging curriculum in schools of social work. *Journal of Gerontological Social Work, 18,* 157–171.

Mason, S. E., & Sanders, G. R. (2004). Social work students' attitudes working with older clients. *Journal of Gerontological Social Work, 42,* 61–75.

Meredith, S. D., & Watt, S. (1994). The Gerontology Development Project: Infusing gerontology into social work curriculum. *Gerontology and Geriatrics Education, 15*(2), 91–100.

Olson, C. J. (2002). A curriculum module enhances students' gerontological practice-related knowledge and attitudes. *Journal of Gerontological Social Work, 38*(4), 85–101.

Owens-Kane, S. (2007). Mosaic of difference: Enhancing culturally competent aging-related knowledge among social workers. In C. Tompkins & A. Rosen (Eds.), *Fostering social work gerontology competence* (pp. 475–492). New York: Haworth Press.

Paton, R. Sar, B., Barber, G., & Holland, B. (2001). Working with older persons: Student views and experiences. *Educational Gerontology, 27*(2), 169–183.

Peterson, D. A., & Wendt, P. F. (1990). Employment in the field of aging: A survey of professionals in four fields. *The Gerontologist, 30,* 679–684.

Prochaska, J. O., & DiClemente, C. C. (1992). Stages of change and the modification of problem behaviors. In M. Hersen, R. Eisler, & P. Miller (Eds.), *Progress in behavior modification* (pp. 184–214). Sycamore, NY: Sycamore Press.

Ranney, M., Goodman, C., Tan, P., & Glezakos, A. (2007). Building on the life-span perspective: A model for infusing geriatric social work. In C. Tompkins & A. Rosen (Eds.), *Fostering social work gerontology competence* (pp. 83–96). New York: Haworth Press.

Ranney, M., Min, J. W., Takahasi, N., & Goodman, C. (2007, October). *Statewide adoption of geriatric social work competencies.* Paper presented at the 53rd annual meeting of the Council on Social Work Education, San Francisco.

Reinardy, J., & Zoff, S. (2006). Strategies for implementing and sustaining curricular change in social work education. In B. Berkman (Ed.), *Handbook of social work in health and aging* (pp. 1033–1040). New York: Oxford University Press.

Richardson, V. E. (1999). *Teaching gerontological social work: A compendium of model syllabi.* Alexandria, VA: Council on Social Work Education.

Robbins, S., (2003). *Organizational behavior.* Upper Saddle River, NJ: Prentice Hall.

Rogers, E. M. (1962). *Diffusion of innovations.* New York: The Free Press.

Rogers, E. M. (1995). *Diffusion of innovations* (4th ed.). New York: The Free Press.

Rogers, E. M. (2002). Diffusion of preventative innovations. *Addictive Behaviors, 27*(6), 989–993.

Rosen, A. L., & Zlotnik, J. L. (2001). Demographics and reality: The "disconnect" in social work education. *Journal of Gerontological Social Work, 36*(3/4), 81–97.

Rosen, A. L., Zlotnick, J. L., & Singer, T. (2002). Basic gerontological competencies for all social workers: The need to "gerontologize" social work education. *Journal of Gerontological Social Work, 39*(1/2), 25–36.

Schank, B., & Hermann, W. R. (2007). Geriatric enrichment: Guaranteeing a place for aging in the curriculum. In C. Tompkins & A. Rosen (Eds.), *Fostering social work gerontology competence* (pp. 63–82). New York: Haworth Press.

Scharlach, A., Damron-Rodriguez, J., Robinson, B. & Feldman, R. (2000). Educating social workers for an aging society: A vision for the 21st century. *Journal of Social Work Education, 36,* 521–538.

Schneider, R. L. (1984). *Gerontology in social work education: Faculty development and continuing education.* Alexandria, VA: Council on Social Work Education.

Schneider, R. L., Decker, T., Freeman, J., & Syran, C. (1984). *The integration of gerontology into social work educational curricula.* Alexandria, VA: Council on Social Work Education.

Singleton, J. (2007). Infusing gerontology throughout the BSW curriculum. In C. Tompkins & A. Rosen (Eds.), *Fostering social work gerontology competence* (pp. 31–47). New York: Haworth Press.

Tan, P. P., Hawkins, M. F., & Ryan, E. (2001). Baccalaureate social work student attitudes toward older adults. *The Journal of Baccalaureate Social Work, 6,* 45–55.

Waites, C., & Lee, E. O. (2007). Strengthening aging content in baccalaureate social work curricula: What students have to say. In C. Tompkins & A. Rosen (Eds.), *Fostering social work gerontology competence* (pp. 47–62). New York: Haworth Press.

Watt, S. (1996). *Final report: Gerontology Development Project.* Hamilton, Ontario, Canada: McMaster University School of Social Work.

Watt, S., & Meredith, S. (1995). Integrating gerontology into social work education programs. *Educational Gerontology, 21*, 55–68.

Weinreich, D. M. (2003). Service-learning at the edge of chaos. *Educational Gerontology, 29*(3), 181–195.

Whitaker, T., Weismiller, T., & Clark, E. (2006). *Assuring the sufficiency of a frontline workforce: A national study of licensed social workers.* Retrieved January 25, 2008, from http://workforce.socialworkers.org/studies/aging/aging.pdf

CHAPTER 6

Lessons Learned for Community Partnerships

The Hartford Partnership Program for Aging Education

Patricia J. Volland and M. Elizabeth Wright

Over the course of time, university–community partnerships have come in many shapes and sizes, with a wide range of objectives on the part of the stakeholders. When engagement between university and community functions optimally, all parties stand to gain from a mutually rewarding exchange of resources, and the long-range winner is society at large. Some partnerships have a research focus, sending faculty and students into the community to conduct participatory-based research; others concentrate on specific projects the university engages in with under-served communities to tackle problems such as economic development or health issues, and a number bring the university and community to-gether for service-based learning opportunities that offer substantial benefits to society and to those who are being educated (Fisher, Fabri-cant, & Simmons, 2004; Martin, Smith, & Phillips, 2005; Pew Part-nership for Civic Change, 2003).

Fisher and colleagues (2004) single out social work partnerships be-tween university and community as another type of category, a *mega-category*, which may encompass all the aforementioned objectives: participatory-based research, community development, and service learn-ing. Social work, because of the unique nature of the profession, its long history of community participation, and its educational model of send-ing students into the community for field practicum experiences, has ce-mented ties between institutions of higher education and local communities on multiple fronts. As a result, social work institutions have a distinctive capacity for developing university–community partnerships arising from the profession's experience in working with multiple disciplines and forging community ties (Fisher et al.). University–community partnerships in social work have their roots in the 19th century, with the notable example of the role of the University of Chicago alongside Jane Addams in the opening of Hull House to serve the low-income population on Chicago's west side (Martin et al., 2005).

A significant body of literature has detailed the rise of university–community partnerships to greater prominence in current times, driven by an increased consciousness of the need for scholarly engagement with community, social, and political change that began in the 1960s, and the increased urbanization of university settings (Boyer, 1990; Cherry & Shefner, 2004; Fisher et al., 2004; Martin et al., 2005). The establishment of the Office of University Partnerships by the U.S. Department of Housing and Urban Development in 1994 marked a significant growth in the funding and initiation of partnerships, bringing colleges and universities together with their communities to address urban problems through its Community Outreach Partnership Center. Private funding has also played a significant role in the establishment of university–community partnerships, in combination with government funding and independently. With respect to innovative collaborations, Martin and colleagues (2005) have described a *new governance perspective* that brings together private sector organizations, educational institutions, different levels of government, and the public to solve problems within the context of community needs.

University–Community Partnerships in Social Work and Aging

Interactions between social work programs and the community have played an important role in educating students of social work since the beginning of the profession; the preference for practice-based training over theory and research predominated as early as the late 19th century (Volland & Berkman, 2004). Although the pendulum has shifted back and forth over time regarding the appropriate balance between academic learning and apprenticeship, field education continues to play a vital role in training new cohorts of social workers. In its Educational Policy and Accreditation Standards (EPAS), the Council on Social Work Education (CSWE, 2008) has emphasized the importance of a pedagogical approach that balances academic learning and field experience: "It is a basic precept of social work education that the two interrelated components of curriculum—classroom and field—are of equal importance within the curriculum, and that each contributes to the requisite competencies of professional practice" (CSWE, p. 8).

Currently, strategies to increase collaboration between academic course work and field instruction to improve the overall educational model have gained ground. This movement has been driven by the recognition that a more interactive relationship brings benefits to educators, community agencies, and students alike, as well as by perceptions of a broadening disconnect between social work programs and the practice community (Diwan & Wertheimer, 2007). Recent initiatives have fallen largely into two major categories: (1) research-based collaborations that center on scholarship addressing direct practice or policy issues and (2) collaborations that focus on gerontological curriculum change and opportunities for aging specialization. Examples of these types of initiatives include university–community partnerships where students have studied the role of social work in reducing caregiver strain to improve end-of-life care (Townsend et al., 2007), and intervention strategies to develop and implement gerontological competencies and content in BSW and MSW curricula (Chapin, Nelson-Becker, Gordon, Landry, & Chapin, 2007).

This chapter focuses in particular on one partnership model in geriatric social work, which has its foundation in collaboration between social work education and the practice community. The Hartford Partnership Program for Aging Education (HPPAE; formerly the Practicum Partnership Program) provides a model for university–community partnerships designed to offer experiential learning opportunities for MSW students through a rotational model of field education. Administered by the Social Work Leadership Institute (SWLI) at the New York Academy of Medicine (NYAM), this program serves an urgent need for our society: preparing social workers to meet the challenge of an aging population by recruiting and training students to the field of geriatrics (Volland & Berkman, 2004).

Since 1998 the HPPAE has been at the forefront of national efforts to build university–community partnerships that offer social work graduate students a distinctive training opportunity to become expert in the field of aging. The partnerships that are at the foundation of this initiative are responsible for the integration of academic learning with multiple practice experiences in settings serving a diverse population of older adults across a continuum of care. As of 2008 the HPPAE has been implemented in 33 states with a total of 72 programs. Over 1,000 MSW students have graduated from the HPPAE, and it is anticipated that by 2011 this number will be at least 2,500. In a 2008 evaluation report of findings from two cycles of funding of 35 HPPAE sites, 80% of students intended to work in the field of aging after graduation. These students also strongly agreed that acquiring work experience in more than one field agency was beneficial and that the rotations helped them learn about a range of services for older adults (NYAM, 2008a).

The SWLI is currently embarked on a grassroots effort to expand the program to other schools and departments so that even more students will have the opportunity to acquire the knowledge and discover the rewards of a career in aging. This "normalization" strategy is designed to allow existing HPPAE programs to work together with potential adopters of the program within regional hubs for support and exchange of knowledge. This effort will be promoted with a variety of materials, including a comprehensive HPPAE manual that will provide schools and departments with technical advice, fund-raising strategies, and other assistance as needed.

The HPPAE model has six essential components, the first and foremost of which is (1) the development of a strong university–community partnership, (2) competency-based education, (3) rotations, (4) focused recruitment of students to the field of aging, (5) an expanded role for field instructors, and (6) leadership development. The members of an HPPAE university–community partnership have primary responsibility for program planning and oversight, aging-focused curriculum development, student recruitment, fund-raising, and evaluation. The development of university–community partnerships and the implementation of the rotational model of field instruction are inextricably linked because the genesis of the HPPAE model requires extensive collaboration between the university and the local network of community-based agencies.

In reviewing the development and achievements of the HPPAE and the distinguishing features of its educational model, the aim is to provide lessons learned from the experiences of the universities and communities that have come together to make these partnerships not just a reality but also a success. Discovering the underpinnings of successful university–community partnerships in social work education has broad relevance for any educational body that seeks to engage with the community and work as allies with community stakeholders for societal benefit (Fisher et al., 2004). Although the focus of this initiative is on preparing MSW-level graduates for careers in geriatric social work, other partnership initiatives in social work, as well as other professional disciplines, can benefit from studying this model. The HPPAE will continue to provide a wealth of learning opportunities as the program expands and as more social work education programs adopt this approach to educate MSW students. Long-term engagement, a hallmark of a successful partnership, depends on the creation of new collaborations and the duration of existing ones to form the university–community bonds that strengthen field education opportunities for social workers and prepare them to be at the front line of aging care.

Designing Rotational Field Models: A Brief Overview of Benefits and Challenges

Certain characteristics of university–community partnerships are universal, not just within social work specializations but also across professional disciplines. Some of these characteristics are benefits, such as a mutually rewarding exchange of resources and increased student and faculty engagement in community life; and some are obstacles, such as the distrust that may exist between "town and gown" and real or perceived power imbalances among the parties involved (Cherry & Shefner, 2004; Martin et al., 2005; Zendell, Fortune, Mertz, & Koelewyn, 2007). At the same time, certain aspects of the HPPAE are specific to the mission of designing an aging-focused curriculum through the integration of classroom learning with a rotational model of fieldwork, and will also be delineated.

In the course of the HPPAE expansion, and from the experiences of different sites in establishing their own programs, some of the universal benefits and challenges of these partnerships have come to light. Benefits include enhanced status of the university in the eyes of the community and vice versa, an enriched educational experience for students aligned with current practice issues, expanded social relevance for the university and its students, and increased student motivation to attend to the needs of underserved communities. Obstacles that are common to university–community relations also emerged: a general mistrust regarding the university's agenda to pursue its own needs with a lack of regard for community benefit, the aforementioned issue of power imbalance where the university may have greater economic and political resources, and a disconnect between the ivory tower of academia and the real world of community practice (Cherry & Shefner, 2004; Fisher et al., 2004; Pew Partnership for Civic Change, 2003).

Overcoming the inherent challenges to implementing a robust and lasting university–community partnership requires "a systematic approach and tenacious attention to developing trust, collaboration, and shared vision of potential" (Zendell et al., 2007, p. 156). In the case of the HPPAE, graduate social work programs, their governing universities, the community agencies that serve older adults and society at large have accrued multiple benefits. The lessons learned from the HPPAE and its innovative field education model have the potential for translation to other fields of practice, in particular the deployment of strategic approaches to partnership building that ensure commitment to the same goals and a shared sense of purpose among all partners.

Steps to Implement a Vital and Sustainable University–Community Partnership

A thorough understanding of the potential benefits and challenges of any given partnership is essential to designing a functioning relationship among the key stakeholders. The university–community partnership behind the HPPAE educational model has a complex charge. Beyond the requirements of the essential components that form the basis of the program, the role of the partnership extends to establishing a program structure that clarifies roles and responsibilities of all those involved. The partnership members must set up an even-handed distribution of authority, plan for sustainability, design and implement evaluation systems, ensure sufficient aging content in the academic curriculum, obtain university support for the program, and expand innovative learning opportunities for a diverse range of students.

Building an Optimally Functioning Partnership

For any body of higher learning with plans to implement an educational- or research-oriented collaboration internally or within a larger community, a wealth of experience and knowledge is available concerning how to set up an optimally functioning partnership that will provide students with a broad array of learning opportunities. One of the first things that must be addressed is formulating the partnership as a relationship in which all parties commit to the project's success; recognize the varying roles and interests of the partnership members; define short-, medium-, and long-term goals; and acknowledge that the partnership as a whole is greater than the sum of its parts (Fortune & Kaye, 2008).

Evaluations of the HPPAE suggest that it is best to configure the governing group at its individual site as a consortium (Lawrance, Damron-Rodriguez, Rosenfeld, Sisco, & Volland 2007; NYAM, 2008b). Putting in place a framework that emphasizes collaboration facilitates an effective working relationship between the social work education program and community service agencies, while avoiding the pitfalls of struggling to achieve goals independently of one another. Several challenges to setting up a collaborative framework have been noted, including potential conflicts between the mission to educate students and the agencies' primary need to serve clients, the de facto placement of power through the ownership of the program by the school/university, and the ever-present limitations on the time and energy of the participants, particularly the agency-based field supervisors (Zendell et al., 2007).

The extra effort required to implement the rotational model of field instruction illustrates the potential tension between the educational and service missions as well as limitations on time and energy. In some instances, this model has presented a hurdle for the agencies that are accustomed to having a student intern over the full academic year. However, the agencies accrued benefits from this model as well, in so far as it facilitated interaction across service systems that led to valuable exchanges and improved services to older adults through student participation in the agencies' work (Lawrance et al., 2007; Zendell et al., 2007).

To overcome these and other challenges, while reinforcing the potential benefits to all parties, the partnership must take a strategic approach to its own method of design and functioning. In the initial phase, detailed attention must be given to the membership, leadership, and structure of the partnership. Because of the flexibility inherent to the HPPAE, schools or departments may tailor the partnership and the essential components of the program to their own and the community's needs. Different social work programs have adopted a variety of approaches in developing a partnership model that takes into account the specific characteristics of the academic setting and the local network of aging services. Regardless of the particular strategies and organizational tactics employed by a specific site, all successful partnerships have certain elements in common: In particular, all participants must have a clear sense of the program's mission and a shared voice in the decision-making process, ensuring that all parties are equally committed to the goal of building a strong program (Lawrance et al., 2007; Zendell et al., 2007; NYAM, 2008b). The various elements contributing to the success of the partnership are equally valid for other areas of specialization in social work or in other disciplines undertaking similar collaborative efforts.

Membership

One of the first steps in developing an HPPAE partnership is to decide on community agency membership. Most often this begins with the group of agencies serving older adults that the school or department already has a working relationship with—and when necessary, persuading these agencies to commit to the rotational model of field instruction. Starting with a nucleus of support from established relationships provides a foundation for expansion to include other agencies that will make available for students the widest possible range of practice opportunities with diverse older adults. Recommendations may come from the founding agency partners, faculty and students, or from older adults themselves (NYAM, 2008b).

A vital aspect of the HPPAE rotational model is that agencies represent a broad spectrum of the continuum of care and include varied services such as health, mental health, wellness, and preventive care; housing; legal assistance; and advocacy (Lawrance et al., 2007). Typical examples of the types of agencies that assume a partnership role are hospital systems, senior centers and services, assisted-living facilities, skilled nursing homes, adult day health programs, nonprofit organizations with an aging focus, local area agencies on aging, adult protective services, and advocacy organizations. Bringing a diverse range of community agencies into the partnership allows students to become knowledgeable of the complex array of services and providers that constitute the aging network.

The process of developing the membership base should also take into account the need for student field experience in work settings that provide exposure to micro and macro levels of practice to broaden the student's perspective on the profession and lay the groundwork for subsequent professional development. The incorporation of macro learning in field experience ensures the development of aging-focused competencies in public policy, advocacy, research, and evaluation. These macro practice behaviors broaden the clinical social worker's perspective on practice and are skills that may be called upon as needed in the future (Mertz, Fortune, & Zendell, 2007). Even though a substantial majority of social work students ultimately choose to pursue a clinical or direct practice concentration, all students need to be well grounded in both types of learning. These domains of knowledge tend to reinforce one another, regardless of the student's ultimate career choice.

Another important consideration is including agencies that serve historically disadvantaged populations. The administrators at many HPPAE schools have made systematic efforts to include agencies that represent underserved populations, and they believe students need to acquire culturally competent gerontological experiential training. Ensuring practice competencies with culturally diverse elders will acquire even greater importance in the coming decades, given the overall demographic trends of the aging population.

As pointed out earlier in this chapter, agency recruitment to the partnership is most successful if the partnership is structured to be inclusive, and all participants understand how they may benefit from participation. Although agencies may have to adapt to altering the traditional 1-year placement, beneficial interagency collaborations develop over time from the interactions generated by the rotational model, and new initiatives or grant-funded activities may result from these collaborations (Zendell et al., 2007). At the same time, an overarching commitment to the cause is called for, such as the belief that preparing students to specialize in aging will bring rewards to the students and the older adults they will serve. Such shared resolve may become even more important in the near future, as agencies struggle with reduced funding and staffing typically needed to ensure the quality of students' learning experiences.

Deciding whom to involve in the partnership logically focuses on the inclusion of agency partners as a first step. Broad support for the partnership should also be advanced through strategic inclusion of consortium members in the social work program and the university at the earliest stages of partnership development (NYAM, 2008a). The engagement of deans or directors and other interested parties demonstrates to the core constituents of the partnership the university's commitment to the program and can subsequently be important to its sustainability. In sum, university support for the HPPAE program must come from all levels of administration, faculty (including adjunct and field faculty), directors of field education, and students. Such strategies would be critical for any social work specialization or similar types of programs in other disciplines that are working to develop a community–university partnership.

Size and Structure

When starting a new program, the founding partnership members from the educational institution and the agencies must work together to make important decisions about the number of participants as well as how the partnership will be structured. Experience has demonstrated that the number of participants should be large enough to accomplish the work at hand but not so unwieldy that meaningful relationships are difficult to maintain (Zendell et al., 2007). In the HPPAE model, the number of agencies varies by site; in the demonstration sites, it ranged from 6 to 21 participants, with minor year-to-year variations. The structure of the partnership differed significantly from one site to another, as did decisions about how often to meet, either in person or by other means, and what communication tools best served program start-up and implementation needs. In the demonstration sites, governing structures typically included university faculty with aging expertise, field education directors, and senior staff (often CEOs) from the agencies (Lawrance et al., 2007; Zendell et al., 2007). Field instructors—in agencies and in academic settings—have been vital to the structure and functioning of the partnership as well, as the success of a program depends on the integration of academic learning with multiple field placements that provide the real-life exposure to social work with older adults in a variety of venues (NYAM, 2004). Depending on the site, representation further included deans, development officers, various levels of agency management, and agency supervisors.

The size and structure of partnerships have varied markedly from one HPPAE site to another; in one instance the consortium was composed of only field instructors, whereas most others had broader representation with an organizational structure composed of governance bodies, committees, and task forces. In spite of these variations, one lesson that emerged across sites is the centrality of support for the partnership from all levels of the participating organizations, that is, from the highest levels of management through midlevel supervisors to those directly carrying out the work of the program (Zendell et al., 2007). Commitment from all levels ensures support from the academic institution and community members who must work together in a unified manner to accomplish the complex and time-intensive task of implementing the program. The need for time devoted to strategies to obtain acceptance from key community stakeholders holds true for partnerships in other areas of social work specialization.

Leadership

Visionary leadership on the part of the university and the agencies is essential to the development of a strong HPPAE program. Talents in coalition building, skilled project management, articulation of the importance of the mission, and sheer determination have all been cited as necessary leadership qualities to bring all parties together and overcome dissent or competition among the participating groups. As mentioned previously, although structures and models of communication vary substantially from site to site, the need for consistent, dedicated leadership is universally required for a successful program, as captured by feedback from participants:

> The PI [principal investigator] made a deep investment in the education for the students and the connection between the institutions and the community. And that's why it's hard not to join once they ask you to help out. It's hard not to help her, [she's a] good leader.
>
> She [the PI] has always been out there advocating for it and negotiating with those forces that weren't totally supportive of it in the beginning.
>
> She had a passion that was consensus-building. (NYAM, 2004, p.4)

The implementation of shared leadership is another often noted attribute of a successful partnership. The university exerts a large degree of control over the program because the grant is awarded to the university, and the partnership needs a stable core of leadership to bring the program to fruition. Nonetheless, it is in the interest of the university to share leadership with the community partners, recognizing the pivotal role that the agencies play in educating social work students. Sharing leadership also serves to redress the sense on the part of the communities that the university has some kind of ulterior motive and is designing a program primarily for its own benefit.

Shared leadership can be achieved through the structure of the consortium and by ensuring that committees and task forces have cochairs from the university and a partner agency. Committees are important vehicles for power sharing and are assigned tasks that are often of specific interest to particular stakeholders. In sharing leadership, agencies are able to participate in major decisions, refuting any notion that they are second-class citizens in the program's overall scheme, and that their input is not important to its development.

Through shared and visionary leadership, individuals can be recruited for appropriate roles, flexibility can be incorporated in the model, and leadership can be sustained over the long term. The initial implementation of an HPPAE program is a time- and labor-intensive effort that requires a devotion to the cause that can be inspired and maintained through a fair distribution of authority and responsibility.

The University–Community Partnership and the Rotational Model of Field Instruction

The rotational model is one of the distinguishing features of the HPPAE and is the centerpiece of providing students with broad exposure to aging services across a continuum of care. From its inception, the HPPAE has promoted the use of rotational field instruction in response to critiques of the weakness of the traditional field education model in preparing social workers for the demands of contemporary practice (Ivry, Lawrance, Damon-Rodriguez, & Robbins, 2005; Reisch & Jarmon-Rhode, 2000; Volland & Berkman 2004). Much of the literature has noted that social workers benefit from working with different field instructors in dissimilar settings, thereby exposing them to a variety of service settings, functional ability of older adults, practice challenges, intervention methods, and interdisciplinary team practices (Ivry et al.).

The rotational approach has encountered some resistance because of concerns about a lack of continuity and depth of learning. However, the HPPAE has demonstrated that student satisfaction with the rotational model is high and that agencies and faculty also stand to gain from the interactions generated by rotations (Lawrance et al., 2007). The benefits of rotation outweigh the potential detriments for a number of reasons, primarily because of the breadth of the student experience. First, students become more knowledgeable and better prepared to confront the challenges of a complex service system for older adults, both on the clinical level and from the policy standpoint. Second, a variety of field placements exposes individual students to the diversity of the older adult population in terms of race/ethnicity, gender, social class, and sexual orientation and the continuum of health from well to frail. Finally, a range of field placements allows students to experience different supervisory styles and workplace cultures and to have interdisciplinary contacts (Ivry et al., 2005).

University-community partnerships often need to be flexible in their approach to designing the rotational model according to the characteristics of their local aging network, the school itself, and the students. Over the course of the HPPAE expansion, from 1999 to the present, variations in the rotational model have been a hallmark of program design. Overarching categories of differences include duration, length, timing, and number of settings, as well as student experiences with agency setting, functional level of clientele, and micro (i.e., clinical) versus macro (i.e., administrative or policy advocacy) experience. Another source of variation emanates from internal rotations within a large agency system versus external rotations where students are assigned to different agencies over the course of the year. Flexibility is in fact necessary to ensure that each individual program can design a rotational model well grounded in competency-based education and congruous with agency resources. A strategic approach to designing the rotational model ensures that students have the most productive learning experience within the possibilities and constraints of a given program setting.

From a structural point of view, an important aspect of the rotational model is determining the number of field instructors who will oversee the student's work and whether the supervisory field instructor is agency based or university based (Robbins & Rowan, 2008). The following variations have been used by different sites:

- One primary agency-based field instructor with task supervisors or preceptors in additional programs or agencies
- Two or more agency-based field instructors, one for each rotation
- A university-based field instructor with task supervisors or preceptors in agencies

To provide the desired range of experiences for the student, one of the chief tasks of the university–community partnership is bringing the appropriate agencies on board. The partnership must persuade existing agencies that a departure from the previous way of doing business is desirable, while also bringing new agencies into the fold that will offer innovative learning experiences for the students. Therefore, the program must be structured so that advantages are clear for the agencies and their personnel and that incentives are strong enough, especially where field instructors are concerned, to expand a network that encompasses a range of student learning opportunities.

The partnership working as a team must establish continuity among the varied placements and ensure that motivated, high-quality students committed to the practice of aging make a real contribution to the work of the agency while also benefiting educationally. Additionally, agency understanding of the rewards involved in equal partnering, the prospects for collaborative research and teaching ventures, and the enhanced prestige from their participation in the programs provide impetus for a successful collaboration.

An Expanded Role for Field Instructors

Regardless of the type of placement in various social work specializations, field instructors have one of the most challenging and important roles in providing students with rich educational experiences. Within the HPPAE rotational model, they take on the following additional responsibilities:

- Direct and coordinate student learning across programs and agencies
- Participate in the university–agency partnership activities
- Participate in HPPAE integrative seminars as leaders, expert commentators on case situations, and instructors
- Consult on education and training in field agencies

In addition, field instructors may be asked to serve as guest speakers in the classroom or as adjunct instructors for aging courses, and to participate in educational activities, such as student brown bag lunches focused on specific geriatric social work practice and policy issues.

For field instructors to assume this expanded role, the partnership must actively work to secure release time for field instructors to commit to the rotational model and ongoing student instruction and supervision. The agencies need to recognize that over the long term, additional time and resources will be minimized once the program is up and running, especially where a strong consortium assumes the management of most tasks (Robbins & Rowan, 2008).

Field instructors bring with them their years of practice experience and in-depth knowledge of service systems for older adults, which are important contributions to the educational experience of student interns. They are also instrumental in recruiting students to the field of aging by offering living proof that working with older adults is rewarding. However, field instructors often carry large caseloads and may have difficulty balancing the demands of the job with the commitment to student education, especially when faced with growing workloads because of budget cuts and the current economic downturn. Thus, partnership leaders must take an active role in obtaining the support of agency directors to facilitate the time and work commitment of field instructors to the HPPAE program.

Many field instructors welcome their expanded role and see the value in the rotational model of fieldwork, in spite of the increased workload this entails. They recognize that they are providing a valuable service to the students, their agency, and the aging population in their community. At the same time, partnership leaders need to acknowledge field instructors' status as the unsung heroes working at the front line of aging care and take concrete steps to make sure they get the recognition they deserve (NYAM, 2004). Writing letters of recognition for services rendered, ensuring a meaningful role in the partnership, issuing invitations to university events and programs, offering continuing education opportunities, and providing positive feedback about the program and its successes are some of the means available to highlight the important contributions of field instructors.

Most field instructors find participation in the HPPAE to be a rewarding experience and have commented in focus groups on the many positives that have resulted from their involvement in the program (Lawrance et al., 2007; NYAM, 2004). The HPPAE has generated noticeable energy and camaraderie among geriatric social work practitioners and greater visibility within the broader social work community. Field instructors derive satisfaction from playing a central role in preparing new cohorts of social workers specialized in working with older adults and acknowledge that student interns help with providing extra time and attention to clients.

Even with substantial support from agency and field instructors of the university–community partnership and the rotational model of field education, constant attention needs to be devoted to the alignment of the university mission with the agency mission. Part of this alignment involves dispensing with the academic ivory tower mentality and ensuring that a common language is spoken among all partners (Fortune & Kaye, 2008). HPPAE programs have strived to be inclusive and to emphasize reciprocity and exchange. Yet more work is needed to ensure that field instructors are equal partners and to gain additional information on agency perspectives regarding the rewards, benefits, and challenges of participating in the HPPAE model (Damron-Rodriguez, Malks, Lawrence, Edsall, & Trimble, 2007).

The University–Community Partnership and Other HPPAE Essential Components

In addition to the critical role the university–community partnership plays in bringing the HPPAE rotational model of field instruction to life, it also is largely responsible for the integration of competency-based education in the curriculum, the recruitment of students to the field of aging, and program elements that will assist academics, students, and agency personnel to become tomorrow's leaders in social work. Each of these components can only be achieved by setting clear-cut goals and ensuring that the university and the agencies are working in unison toward their accomplishment, which is true for ensuring the success of the rotations and an expanded role for field instructors.

The development of competency-based education is described in detail in chapter 2. In the HPPAE model, the key elements of competency-based education are adoption of the Geriatric Social Work Competency Scale II, establishment of student learning goals based on these competencies, ongoing assessment of student skill level, and integration of class and field learning through a competency-based curriculum (Damron-Rodriguez & Brownell, 2008). In some instances social work programs may lack sufficient courses or field placements with an aging focus and have too few faculty members with gerontological expertise. An advantage of the HPPAE model is that this shortfall can be overcome by offering specialized integrative seminars that link academic and field training, using the competencies as an organizing principle (NYAM, 2008a). These seminars are often held in the consortium agencies for students to acquire firsthand knowledge of a broad range of agency services and programs. This integration of field and classroom learning is grounded in competency-based education and focused on best practices (Ivry et al., 2005). A strong university–community partnership facilitates this interchange, providing students with a rich learning experience and an in-depth understanding of geriatric principles in real-world settings.

Student recruitment to the HPPAE program is another area where interaction among faculty, administrators, students, and field instructors is critical. Recruitment to the field of aging is an ongoing challenge because of persistent biases and assumptions associated with older adults and geriatric work. As with all the other essential components, successful recruitment requires that the university and the agencies work together to highlight the program benefits. Recruitment may begin as soon as a student is accepted to the MSW program, and the opportunity to join the HPPAE is reinforced by the attractiveness of student stipends and the rotational model of learning. Building a close relationship between the admissions office and the field education office will aid in cultivating students' interest from the earliest stages of their graduate education.

An important aspect of student recruitment that has come to light over the course of the HPPAE's implementation and growth is the relative diversity of the student body and the trends that have emerged from data collection. In the 11 initial demonstration sites across six schools, diversity characteristics of the Practicum Partnership Program (now HPPAE) students as compared with the national MSW student population were quite favorable. For example, 50% of these HPPAE Cohort 1 students were Caucasian compared to 68% nationally, 18% were African American compared to 15% nationally, and 14% were Hispanic/Latino/Latina compared with 6% nationally. Subsequent data collection, however, has showed a significant decline in HPPAE student diversity, probably because of the expansion of HPPAE programs to less-urban environments and less-ethnically diverse populations than those of the demonstration sites. Certainly this trend bears further investigation and will need to be an area of focus for HPPAE programs' going forward. Attention to the diversity of the student population is critical given the projection that elders of color will form 33% of the older population by 2030 (Administration on Aging, 2008).

Agencies and field personnel have a significant influence on recruitment in geriatric social work because HPPAE students may include not only those who are already committed to this field but also those who are still deciding about their area of ultimate specialization. Students may become interested in the program because of the opportunity to have a broad range of work experience or the program's strong community focus:

I've known a number who come in who really aren't sure, frankly. They were attracted by . . . sometimes I think it's the additional rigor of the program. . . . I can't think of anyone who didn't end up falling in the love with the population and wanting to stay in this field. . . . so if it takes a more rigorous program or a stipend or whatever it is to attract them in, that's ok. (NYAM, 2008b, p.13)

Leadership, the most recently included essential component of the HPPAE model, goes hand in hand with recruitment to the field of aging because leaders in social work act as ambassadors for the program whether they are students, academics, or field personnel. As with the other components, leadership initiatives are most effective when the university works closely with the community to perform outreach, to articulate the benefits of the partnership, and to communicate the societal imperative of developing a comprehensively prepared workforce to attend to the needs of an aging population.

The SWLI, the founder of the HPPAE, has established a Leadership Academy in Aging to address the need for deans and directors to strengthen their leadership and management skills in the field of geriatric social work. In so doing, not only will they communicate the benefits of gerontological social work, but they will also forge stronger ties between the academic community and social work practitioners in the field, with the goal of increasing the ranks of social workers from culturally diverse backgrounds who specialize in aging and eventually become leaders themselves.

Students and field instructors also have an important role to play as leaders. SWLI is actively pursuing initiatives to engage these groups in learning about the components of leadership and providing opportunities where these skills can be put into practice. All these groups working together—from field, academic, and student perspectives—are necessary to make social work a recognized and powerful agent for change in addressing the societal need for an expanded geriatric social work workforce.

Conclusion

The basic principles for setting up a successful, productive university–community partnership are relatively uncomplicated, even if the work the partnership must accomplish to bring these projects to life involves numerous participants and a complex set of tasks. These guiding precepts have been summed up accurately and succinctly to include five leading elements: communication, collaboration, support, flexibility, and vision (Pew Partnership for Civic Change, 2003). Keeping these five principles in the forefront of all interactions is essential to overcoming the barriers previously described, such as skepticism toward the educational institution's motives and the historical tensions between the university and the community. If an open and collaborative manner of working is coupled with an understanding and appreciation of the nature of the community and a commitment to long-term engagement, significant advances can be accomplished in a variety of disciplines, beyond the social work arena and with different populations, even with limited external funding.

In the case of the HPPAE, the skills required to build and sustain a robust university–community partnership have been put to the test many times, with positive outcomes demonstrated by the increasing number of social work students who have participated in the program and the many graduates who have gone on to work in the field of aging. Since its inception in 1998 the HPPAE has grown steadily, in large part because of the strength of the many university–community partnerships that have brought these programs to life. A strategic plan is under way for the HPPAE to become more widely adopted by graduate schools of social work, through networking among schools, the efficient sharing of knowledge, and proof of the efficacy of this model in preparing new cohorts of gerontological social workers via the continuing evaluation of the program.

An HPPAE partnership succeeds when it overcomes the obstacles that have traditionally hindered relations between the university and the community to establish a permanent and committed network of like-minded professionals who share responsibility for the program's mission and goals. Looking to the future, as the program continues to expand to other social work programs, the rewards will continue to accrue for the university and the community through a beneficial exchange of resources, greater community interaction, new professional opportunities, and so on. The greatest reward of all, however, will be knowing that the achievements of these university–community partnerships will allow students to engage in rewarding careers in the field of aging and help older adults lead productive, independent lives.

References

Administration on Aging. (2008). *A profile of older Americans: 2008.* Washington, DC: U.S. Department of Health and Human Services.

Boyer, E. (1990). *Scholarship reconsidered: Priorities of the professoriate.* Princeton, NJ: The Carnegie Foundation for the Advancement of Teaching.

Chapin, R., Nelson-Becker, H., Gordon, T., Landry, S. T., & Chapin, W. B. (2007). Responding to the Hartford Geriatric Social Work Initiative: A multilevel community approach to building aging competency. *Journal of Gerontological Social Work, 50*(1), 59–74.

Cherry, D. J., & Shefner, J. (2004). Addressing barriers to university–community collaboration: Organizing by experts or organizing the experts? *Journal of Community Practice, 12*(3), 219–233.

Council on Social Work Education. (2008). *Educational policy and accreditation standards.* Retrieved November 30, 2008, from http://www.cswe.org/NR/rdonlyres/2A81732E-1776-4175-AC42-65974E96BE66/0/2008EducationalPolicyandAccreditationStandards.pdf

Damron-Rodriguez, J., & Brownell, P. (2008, February). *Practicum partnership program orientation: Competency-driven field education.* Presented at the Hartford Partnership Program for Aging Education Orientation/Training Annual Meeting, New York.

Damron-Rodriguez, J., Malks, B., Lawrence, F. P., Edsall, J., & Trimble, M. (2007, October). *Aging agencies and university partnering in field education: The PPP model.* Paper presented at the 53rd annual meeting of the Council on Social Work Education, San Francisco.

Diwan, S., & Wertheimer, M. R. (2007). Aging services or services to the aging? Focus of a university–community curriculum development partnership to increase awareness of aging issues in social work practice. *Journal of Gerontological Social Work, 50*(1), 187–204.

Fisher, R., Fabricant, M., & Simmons, L. (2004). Understanding contemporary university–community connections: Context, practice, and challenges. *Journal of Community Practice, 12*(3), 13–34.

Fortune, A. E., & Kaye, L. W. (2008, February). *University-community partnerships.* Presentation at the Hartford Partnership Program for Aging Education Orientation/Training Annual Meeting, New York.

Ivry, J., Lawrance, F. P., Damron-Rodriguez, J., & Robbins, V. C. (2005). Fieldwork rotation: A model for educating social work students for geriatric social work practice. *Journal of Social Work Education, 41*(3), 407–425.

Lawrance, F. P., Damron-Rodriguez, J., Rosenfeld, P., Sisco, S., & Volland, P. J. (2007). Strengthening field education in aging through university–community agency partnership: The Practicum Partnership Program. *Journal of Gerontological Social Work, 50*(1), 135–154.

Martin, L. L., Smith, H. P., & Phillips, W. (2005). Bridging "town & gown" through innovative university–community partnerships. *The Innovation Journal: The Public Sector Innovation Journal, 10*(2), Article 20. Retrieved August 16, 2008, from http://www.innovation.cc/volumes-issues/martin-u-partner4final.pdf

Mertz, L., Fortune, A., & Zendell, A. (2007). Promoting leadership skills in field education: A university–community partnership to bring macro and micro together in gerontological field placements. *Journal of Gerontological Social Work*, 50(1/2), 173–186.

New York Academy of Medicine. (2004). *Unsung heroes at the front line: The PPP from perspectives of agency representatives.* New York: Author.

New York Academy of Medicine (NYAM). (2008a). *Hartford Partnership Program for Aging Education (HPPAE) student summary multi-site report.* New York: Author.

New York Academy of Medicine (NYAM). (2008b). *Implementation of the Hartford partnership program for aging education: Lessons from the field.* New York: Author.

Pew Partnership for Civic Change. (2003). *University + community research partnerships.* Charlottesville, VA: Author.

Reisch, M., & Jarmon-Rhode, L. (2000). The future of social work in the United States: Implications for field education. *Journal of Social Work Education, 36*, 201–213.

Robbins, V. C., & Rowan, N. L. (2008, February). *Rotations in field work.* Presentation at the Hartford Partnership Program for Aging Education Orientation/Training Annual Meeting, New York.

Townsend, A. L., Ishler, K. J., Vargo, E. H., Shapiro, B. M., Pitorak, E. F., & Matthews, C. R. (2007). The FACES project: An academic-community partnership to improve end-of-life care for families. *Journal of Gerontological Social Work, 50*(1), 7–20.

Volland, P. J., & Berkman, B. (2004). Educating social workers to meet the challenge of an aging urban population: A promising model. *Academic Medicine, 79*, 1192–1197.

Zendell, A. L., Fortune, A. E., Mertz, L. K. P., & Koelewyn, N. (2007). University-community partnerships in gerontological social work: Building consensus around student learning. *Journal of Gerontological Social Work, 50*(1), 155–172.

PART III

Creating Structures and Supports for a National Initiative

CHAPTER 7

Common Goals, Diverse Locations

A Collaborative Virtual Team Model

**Suzanne St Peter, Ashley Brooks-Danso,
and Julia Meashey**

Collaboration across diverse programs and organizations at geographic distances is often challenging and problematic. Nevertheless, working together across multisite, multiprogram initiatives can yield substantial benefits for the participants and the programs' goals (Gillam & Oppenheim, 2006; Hardy, Phillips, & Lawrence, 2003; Powell, Piccoli, & Ives, 2004). In addition, the use of modern technology can accentuate the advantages of interorganizational collaboration and minimize the difficulties. A group of individuals collaborating across organizations using technological media such as conference calls, e-mail, and Web-based meeting software is designated as a *virtual team* (Bell & Koslowski, 2002; Zigurs, 2003). As part of a multisite, multiprogram initiative, the principal investigators (PIs) and program coordinators of the Hartford Geriatric Social Work Initiative (GSWI) have experienced the challenges and benefits associated with working as virtual teams.

This chapter begins with a brief background of virtual teams. Next, the rationale for and development of the GSWI Program Coordinator Virtual Team is presented. The team's experiences with virtual, interorganizational collaboration are then discussed, including obstacles, effective strategies to address these challenges, and lessons learned. Last, a collaborative virtual team model is provided, which can be replicated by other multisite/multiprogram initiatives in social work or other disciplines, regardless of the substantive area.

Virtual Teams

Most definitions of virtual teams include the basic elements of geographic dispersion, electronic communication, common goals, and diverse members (Bell & Koslowski, 2002; Gillam & Oppenheim, 2006; Zigurs, 2003). Griffith, Sawyer, and Neale (2003) distinguish between pure virtual teams, in which members never meet face-to-face, and hybrid virtual teams, in which the majority of interaction takes place via electronic communication, yet members meet in person from time to time. Most individuals in the nation's workforce are members of virtual teams, whether working in corporate, government, nonprofit, or academic environments. A 2002 study suggested that by 2004, more than 60% of corporate employees would be working in some manner of virtual teams (Kanawattanachai & Yoo, 2002).

Yet at the core, per Lurey and Raisinghani (2001), "virtual teams are first and foremost teams. As such, they must have a shared purpose to foster the need for members to work together" (p. 532). Accordingly, the GSWI program coordinators are a team—a geographically dispersed, hybrid virtual team working primarily via electronic communication to achieve the same goal: preparing gerontologically competent social workers to improve the health and well-being of older adults nationwide.

Development of the GSWI Program Coordinator Virtual Team

The four core GSWI programs—Hartford Faculty Scholars (HFS), Hartford Partnership Program for Aging Education (HPPAE), Hartford Doctoral Fellows (HDF), and CSWE National Center for Gerontological Social Work Education (Gero-Ed Center)—are located at six organizations across the country. The programs' dispersed locations developed organically as a result of the GSWI's funding process, in which the John A. Hartford Foundation sought experts in the fields of gerontology, social work, and higher education to provide leadership for the four primary programs. Within this broad category, the PIs were selected for their specific expertise in practicum/field, research, curriculum change, and doctoral student development. The foundation is also strategic in directing funding to professional associations, not single academic departments, to build institutional capacity and sustainability for the field as a whole. As a result, the PIs and administrative personnel are located at a diverse mix of academic institutions and nonprofit organizations.

During the first years of the GSWI, initial steps to ensure consistency and collaboration among the four programs involved monthly conference calls and annual in-person strategy meetings with the PIs. In 2006, with all programs wholly operational and fully staffed, the program coordinators formed a virtual team to increase interorganizational collaboration, specifically at the day-to-day, operational level. Although the PIs' high-level vision, substantive expertise, and macro administration of their programs are critical, the program coordinators' midlevel management, daily administration, and operational savvy are also vital to the success of each program and to the GSWI as a whole (Burgelman, 1983; Wooldridge & Floyd, 1990).

The program coordinators first met at a national gerontological social work conference, which served as a platform for the exchange of information about their programs. A primary discussion topic was data collection and analysis, and the duplication of efforts among the programs was immediately evident: Several program coordinators were collecting the same data points and conducting similar analyses. This initial face-to-face meeting highlighted the need for improved coordination of such tasks and it generated enthusiasm, both of which enabled the team's relationships to develop more quickly (Kimble, Li, & Barlow, 2000). As a result, the program coordinators decided to maintain and expand this initial collaboration, communicating about every 6 weeks via conference calls to provide program updates and collaborate on joint projects that would enhance the GSWI's overall effectiveness.

Accordingly, the GSWI program coordinator group made the transition naturally into a virtual team: Staff are diverse in terms of age, ethnicity, and sexual orientation; geographically dispersed across the nation; employed in dissimilar types of organizations (academic, nonprofit membership); communicate primarily via telephone and e-mail; and share the common purpose of increasing effective, efficient collaboration among the four GSWI programs. Although the geographic distribution of the programs necessitates working as a virtual team the majority of the time, the program coordinators continue to schedule face-to-face meetings and informal gatherings at national conferences. This consistent, albeit infrequent, in-person interaction catalyzes continued relationship building among team members and fosters an expanded commitment to the GSWI's shared goals, as described in the foreword (Gillam & Oppenheim, 2006; Powell et al., 2004; Zigurs, 2003).

The Virtual Team: Encountering Challenges

As noted previously, multiple barriers to effective collaboration are inherent in multiprogram, multisite initiatives by nature of their composition. The geographic separation of the program sites, whether across town or across the country, impedes frequent, informal face-to-face communication and may lead some team members to feel isolated (Gillman & Oppenheim, 2006). Despite the benefits of electronic communication among disparate sites, technological problems, such as server failure, interruption of the e-mail service provider, and incompatible software, can inhibit fast, efficient transfer of information between parties (Kimble et al., 2000). Organizational and functional culture differences at the separate locations further complicate communication and mutual understanding (Gibson & Gibbs, 2006). Challenges specific to the GSWI programs as well as effective strategies to address these obstacles are described in the following sections. These strategies are transferrable to other areas of social work education involving national collaborations and other disciplines.

The GSWI is a complex entity encompassing four programs located at six geographically dispersed, organizationally and culturally divergent settings. Current personnel include three principal and two co-PIs; a faculty-level project PI and codirector; a coordinating center program officer; and 16 staff, 9 of whom are members of the program coordinator virtual team (see Table 7.1). Although most of the cross-program collaboration takes place among the program coordinators, effective collaboration can improve the work environment and sense of cohesion among all levels of staff.

Dispersed Geographic Locations

The program coordinators are located in five cities across the country, with the majority on the East Coast. Only one office is on the West Coast. This bicoastal arrangement has the obvious coordination issues of scheduling across multiple time zones and arranging meeting times during standard business hours. The varied locations challenge the program coordinators to get to know each other and work together as a team irrespective of the fact that they may have only met face-to-face on a handful of occasions.

Program Structures

PIs and staff at the four programs are distributed across five schools of social work, two nonprofit professional membership associations, and one nonprofit research and policy organization. Specifically, the HFS and HDF programs are housed in academic institutions and the Gerontological Society of America (GSA). The HPPAE is situated at a research and policy organization—the New York Academy of Medicine (NYAM)— and the Council on Social Work Education (CSWE) Gero-Ed Center personnel are based at three separate locations: a professional membership association (CSWE) and two schools of social work.

Additionally, GSWI Coordinating Center staff, located in the membership association of GSA, serve a dual role of administrative and financial coordination for the scholars and fellows programs, and overall GSWI communication coordination, adding to the complexities of cross-program collaboration. Overall organizational, functional, and cultural differences exist between the schools' academic environment and the nonprofit organizations' work environment. Additionally, within the academic and nonprofit environments, each of the six locations operates in its own context of organizational, functional, and cultural norms.

In academic settings, lines of authority are typically hierarchical, tied to faculty rank, and staff seniority. Faculty PI and program staff roles and responsibilities are clearly defined, based on a distinct hierarchy, with faculty having authority and supervising and assigning work to staff. Strategic decisions are made by the faculty PI around the specific goals of the project but within the larger context of the social work program and institution in which it is housed. The faculty PIs tend to have numerous other academic responsibilities, such as teaching and participation in governance, which may constrain their ability to focus primarily on project demands and provide daily supervision, possibly resulting in staff's working on a relatively independent basis. Oftentimes, an academic environment offers greater flexibility of work hours than is generally possible in nonprofit settings. Yet, in one GSWI program, staff in the partner nonprofit organization has a 35-hour work week, whereas

Table 7.1
HARTFORD GSWI PROGRAMS

Program Name	Staff Positions	Leadership
GSWI Coordinating Center	*Program manager* *Program coordinator* Administrative assistant	Linda Harootyan, program officer; deputy executive director, GSA
Gero-Ed Center	Alexandria, VA: *Codirector* Program assistant Administrative assistant Project assistant, Master's Advanced Curriculum (MAC) Project Seattle, WA: *Director* Program coordinator	Julia Watkins, Co-PI; executive director, CSWE Nancy Hooyman, Co-PI; Endowed Professor of Gerontology and dean emeritus, University of Washington Sadhna Diwan, MAC Project PI; associate professor, San José State University
HPPAE	*Program officer* *Program strategy associate*	Patricia Volland, PI; director, Social Work Leadership Institute and senior vice president of administration and finance, NYAM
HFS Program	*Program manager* (Located at GSA) *Program evaluator*	Barbara Berkman, PI and national program director; Helen Rehr/Ruth Fizdale Professor of Health and Mental Health, Columbia University
HDF Program (includes Pre-Dissertation Award)	*Program manager* (Located at GSA) *Program manager* (On site) *Research associate*	James Lubben, PI and national program director; Louise McMahon Ahearn University Chair, Boston College Carmen Morano, Codirector, Pre-Dissertation Award Program; senior faculty fellow and associate professor, Hunter College

Note. Staff positions participating in the virtual team are in italics.

Location	Program Description/Components
The Gerontological Society of America 1220 L St., NW Suite 901 Washington, DC 20005	Fiscal and administrative coordination of Hartford Faculty Scholars and Doctoral Fellows Programs Coordinates GSWI interprogram communication, including program coordinator virtual team GSWI e-newsletter: Ripples GSWI Web site: http://www.gswi.org

Council on Social Work Education 1725 Duke Street Suite 500 Alexandria, VA 22314 and University of Washington School of Social Work 4101 15th Ave. NE Seattle, WA 98105	Fiscal and administrative coordination
	
	Gero-Ed Center Web site: http://www.gero-edcenter.org
	
	Gero-Ed Track at the CSWE Annual Program Meeting
	
	Curricular development/faculty training programs:
	    Curriculum Development Institutes (CDIs)
	    BSW Experiential Learning (BEL)
	    Specialized Gerontology Program
	    MAC Project
	Curricular infusion eLearning courses

New York Academy of Medicine Room 564 1216 Fifth Ave. New York, NY 10029	Fiscal and administrative coordination Peer review Trainings and educational materials Marketing and communications Reporting and oversight Dissemination (presentations and publications)
Columbia University School of Social Work 1255 Amsterdam Ave. New York, NY 10027	Development and facilitation of programs for scholars including orientation, research, leadership, teaching, and policy institutes Program data collection and evaluation Coordination of National Research Mentor Program for scholars
Boston College School of Social Work McGuinn Hall 315 140 Commonwealth Ave. Chestnut Hill, MA 02467 Hunter College School of Social Work Brookdale Center on Aging 129 E. 79th Street New York, NY 10021	Development and facilitation of programs for doctoral fellows and recipients of the Pre-Dissertation Award, including orientation, professional development, and research intensives Program data collection and evaluation Coordination of Academic Career Advisor Program

their academic colleagues work 40 hours per week (yet, admittedly, enjoy greater work-hour flexibility). These issues, although seemingly minor, create disparate norms about the length and nature of the work week and responsibilities on weekends and evenings.

In contrast to academic settings, the nonprofit organization work environment, particularly in membership organizations, requires staff positions that are broad in scope. Challenged by the need to be highly efficient with limited resources, including personnel, staff positions in nonprofits frequently require individuals to operate as generalists, constantly thinking how the work of the organization might benefit the GSWI as a whole or vice versa. Although some program personnel in membership organizations focus primarily on the GSWI activities, they also must bring the GSWI's goals and perspectives into the larger context of the membership organization's mission and goals. For instance, in a national membership organization such as GSA, decisions are made based on membership needs, which are considered the heart of the organization. In most cases, competing demands exist among the membership and, therefore, within the organization. Additionally, as a result of their membership's national interests, and because of their close proximity to Washington, DC, program staff at the Gero-Ed Center and the GSWI Coordinating Center are frequently called upon to represent their organizations and the GSWI on national committees and in meetings on broader issues within and beyond geriatric social work, thus placing additional demands on staff time that may not be visible nor appreciated by personnel in academic settings.

Administrative Complexities

The term *program coordinator* was developed as a general identifier for the variety of program staff working to coordinate their programs. However, staff titles vary among the work environments and the programs. Actual titles of the program coordinator virtual team staff members range from program manager to research associate to program officer to codirector (see Table 7.2).

In some cases, program personnel have backgrounds in social work and have taught in an academic setting. Others are part-time students either in social work or other fields such as public policy or gerontology. There are also individuals without social work backgrounds who have an interest in human services (i.e., nursing, business, psychology, or gerontology). In addition, program coordinators' responsibilities and relationships with the PIs vary. In some instances, staff operate as a collegial team with faculty PIs; although the PI retains the final decision-making authority, some decisions are shared. In other cases, staff operate in a largely support-based capacity, with decision making assumed by the PI with limited staff input.

These differences in settings and staffing classifications and configurations can hinder collaboration efforts. For example, the disparate titles given to program staff can make it difficult to determine who manages a particular program. Role confusion can lead to misperceptions regarding an individual's authority and responsibilities within the organization. And, as discussed next, the complexity and seemingly arbitrary nature of staff titles and roles hinders the social work education community's understanding of the individual programs and the overall GSWI.

Program Coordinator Differences

The program coordinators recognized the need to work in partnership as a group, in addition to the PIs' collaboration. All coordinators agreed to increase communication via scheduled conference calls and to develop scholarly presentations for national conferences. Even with such collective agreement and commitment, however, dissimilarities in personalities and work styles can inhibit a team's best intentions (Boumgarden & Campagna, 2007). For example, as with nearly all teams some program coordinators are more assertive and outspoken than others, resulting in an unequal representation of individual programs on conference calls. Differences also occur in writing and work styles; some coordinators prefer to complete joint conference presentations several weeks in advance of the presentation date, whereas others work better under deadline pressure and are comfortable finalizing the presentation days before the due date.

The Social Work Education Community's Perceptions

There has been a significant amount of confusion in the broader social work education and gerontology communities regarding the distinctive goals of each GSWI program. As noted in the foreword, each program

Table 7.2
GSWI PROGRAMS: LOCATION AND ORGANIZATION TYPE

Program	Location
Gero-Ed Center:	
Location A	CSWE
Location B	University of Washington School of Social Work
HPPAE	Social Work Leadership Institute, NYAM
HFS Program:	
Fiscal and Administrative Coordination	GSWI Coordinating Center, GSA
Program Development and Facilitation	Columbia University School of Social Work
HDF Program:	
Fiscal and Administrative Coordination	GSWI Coordinating Center, GSA
Program Development and Facilitation	Boston College School of Social Work
GSWI Coordinating Center	GSA

Organization Type	City, State	Staff Position Responsible for On-Site, Daily Administration
Nonprofit, national professional membership organization	Alexandria, VA	Codirector A
Public higher education institution	Seattle, WA	Codirector B
Nonprofit health advancement organization	New York	Program officer
Nonprofit, national membership organization	Washington, DC	Program manager
Private higher education institution	New York	Program evaluator
Nonprofit, national membership organization	Washington, DC	Program manager
Private higher education institution	Boston, MA	Program manager
Nonprofit, national membership organization	Washington, DC	Program manager

has a distinct mission, goals, and target audience (social work students, faculty, researchers, and field supervisors). Additionally, each program has unique criteria for selection, application deadlines, and funding opportunities. Despite an intensive communication strategy for the GSWI, described in chapter 8, members of the social work and gerontology communities still hold misconceptions about each of the initiatives.

Prior to instituting collaboration among the program coordinators, confusion regarding program distinctions was evident among program staff as well. Lack of collaboration and information sharing among the coordinators in the first years of the initiative significantly contributed to the problem and, as a result, arguably reduced the overall impact of the GSWI. Additionally, this lack of understanding and communication between GSWI programs served to further the misunderstanding among broader social work and gerontological constituencies.

Strategies to Overcome Challenges

Dispersed Geographic Locations

The program coordinator virtual team's *interaction mode* can be construed as being face-to-face and electronically mediated (Jarvenpaa & Leidner, 1998): By committing to meeting in person two to three times per year at national conferences, the majority of communication takes place virtually, but relationships are further developed via face-to-face interactions. Ideally, such face-to-face interaction, which is typically short in duration, would occur outside the context of national conferences where staff face other demands. However, lacking the resources to meet in person at other times than at these national venues, the coordinators have prioritized these meetings and worked to fit them into their busy conference schedules.

Program Structures

One strategy used to address the challenges of this complex, multiorganization initiative has been consistent communication to describe and understand not only the different programs but also the dissimilar roles that each program coordinator has in his or her organization. Collaboration among the GSWI program coordinators has increased their own staff's understanding of these variations and served to highlight the importance of taking account of them in collaboration and communication efforts across programs. For example, through the planning process of collaborative presentations at national conferences, not only has the broader professional community been made more aware of the GSWI, but also the staff have learned more about each program's structure and specific goals and achievements.

Administrative Complexities

As the program coordinators worked together during two to three conference meetings and on eight to nine conference calls each year between 2006 and 2008, the administrative differences related to title and specific roles became less important than the similarities in providing the day-to-day operational-level support for the GSWI programs. In working together to develop presentations for national conferences, the coordinators not only learned more about their similarities, but were able to educate the broader social work community about each coordinator's role in ensuring the success of the overall GSWI mission. Ultimately, the heightened mutual understanding of each other's roles in the administrative environment led to a better understanding of the GSWI for the broader social work education community.

Program Coordinator Differences

An effective strategy for coping with differences in team members' personalities and work styles is first to openly acknowledge them and then take steps to understand each other's individuality and background (Boumgarden & Campagna, 2007). To illustrate, staff from one GSWI program attended a retreat with the primary purpose of acknowledging and understanding differences. In one of the exercises, each of the six staff, including two members of the Program Coordinator Virtual Team, described whether they avoid or embrace conflict in the workplace. The insights gained in each other's aversion to or inclination for conflict created a deeper understanding of each staff member, resulting in decreased miscommunication and increased empathy for others and their different styles.

Participation in virtual team activities also helped staff who had previously worked in relative isolation understand the big picture and the importance of their roles in GSWI's influence on the social work education community. This created a sense of excitement and connection and helped establish a positive extended social network that is critical for job satisfaction (Haley-Lock, 2007).

The Social Work Education Community's Perceptions

Communication among program coordinators and dissemination of consistent messages regarding each program's mission and purpose have become the primary means to address misunderstandings among social work and gerontology communities regarding the GSWI's goals and scope. Communicating on a regular basis has better equipped the program coordinators to field and route questions about other GSWI programs. Armed with a better understanding of and information about the latest projects, the program coordinators now have a broad knowledge base from which to address questions and make referrals. This streamlined front has reduced confusion and increased the visibility and understanding of the GSWI's overall mission.

The enhanced communication among program coordinators has fostered the dissemination of their work in national professional conference settings, thus adding to the visibility that the PIs bring to the GSWI. This collaboration on presentations at conferences has contributed to the broader understanding among social work and gerontology faculty, students, and practitioners about the opportunities available to them through the GSWI. Additionally, this leadership capacity building among the program coordinators has served to expand their own professional development opportunities.

As mentioned earlier, collaborative presentations among the GSWI program coordinators have educated the broader professional community about the GSWI's distinctive approach in targeting social work students and faculty and curriculum and field education to create a national gerontological movement. As a result, several faculty members have approached the coordinators, seeking information on how to replicate the GSWI model in other substantive areas in social work. Highlighting not only the details of each program but also how the program coordinators collaborate has contributed to the GSWI's overall influence on the social work education community.

Use of Technology

Technology remains the primary means to facilitate increased communication among the disparate sites. Conference calls are a quick and relatively economical way to stay in touch. The conference call allows for clear, instantaneous communication. Unlike e-mail, it allows coordinators to distinguish personal styles and some nonverbal signals such as voice tone. Conference calls have been used as a method of introduction, are more personal than e-mail, and are used regularly for program updates and brainstorming, which is essential to projects requiring cross-program collaboration such as those related to national conferences and presentations.

Web-enhanced conference calls are particularly useful when new information is available or new skills are being taught. For example, a Web-enhanced call was used to introduce new program staff and update seasoned program staff on information and materials available on the John A. Harford Foundation's Bandwidth Web site (http://www.bandwidthonline.org/). As part of the GSWI's overall communication strategy, the site provides useful tools for faculty and doctoral student participants in GSWI programs that promote consistency in messaging and branding items used by programs and recipients.

E-mail, of course, is the most frequently used electronic means of communication in cross-program collaboration between different sites at geographic distances. It remains the quick, easy way to relay messages and gather succinct information. Although slightly less personal, it is an excellent way to supplement conference calls. Some programs have even experimented with instant messaging to aid in communication and build rapport.

As cross-program collaboration continues to gain in importance and telecommuting becomes more widespread, especially in the face of rising fuel and travel costs, program staff in a wide range of settings will need to rely even more heavily on the use of technology. Because of the types of relevant technology, ease of access, and the economical aspect of this mode of communication, telecommuting will not only gain in popularity but will likely drive technological innovations that will contribute to successful cross-program collaborations of the future (Gillam & Oppenheim, 2006).

Lessons Learned

The lessons learned that are described here are relevant to cross-program collaborations, regardless of the substantive areas or disciplines involved. Meeting face-to-face in the initial, formative stages of a project is optimum to developing interpersonal relationships among virtual team members (Powell et al., 2004). Perhaps by nature of the program coordinators' personalities in the GSWI virtual team, the members have developed trust and are committed to continuing to advance their effective professional relationships. However, development of the team in the beginning months of the GSWI, including an in-person meeting to set goals and action plans, would have increased cohesion among members at an earlier point and reduced some of the communication challenges experienced during the first few years.

For virtual teams to succeed, program staff must have a shared purpose and a common vision (Lurey & Raisinghani, 2001). This common vision can be obscured by disparities in location and issues of role confusion. One lesson learned from the GSWI is that multisite, multiprogram teams must always consider the importance of the environment where the majority of the work is taking place. Clearly, the different organizational and functional cultures inherent in each program location are primary challenges to the effectiveness of interorganizational collaboration. This is also a key issue to consider in understanding the daily operations of the individual programs. Therefore, although each program is working toward the goals of the overall GSWI, each program is operating within its own environment with its corresponding priorities, implicit culture, and communication norms. It is critical for staff to understand that although their organizations' missions may differ from one another, the GSWI's overall mission is the same. By recognizing this fact, the scale of individual differences between programs begins to lessen, and collaboration becomes much easier.

Although these dissimilarities create their own set of challenges, they are also beneficial. The collaboration among the program coordinators working within diverse settings also provides new perspectives and approaches to projects that enhance the effectiveness and overall mission of the GSWI. For example, for several years the GSWI has hosted an exhibit booth at various national conferences. This booth was always managed by the GSWI coordinating staff and through their close connection with the HFS and HDF programs, the booth was staffed primarily by the scholars and fellows, who often lacked information and were unable to answer questions about the other two GSWI programs. The program coordinators collaboratively suggested that the responsibility for staffing the booth be dispersed among all programs to relieve the GSWI coordinating staff from sole responsibility and to decrease such information gaps. This new strategy has worked successfully for the past 2 years.

The acceptance and encouragement of high-level administration is crucial to the continuing operation and success of efforts to create positive changes by midlevel staff (Hooyman, 2006). The GSWI PIs have provided such backing to the coordinators' virtual team. All the PIs have supported their coordinators' taking the time to meet at national conferences, conducting conference calls, and working on projects that often benefit the GSWI as a whole but perhaps not the PI's individual program specifically or immediately. Another advantage is that the reduced duplication of effort brought about by the program coordinators' collaboration and information sharing has also diminished the PIs' workloads. An example of this is the availability of data analyses conducted by other PIs or coordinators, which, without the coordinators' virtual team, would probably have to be developed by each individual PI.

A Collaborative Virtual Team Model

Based on the experiences of the GSWI Program Coordinator Virtual Team, other multisite, multiprogram initiatives may gain from incorporating the following strategies in their operations plan, which will enhance collaboration, communication, and, ultimately, the probability of successful programmatic outcomes:

◆ **Encourage and support operational-level staff to collaborate on a regular basis, especially early in the initiative's formation.**
   Presuming that resources are adequate, a face-to-face meeting of the operational-level program staff from all participating programs should occur in the initiative's formative stages. By meeting in the start-up phase, personnel immediately begin to develop cooperative working relationships and appreciate the diverse backgrounds they bring to the team. Typically, enthusiasm and commitment to the program's mission and goals are high, and staff will more readily

incorporate such team collaboration as part of their usual work-load rather than viewing it as an added responsibility or task. Face-to-face gatherings, although not always possible, are a best practice to improve virtual team success, because such personal contact establishes supportive relationships, which are critical to a team's effectiveness and sustainability (Lurey & Raisinghani, 2000).

As noted under "Lessons Learned," obtaining each PI's acceptance of and support for such an operational-level virtual team is critical to ensure cohesion among the different programs. Additionally, PIs may need to encourage their program coordinators to join and contribute to the team, emphasizing the benefits of collaboration, such as continuity of data collection and analysis and elimination of duplication of efforts. The PIs' own modeling of interorganizational collaboration can also support the operational staff's motivation to work as a team.

♦ **Use available technology to develop and maintain a virtual team.**

In this information age, technology is taken for granted on the one hand, yet also not fully employed on the other. Most, if not all, multisite, multiprogram initiatives will possess all the hardware necessary for virtual communication: desktop or laptop computer, Internet service provider, Web browser, and telephone. In addition to these basics, program staff should research and obtain appropriate services and software to enhance the use of this equipment.

Although the use of e-mail can be overwhelming at times because of the number of messages received, it allows near-simultaneous communication between two or more individuals. Strategies to enhance e-mail usage and minimize overload include designating folders for initiative- and team-related discussions, creating an e-mail distribution list for virtual team members, using a keyword in all team-related subject lines, using chat platforms, and, depending on the number of team members, developing an electronic mailing list (e.g., e-list or electronic list server). Such a list allows members to send an e-mail to all other members using one central address, to review all previous messages sent to the e-list, and to store all messages separately from their personal e-mail system.

Conference calls are perhaps the best-known and easiest method of voice-to-voice virtual communication. If organizations do not own or do not have the resources to purchase in-house conference call software and equipment, multiple conference call centers are available in nearly all communities. Conference call centers are service companies that provide the technology and support to conduct conference calls without purchasing in-house equipment. Using such a service is an inexpensive, user-friendly way to conduct multiple-party telephone calls.

The next step up in virtual communication, online meeting providers, enables multiple users to view one or more users' computer screens, usually concurrent with a conference call. Collaborative projects progress much faster when all parties involved in tasks such as designing a marketing brochure or informational flyer or setting a conference schedule can see the document(s) simultaneously. Control of the call and whose computer screen is being shown can be moved from participant to participant during the call. One of the GSWI programs subscribes to and receives quality service from GoToMeeting, a popular, well-reviewed, online meeting (or Web conferencing) service.

◆ **Acknowledge differences in organizational variables (culture, purpose/function, and process) and diversity among individual team members—and the resulting challenges to successful collaboration.**

Members of virtual teams will be best served by acknowledging openly the differences in their organizations' culture, purpose, and processes. Making them explicit can minimize misunderstandings about dissimilarities in workload demands and work styles. It is especially helpful to view each member of the team within the context of the purpose of his or her immediate work environment to avoid jumping to the conclusion that one's perspective is directly the result of one's personality. Boumgarden and Campagna (2007) conceptualize a worker as responding in a work environment first in reaction to the organization's purpose, then in response to the processes set forth by the organization, and last in reaction to his or her own personality.

For example, if data is needed for a specific team project and one member is hesitant to provide this information, it is easy to conclude that this person is being difficult. However, in an academic setting, this information may be considered the intellectual property of the faculty or institution involved in the project, and it may not yet have been released for public consumption. The release of such data usually follows a standard process set forth by the university and/or professor who has ownership of it. This example illustrates how a request for data may in some cases lead to hesitation by a staff member not because the person is trying to be difficult but rather because of the larger context of his or her work environment.

In addition to the disparate work environments, acknowledging and respecting the diversity and multiple identities of individual team members—such as variations in gender, race, ethnicity, age, or sexual orientation—are essential to building and maintaining team continuity (Schomer, 2000). Perhaps even more so in a virtual team, bringing the differences among individuals to the surface is important because team members infrequently interact face-to-face where nonverbal cues may assist the communication process and understanding. The use of language can be especially critical to conveying respect for individuals' diverse social identities and locations during e-mail and phone communication. Viewing such diversity as richness and strength rather than as potential sources of conflict will help minimize misunderstandings and increase team productivity and satisfaction.

◆ **Develop and maintain a feedback loop: Ensure communication between midlevel operational program staff and PIs.**

Maintaining consistent communication among program staff and the GSWI's PIs helps ensure that essential information is provided to both parties. This in turn enables the program coordinator and the PI to function in the most effective and efficient way possible. Through the program coordinators' participation in the virtual team, they are able to keep the PIs updated on the various GSWI programs; this may then inform the discussion among the PIs at their annual meeting. By the coordinators' sharing information, the PIs can stay abreast of ongoing developments among the programs with a minor investment of their time. Communication should, however, go both ways. As mentioned previously, the PIs have an important role in modeling collaboration and sharing their knowledge and expertise. Therefore, it is equally important that the PIs continue to support and encourage program coordinators by keeping them abreast of the overall goals and strategies that drive the initiative.

Conclusion

The GSWI's effect on social work education has been magnified through cross-program collaboration. The virtual team model has contributed to the success, effectiveness, and sustainability of the GSWI, despite the many challenges of working across diverse organizations, geographic locations, and program structures. Moreover, the GSWI is a model germane to other multisite/multiprogram initiatives in social work or other disciplines. Four strategies are essential for any cross-program collaboration:

1. Encouraging and supporting operational-level staff to collaborate on a regular basis and early in the initiative's formation.
2. Using available technology to develop and maintain the virtual team.
3. Acknowledging differences in organizational culture, purpose/function, and process as well as the resulting challenges/barriers to successful collaboration.
4. Developing and maintaining a feedback loop to ensure communication between midlevel operational program staff and PIs.

The positive benefits accruing from the time and resources devoted to building a virtual team among program coordinators and other administrative staff serve as powerful reminders of the importance of supporting and strengthening the contributions of all members of organizations seeking to bring about profound and sustainable changes. This reminder may seem simple and self-evident. In reality, however, attention to strategies to maximize the contributions of all staff in a multisystem initiative may be overlooked in the pressure to meet deadlines, produce deliverables, and respond to expectations of PIs and stakeholders. The virtual model presented here is but one example of a strategy to maximize the contributions and the workplace satisfaction among administrative staff and, in the long term, to improve the quality of gerontological research, teaching, and practice.

References

Bell, B. S., & Kozlowski, S. W. (2002). A typology of virtual teams: Implications for effective leadership. *Group & Organization Management, 27*(1), 14–49.

Boumgarden, P., & Campagna, R. (2007, April). *Team building workshop.* Paper presented at the staff retreat of the Council on Social Work Education Gero-Ed Center, St. Louis, MO.

Burgelman, R. A. (1983). Corporate entrepreneurship and strategic management: Insights from a process study. *Management Science, 23*(12), 1349–1363.

Gibson, C. B., & Gibbs, J. L. (2006). Unpacking the concept of virtuality: The effects of geographic dispersion, electronic dependence, dynamic structure, and national diversity on team innovation. *Administrative Science Quarterly, 51,* 451–495.

Gillam, C., & Oppenheim, C. (2006). Review article: Reviewing the impact of virtual teams in the information age. *Journal of Information Science, 32*(2), 160–175.

Griffith, T. L., Sawyer, J. E., & Neale, M. A. (2003). Virtualness and knowledge in teams: Managing the love triangle of organizations, individuals, and information technology. *MIS Quarterly, 27,* 265–287.

Haley-Lock, A. (2007). Up close and personal: Employee networks and job satisfaction in a human service context. *Social Service Review, 81*(4), 683–707.

Hardy, C., Phillips, N., & Lawrence, T. B. (2003). Resources, knowledge, and influence: The organizational effects of interorganizational collaboration. *Journal of Management Studies 40*(2), 321–347.

Hooyman, N. R. (2006). *Achieving curricular and organizational change: Impact of the CSWE Geriatric Enrichment in Social Work Education Project.* Alexandria, VA: Council on Social Work Education.

Jarvenpaa, S. L., & Leidner, D. E. (1998). Communication and trust in global virtual teams. *Journal of Computer Mediated Communication, 3*(4). Retrieved August 13, 2008, from http://jcmc.indiana.edu/vol3/issue4/jarvenpaa.html

Kanawattanachai, P., & Yoo, Y. (2002). Dynamic nature of trust in virtual teams. *Journal of Strategic Information Systems, 11*, 187–213.

Kimble, C., Li, F., & Barlow, A. (2000). Effective virtual teams through communities of practice. Retrieved July 10, 2008, from http://papers.ssrn.com/sol3/papers.cfm?abstract_id=634645

Lurey, J. S., & Raisinghani, M. S. (2001). An empirical study of best practices in virtual teams. *Information & Management, 38*, 523–544.

Powell, A., Piccoli, G., & Ives, B. (2004). Virtual teams: A review of current literature and directions for future research. *The DATA BASE for Advances in Information Systems, 35*(1), 6–36.

Schomer, K. (2000). Building multicultural teams. *Siliconindia, 4*(2), 90–91.

Wooldridge, B., & Floyd, S. W. (1990). The strategy process, middle management involvement, and organizational performance. *Strategic Management Journal, 11*(3), 231–241.

Zigurs, I. (2003). Leadership in virtual teams: Oxymoron or opportunity? *Organizational Dynamics, 31*(4), 339–351.

CHAPTER 8

Communications

*Leveraging the Financial Investment,
Expanding the Effect of the Geriatric
Social Work Initiative*

John Beilenson

Forging a Common Identity

Communications is an often overlooked aspect of programmatic-level efforts to improve social work education and practice. Resources necessarily flow primarily to the work of developing new ideas, guidelines, and tools, but investments in disseminating or diffusing these materials are generally modest and can leave these ideas in binders and books on the shelf. This chapter describes the communications and branding efforts, including the successes and the limitations of this work, associated with the Geriatric Social Work Initiative (GSWI). It outlines a straightforward, practical approach to using communications to amplify the impact and uptake of educational or program innovations, and a series of lessons learned about the powerful benefits these strategies and tactics can generate for similar fieldwide efforts, not only in social work but in other disciplines as well. These transferable lessons include the importance of naming programs carefully, the benefits of creating a common brand as a rallying point for internal stakeholders, and the capacity of a straightforward strategic communications planning process to create a sustainable organizing framework for conducting these activities over time.

Described in detail in chapter 1, GSWI comprises a comprehensive series of programs launched with support from the John A. Hartford Foundation in 1998. This effort is designed to create geriatrics-focused education and training programs that improve social work practice and generate more social workers prepared to care for older adults and their families. It uses three core strategies: namely, to cultivate new faculty leaders in gerontological education and research, to develop aging-rich field opportunities in real-world settings, and to infuse gerontological competencies into social work curricula and teaching.

Following GSWI's second round of major grants in 2000–2001, the Hartford Foundation invited Strategic Communications & Planning, a firm in Wayne, Pennsylvania, to work with GSWI principal investigators (PIs) to frame a common set of messages for the initiative as a whole. In 2000 the PIs had participated in a communications training session sponsored by the foundation. Even though some PIs had limited experience with such branding and marketing efforts, they began to recognize the potential strategic benefits of communications, particularly the development of a common message set as a vehicle to define greater clarity around the initiative's vision. For its part, the foundation, represented by the senior program officer for GSWI, was eager to ensure that the whole of its diverse investment in social work was greater than the sum of its parts. Because the foundation was also hoping to generate significant recognition for the initiative, the messaging was part of the broader effort to establish the quality of this work and the issue of geriatrics and gerontology within the social work education community.

Initially, the interest in messaging was not part of a comprehensive strategic marketing or branding exercise. This emergent concern around consistent language, however, did reflect a belief, supported in the literature, that common messaging could add value in a variety of ways. For example, Aaker (1996) states that this work can create "a consistency of meaning . . . through time that can provide ownership of a position . . . and cost efficiencies" (p. 222). Hershey (2005) notes that messaging can create organizational cohesion, a way of "strengthening [a nonprofit] organization inside and out," a way to "instill not only a sense of pride but also a motivational tool for staff and volunteers [or in this case, PIs and their program staff] to live the promise [implicit in these messages] in their day-to-day tasks" (p. 12). Finally, the initial work on messaging introduced an approach to thinking strategically about communications. It was a way to begin to ask GSWI PIs to prioritize their communications objectives, segment their audiences, and develop messages and associated outreach based on a value proposition (i.e., a set of rational, emotional, self-expressive benefits) for those audiences (Kotler & Lee, 2007).

As described in this chapter, the early messaging efforts provided an initial "small win" for the GSWI PI group. This success built the group's confidence and interest in communications and ultimately branding (Weick, 1986). The group effort also provided a mechanism for PIs charged with launching ambitious individual projects to think collectively and collaboratively about their common goals and aspirations. It led to the development of a set of communications approaches, products, and tools that together supported their common and individual program outreach efforts and in doing so, strengthened the PIs' sense of cohesion. Finally, initiative-wide attention to communications created a powerful movement orientation among the PIs and others involved in GSWI, adding energy and lift to this exciting new effort in the field.

Singing from the Same Song Sheet: Common Messaging, Common Names

The initial communications work for GSWI revolved around language. This included the development of a common set of messages for the initiative, a framework for organizing a description of the program, and a set of names for the individual programs that enabled insiders and outsiders to see the relationship of these individual parts to the whole. On the most instrumental level, this work had powerful team-building benefits, enabling the group of lead PIs to learn from each other and collaboratively develop a concrete product that reflected a collective vision and commitment. In addition, the message framework itself turned out to be a useful tool in its own right, providing the structure and language that would ultimately be used in the development of a practical set of communication tools to reach out to broader audiences.

Following the 1998 launch of GSWI, the Hartford Foundation provided modest funding to the Gerontological Society of America (GSA), the major professional association of gerontological researchers, educators, and practitioners, to facilitate communications among the initiative's four programs—Hartford Faculty Scholars (HFS), Hartford Partnership Program for Aging Education (HPPAE), Hartford Doctoral Fellows (HDF), and Council on Social Work Education National Center for Gerontological Social Work Education (CSWE Gero-Ed Center)—and to serve as a de facto resource center for them. This strategy, used by the foundation in most of its major grants in nursing and medicine, had a variety of benefits. For example, funding resource centers in this way

- ♦ enabled key institutional actors in the field, rather than the foundation, to take primary responsibility for coordination and communications among grantees;
- ♦ created capacity in the field, rather than at the foundation, to sustain this work over time; and
- ♦ linked funded efforts with a major professional association that provided helpful legitimacy for new efforts in the field and relationships to other organizational players beyond the grantees themselves.

The first communication strategy used by GSA was a regular monthly phone conference call with the PIs of the four projects. These conference calls focused on upcoming events, project updates, and the considerable logistics surrounding the launch of the various projects. Following their participation in a Hartford-sponsored communications training session, the PIs recognized the need for a common way to talk about their ambitious efforts on behalf of geriatrics and gerontology in social work. The group added messaging to its agenda and invited Strategic Communications & Planning to facilitate a process designed to create a standard set of statements that described the initiative and its constituent grants, the rationale behind this work, and its central benefits.

Too often, educational and nonprofit project staff members under- mine their own efforts by forgetting to pay attention to this messaging process. Various actors involved in an initiative may speak in contra- dictory ways and ultimately confuse key stakeholders. As Hershey (2005) writes:

> To make sure your audience begins to embrace your key messages, you need to consistently make the same points in all of your com- munications. . . . Nonprofits frequently make the mistake of de- vising a dozen complex messages that even their internal audience can't commit to memory. (p. 16)

To avoid this frequent mistake, the first step in this messaging process was a teleconference to introduce the concepts and associated benefits of consistent messaging. Staff at Strategic Communications & Planning then drafted an initial set of messages based on interviews or e-mail corre- spondence with all four PIs. This so-called message framework included

+ a rationale for the initiative,
+ a one-sentence description of the initiative as a whole,
+ four key strategic directions for the initiative, and
+ one-sentence descriptions of the four key initiative grants.

During subsequent conference calls, the group responded to these initial formulations, and the draft went through a series of iterations until it was finalized (see Figure 8.1). The final version hewed closely to the structure of the original messages proposed. However, the group spent considerable effort ensuring that their respective program messages clearly reflected their distinctive aims. The PIs also debated several key words and terms. Notably, they ultimately settled on the phrase "aging-savvy social worker" as shorthand for the kind of gerontologically prepared practitioner they sought to develop. They also claimed the words *navigator* and *expediter* of services to describe a social worker's central coordinating role in the care of older adults and their families.

As part of this process, each PI developed a clear two-word name for her or his program—Faculty Scholars, Doctoral Fellows, Practicum Partnership (now the HPPAE), Faculty Development (for SAGE-SW, the first curriculum grant focused on individual faculty) and GeroRich (now the Gero-Ed Center). This not only created a parallel structure to talk about a complex set of grants but also enabled the PIs, their staff, and associated faculty and students to more easily remember each other's program names and their associated descriptions. The discussion of the program names ultimately prompted a related discussion of GSWI's name. Up to that point, it had been referred to as the Hartford Geriatric Social Work Initiative. In thinking about this strategically, the PI group, with the foundation's concurrence, decided to remove Hartford from the official communications of the initiative. The PIs concurred that removing the foundation's name would create the opportunity for other funders and external partners to join the work, which other foundations later did. However, the foundation and its role in launching the initiative were still described, and the Hartford logo was still included in print and electronic materials.

This concern for messaging, and particularly for naming, reflects an issue nonprofit and educational groups avoid at their peril. Bulky or inappropriate names weigh down a program's communications over time. In contrast, as Wheeler (2006) writes, "the right name is timeless, is tireless, is easy to say and remember, stands for something, and facilitates brand extensions. A well-chosen name is an essential brand asset"

Figure 8.1
INITIAL GSWI MESSAGE FRAMEWORK 2001

- The number of older people, particularly the oldest (85 plus), is growing, and they need more assistance to remain active and independent.

  - Older people, when they need help, receive it mainly from their families or a combination of family care and an assortment of community-based health and social services.

  - Therefore, coordinating care with older adults, their families, and complex service networks is crucial.

- Aging-savvy social workers serve as navigators and expediters, enabling older adults and families to understand and choose among the bewildering array of available health and social services.

  - Social workers empower older adults and families to find the care they need.

  - Social workers also facilitate family support, provide counseling and direct services, and coordinate care delivered through professional systems.

- The John A. Hartford Foundation's GSWI collaborates with social work education programs to prepare needed, aging-savvy social workers and improve the care and well-being of older adults and their families.

- Specifically, the GSWI is

  - Cultivating faculty leaders in gerontological education and research through

    – The HFS program, which supports the career development and research of talented faculty

    – The HDF program, which provides dissertation support, mentorship, and leadership development for promising students

  - Developing excellent training opportunities in real-world settings through

    – The Practicum Partnership Program (now the HPPAE), which is developing and testing innovative, aging-rich field experiences for graduate students that connect communities and schools of social work

  - Creating new gerontological curricula and other teaching tools through

    – The Faculty Development Program (Strengthening Aging and Gerontology in Social Work Education, which is strengthening social work faculty's ability to develop, integrate, and teach aging content in new and existing courses via training, information exchange, and dissemination.

    – The GeroRich project, which is expanding the number, quality, and sustainability of aging-rich learning experiences (in classroom curricula, field practica, lectures, presentations, and other activities) at the undergraduate and graduate levels.

(p. 48). Accordingly, the initiative's program names became part of an integrated framework that could be incorporated easily in materials, a Web site, and even a colorful and adaptable meeting exhibit. For other social work education efforts, even those with a communications budget more limited than that of GSWI, up-front and focused attention to naming and messaging can be a cost-effective strategy that pays significant internal and external dividends.

Strategic Thinking, Audience Segmentation, and Critical Choices

Following the successful development of GSWI messages and program names, the PI group was willing to build on this achievement and began designing a comprehensive strategic communications plan for its work. The commitment to create a strategic plan—and within that plan to concentrate efforts on a single (through admittedly broad) objective and audience segment—gave needed structure to the group's communications efforts. The planning process ultimately served to identify a set of focused outreach strategies and tactics. It allowed the group to think critically about what their target audience (social work faculty, including deans and directors, and students) knew about GSWI and gerontological social work and to identify key moments in the academic year when members of this academic community were most receptive to the initiative's outreach.

In retrospect, the small win produced by developing the message framework was an effective introduction to a more ambitious communications effort that was not initially considered by some of the PIs. The messaging exercise also brought out into the open certain unspoken ideas or agendas that individuals held, particularly their biases about what they thought were critical elements of how best to talk about and describe the initiative and its projects. By acknowledging these differences, the group was then able to seek a clearer, common message, formalize the PI's collective vision, create a greater sense of group cohesion, and help move its communications forward more effectively.

This positive momentum facilitated the launch of a strategic communications plan. In the context of the monthly conference calls, Strategic Communications & Planning introduced a strategic communications framework used by the firm and based on practical and widely held communications principles (Beilenson, 1999; Bonk, Griggs, & Tynes, 1999).

Using these principles, the PI group first sought to identify its key communications objectives and various audiences for the initiative. Initially, the group framed four objectives (see Figure 8.2), but the PIs ultimately settled on a priority objective, namely to "increase awareness and knowledge, and where necessary, change attitudes within the social work education community about GSWI and the essential role social workers play in improving the health and well-being of older adults" (Hartford GSWI, 2002). Rather than seeking to influence the larger gerontology and geriatrics community or older adults and families, GSWI leaders agreed to concentrate their energies in the arena they knew best—the social work education community. This did not mean that they completely ignored other identified objectives. In fact, they pursued reactive or opportunistic efforts to work in the other areas. For example, at the annual meetings of the GSA, GSWI program leaders planned receptions, poster sessions, and other events that showcased social work for an interdisciplinary audience of doctors, nurses, and others focused on aging. Still, this prioritization on social work education provided a helpful focus for the PI group's communication planning and ultimately the main body of its communications work. In retrospect,

---

Figure 8.2
GSWI COMMUNICATIONS OBJECTIVES

Primary Objectives (Building Professional Support)

1. Increase awareness and knowledge, and where necessary, change attitudes in the social work education community about the GSWI and the essential role social workers play in improving the health and well-being of older adults. (Infuse gerontology into social work.)

2. Inform, excite, and mobilize geriatric and gerontological professionals about, and in support of, the GSWI and the essential role social workers play in improving the health and well-being of older adults. (Infuse social work into gerontology.)

Secondary Objectives (Creating Greater Demand)

1. Build awareness among employers and payers (e.g., HMOs, insurers) about the essential role social workers play in improving the health and well-being of older adults and providing cost-effective care.

2. Educate the baby boom generation about the essential role social workers play in improving the health and well-being of older adults.

the single objective could have been further sharpened to enable GSWI leaders to measure progress in influencing social work educators' awareness and attitudes in specific ways.

In the social work education community GSWI PIs segmented their target audience into faculty and staff, administrators (deans and directors), and students (BSW, MSW, and PhD). Using the monthly conference calls with the initiative's leadership, Strategic Communications & Planning conducted an analysis of each of these audience segments, including their values and interests, who influenced them, and where they received information (Kotler & Lee, 2007). This is a critical step in all nonprofit marketing and communications activities, because it forces the marketer, in this case the PI leadership group, to assume a customer orientation to see its work from the audience's point of view and to develop appropriate approaches and outreach (Kotler & Andreasen, 1996).

All the Hartford GSWI leaders needed, in one form or another, to engage junior and senior faculty members to become part of their programs. The group, therefore, decided to concentrate its efforts on this audience segment first, while seeking opportunities to influence deans and directors where possible. In this early phase, the group did not regard students as a primary audience but directly addressed students, particularly doctoral students, in subsequent communications efforts.

With a single objective and a sense of the priority audience (as well as a message framework in place), GSWI's PIs were able to create a solid foundation for communications and outreach. In turn, the group then used this intellectual capital to undergird a comprehensive branding effort and design a set of coordinated strategies and tactics that took the initiative's messages out to its target audience in the service of its main objective. For other change efforts in social work education or other disciplines, it is important to note that the costs of such strategic planning are likely within reach and may even be borne by the change agents themselves. Financial support from the Hartford Foundation enabled GSWI leaders to put together a robust set of outreach activities; however, no- or low-cost tactics that follow a strategic framework with a clear sense of objective, audience, and message can generate important gains as well. For example, a faculty group seeking to build awareness about its graduate social work program among undergraduates at its university would do well to refer to a basic guide to strategic communications (e.g., see Hershey, 2005, or Ratke, 1998). With guides and accompanying materials from such resources, the group could develop a clear, measurable objective (e.g., attract eight new applications from graduating seniors) and interview a handful of juniors to conduct a basic audience analysis. This would help the faculty understand who influences these students, how and where they get their information, and what they think about social work graduate programs. From there, the group could identify key messages about its social work program that resonate with that audience. With this intellectual foundation, group members could brainstorm outreach strategies that use resources and vehicles that are readily available (e.g., one-on-one contacts with promising students, announcements in all upper-level undergraduate social work classes, flyers, e-mails, special event tables, connections to university-wide admissions and the career development office). Thus, without an expert consultant or significant budget, the group can develop a strategic plan that is likely to meet the stated aims of the effort.

Building the Brand: Logo and Graphic Identity

Recognizing the success of the group's initial communications efforts, the Hartford Foundation set aside additional funds to support strategy development, particularly the design of a common graphic identity and logo and, ultimately, a Web site. The foundation's interest in branding was consonant with Hershey's (2005) assertion that such work is critical to differentiating a new product, service, or other offering from others in the marketplace. As she writes, an organization's brand "should be distinctive, appropriate, memorable, and used consistently" (p. 14). The process of developing GSWI's brand continued to reinforce the leadership group's cohesion and created another mechanism for talking about and refining aspects of its collective vision for the initiative.

To begin this part of the work, Strategic Communications & Planning engaged a branding firm with experience in the nonprofit arena. With this firm, the PI group and Strategic Communications & Planning worked through a branding process that included research and discussions related to the key and distinguishing attributes of the initiative, its value-added proposition (the benefits it provided for key stakeholders), and imagery and symbols related to aging and social work. Through a face-to-face meeting and subsequent discussion and review in the monthly conference calls, the PI group settled on a hand-drawn, lavender "ripple" (see Figure 8.33). This symbol eschewed traditional notions of and even indirect connotations surrounding aging. Instead, it focused on the energy and optimism that were GSWI's central attributes along with the desire to overcome stereotypes and create a positive movement around gerontology in the social work education community. The Hartford Foundation senior program officer noted that the ripple captured how one relatively small change (e.g., a single faculty member who infuses gerontological competencies into a course) can have broader effects, spreading outward and affecting peers, students, practitioners, older adults, and countless others (L. Robbins, personal communication, July 8, 2008).

Figure 8.3
THE GSWI RIPPLE LOGO

GERIATRIC SOCIAL WORK INITIATIVE

Additional elements of GSWI's graphic identity also enabled the PIs and others involved with the initiative's programs to see themselves as part of a larger whole. The lavender in the logo served as GSWI's corporate color, but each grant program chose its own subcolor from a predefined color palette that it was expected to use in all its materials. This logo and color scheme were incorporated into a comprehensive graphic identity (including a common typeface) and then transformed into business cards, postcards, PowerPoint slides, and finally a GSWI exhibit. The exhibit included five tall colorful banners—one for GSWI and one for each of the four programs—that could be used separately or together and included language derived from the original messaging work. Over time, this branding was used for a variety of collateral materials including book bags, tote bags, hotel key cards at the annual program meeting (APM) of the CSWE, computer screen savers, memory sticks, pens, and jewelry-quality pins commemorating the Hartford Foundation's 75th anniversary and GSWI's 10th anniversary. These materials ultimately created a common and attractive framework for the initiative's communications, one of the key benefits of the branding process (Aaker, 1996; Andreason, 2005). The ability of GSWI participants to see and use these materials also reinforced their sense of pride and their inclusion in the work and helped to build their identification with the initiative and its larger aims.

Making It Real: Strategy and Outreach

Audience analysis, the development of a common set of messages, the identification of a priority communications objective, and the creation of a versatile and common graphic identity created a strong base for the PI group to build a comprehensive set of outreach strategies and tactics. These communications vehicles served a variety of purposes but, most importantly, provided several mechanisms for translating the collective thinking (i.e., the GWSI's messages) developed by the PIs and delivering it to the social work education community.

To reach faculty members (including social work program leaders) identified as its priority audience, the PI group outlined and then implemented a series of activities:

♦ An organized exhibit strategy. Maintained throughout the year, this strategy ensured that GSWI was represented (and its GSWI banner and associated program banners visible) at key meetings including those of the GSA, CSWE, the Group for the Advancement of Doctoral Education in Social Work, the Society for Social Work Research, and others. The exhibits also made available takeaway products developed by the four GSWI programs, such as pens, mirrors, Post-it notes, calendars, bookmarks, and the Hartford Foundation anniversary pins.

♦ Branded scholarship and program applications and associated materials. These reinforced the initiative's common message among individuals and schools or departments that applied for GSWI programs.

♦ An information-rich, regularly updated Web site. This included a calendar of GSWI events, sections for each of the programs, and segments on career development, funding opportunities, and educational materials that faculty could use to infuse gerontological competencies into their classroom and field courses.

- A regular, monthly e-newsletter, *Ripples*. This ongoing vehicle featured news of interest to a network of more than 500 faculty, administrators, and students committed to gerontological social work.
- Presentations to the annual meeting of social work deans and directors. In these sessions, the PIs intentionally used the initiative's branding, exhibit posters, and message framework to inform these essential academic leaders. Importantly, these presentations recruited deans and directors who had participated in GSWI programs to sing its praises and to talk peer-to-peer with their colleagues.
- *Experience*. This glossy publication to recruit more students into gerontological social work was created once the initiative had been established and its communications focus broadened to include students. It included stories from GSWI participants about their experiences in the programs and in their careers. Costs were defrayed by ads placed by more than 20 social work programs that took an active role in distributing copies of the publication directly to applicants through admissions offices and to matriculated students through career placement offices.
- Information packages for the faculty scholars, doctoral fellows, GeroRich, Gero-Ed, and Practicum Partnership (now HPPAE) programs. These collateral materials used GSWI's branding and served as recruitment and engagement tools for all four programs.

Planning and conducting these strategies continued to be coordinated through monthly conference phone calls by the PIs and annual or biannual face-to-face meetings. These gatherings, with communications as part of their agendas, included the members of the PI leadership group as well as representatives from the Hartford Foundation and Strategic Communications & Planning. Over time, these collectively sponsored efforts, as well as each of the program's presentations, recruitment, and outreach activities, created a consistent and cohesive drumbeat of communications about the initiative. Although it is not possible to accurately measure the direct or even indirect outcomes of these activities, they were nevertheless associated with a number of positive changes in the field. These include a rise in the percentage of programs with faculty with an expertise in aging, an upward trend in the number of geriatric social work dissertations, robust applications to the four GSWI programs, a dramatic increase in the number of presentations on aging (from one to two symposia at the CSWE APM in 2000 to more than 200 presentations in 2005), and growth in the National Association of Deans and Directors Aging Task Force from 25 in 2000 to 106 in 2005, as well as in the Association of Baccalaureate Program Director's Committee on Aging (L. Harootyan, personal communication, August 18, 2005).

Adaptation and Integration

Because the communications and branding effort was launched in 2000, GSWI leaders' collective work around this effort has leveled off, particularly as the initiative's constituent programs established themselves and developed outreach mechanisms of their own. This reflects a natural progression often seen in Strategic Communications & Planning's experience in the field of nonprofit communications during the past 20 years. As nonprofits, or in this case academic leaders, gain experience and confidence with communications and their ability to use and adapt messages and graphic tools, these functions are institutionalized into formal staff roles and responsibilities within their organizations. In GSWI, communications issues are now generally handled through regular meetings of the initiative's program managers, who as operational staff have the day-to-day responsibility for administering their program's work (see chapter 7). Although communications has been a topic at some of the semiannual meetings of the PI group, energetic attention to the issue has waned. For the most part, the communications work has focused on sharing information across the programs, particularly below the PI and program manager level, to ensure that faculty and student participants in GSWI projects have a sense of the other programs and GSWI as a whole.

Indeed, from the experience of GSWI's communication work, one may argue that whereas branding and communications are often initially focused on external aims, their internal benefits can be just as compelling. This is particularly the case for a new effort in the process of establishing a collective identity and cohesive approach to its work.

Programmatically, the initiative has evolved significantly as well. Direct financial funding of some programs has ended, and new programs have been launched. Through these changes, much of the branding has been sustained, particularly the logos and color palettes. GSWI's messaging is still carried on the initiative's Web site and several of the constituent program's Web sites as well. Still, there have been adaptations, with one of the initiative's programs moving away from the original commitment to parallel, two-word names.

This increasing looseness around the names may reflect a natural tension that develops over time between an initiative with a decentralized organization and the ability of its various leaders to consistently use and extend its collective brand and communications. Without a single person or group responsible for the brand's stewardship, its implementation will at times follow the idiosyncratic needs of its various constituents. As Stride and Lee (2007) note:

> Brand development in the charity sector . . . is often conducted in a consultative manner, involving both staff and other stakeholder groups. . . . [Yet] a participative approach to brand management will result in a coherent and consistent brand identity only if considerable effort is made to ensure the key brand values truly encapsulate those values that the charity's stakeholder groups also consider to be of fundamental importance to both themselves and the work of the organization. (p. 118)

GSWI's brand continues to encapsulate the core values of the initiative. However, the initiative itself has matured, and instrumental concerns have superseded the importance of fostering a collective vision. Indeed, close attention to brand consistency is today less important to the initiative's success. Nevertheless, the collective vision remains robust and generally unchallenged. Accordingly, the concern for influencing the social work education community, as initially envisioned by the PI group, remains paramount.

Assessing the Impact of Communications

Finally, in reviewing the GSWI communications effort it is fair to ask, "How well did we do? What has changed?" Good strategic communications practice always includes some form of evaluation (Bonk et al., 1999). Andresen (2006) notes that "good campaigns are tested before they happen, while they are happening, and after they happen. . . . We need to set up a feedback loop that tells us how we're doing" (pp. 249–250).

As noted previously, GSWI on the whole has made progress on a variety of its key aims in the social work education community from increasing the number of geriatric expert faculty and doctoral students and the number of courses and field placements with gerontological competencies to expanding the range of presentations on aging at key national meetings. Communications has certainly played a role in these gains, but it is impossible to tease out the extent to which the cohesive communications and branding strategy contributed to these accomplishments. Indeed, the size and consistency of the foundation's financial investment, the quality work of the programs themselves, and the creation of a network of faculty and others dedicated to this effort are likely the most important drivers of success. Without these components, the communications strategy would have no substance.

Impressionistic responses from GSWI PIs and others in the field suggest that the branding and initial outreach created awareness and a buzz about the new foundation investment. Because of the relatively modest outlay in communications throughout the period, the initiative leadership has not sought to explicitly measure the external impact of the branding and evaluate results of the outreach. How well do people in the field recognize GSWI, its name, or the ripple logo? What associations do they have with the branding and its associated messages or with the field of geriatrics and gerontology? These are appealing, perhaps even worthwhile, questions to pursue but are not currently under consideration. Indeed, the failure to measure the results of this work to date may make it more difficult to build support for more aggressive communications strategy if needed in the future. As Hershey (2005) writes:

> While quantifying the impact of communications efforts can be challenging, it has its rewards. You'll be able to ascertain what's working and what's not so that you can make adjustments to your plan. You'll be able to demonstrate . . . the value of funding a comprehensive communications program. . . . And you'll know that your efforts are making a real difference in reaching your constituents and supporting your . . . mission. (p. 60)

Ultimately, the communications efforts appear to have succeeded in their primary objective. First and foremost, the work was meant to provide a mechanism for a group of distinguished project leaders to come together and think about their common objectives and define and then make real a collective vision. At the beginning of an ambitious multi-year foundation investment, these leaders coalesced around a set of issues beyond the parochial concerns of their individual grants. This successful work served to create a sense of excitement and internal momentum among the leadership group and later among scholars and fellows and other participants in the initiative's various programmatic-level projects. By helping to create a shared sense of purpose and meaning, communications created a significant internal boost for the initiative, supporting the launch of GSWI and its critically important work of changing social work education and improving the care and well-being of older adults.

References

Aaker, D. A. (1996). *Building a strong brand.* New York: The Free Press.

Andreasen, A. (2005). *Social marketing in the 21st century.* New York: Sage.

Andresen, K. (2006). *Robin Hood marketing: Stealing corporate savvy for just causes.* San Francisco: Jossey-Bass.

Beilenson, J. (1999.) *A strategic approach to communications.* Retrieved August 8, 2008, from http://www.aboutscp.com/pdf/071018_Strategic_Approach_to_Comms.doc

Bonk, K., Griggs, H., & Tynes, E. (1999). *The Jossey-Bass guide to strategic communications for nonprofits.* San Francisco: Jossey-Bass.

Hartford Geriatric Social Work Initiative. (2001). *HGSWI communications strategy—80101.* Malvern, PA: Strategic Communications & Planning.

Hershey, C. R. (2005). *Communications toolkit: A guide to navigating communications for the nonprofit world.* Santa Monica, CA: Cause Communications.

Kotler, P., & Andreasen, A. R. (1996). *Strategic marketing for nonprofit organizations* (5th ed.). Saddle River, NJ: Prentice Hall.

Kotler, P., & Lee, N. (2007). *Marketing in the public sector: A roadmap for improved performance.* Upper Saddle River, NJ: Wharton School Publishing.

Ratke, J. M. (1998). *Strategic communications for nonprofit organizations: Seven steps to creating a successful plan.* New York: Wiley.

Stride, H., & Lee, S. (2007). No logo? No way. Branding in the nonprofit sector. *Journal of Marketing Management, 23*(1/2), 107–122.

Weick, K. (1986). Small wins: Redefining the scale of social issues. In E. Seidman & J. Rappaport (Eds.), *Redefining social issues* (pp. 29–48). New York: Society for the Psychological Study of Social Issues.

Wheeler, A. (2006). *Designing brand identity: A complete guide to creating, building, and maintaining strong brands* (2nd ed.). New York: Wiley.

CHAPTER 9

Working With a Private Foundation

Strategies for Institutionalization and Sustainability

James F. O'Sullivan and Nancy R. Hooyman

The John A. Hartford Foundation's commitment to social work education is unprecedented and unparalleled. Indeed, few professions have received the concentration of external resources of the scale made available by the Hartford foundation to social work education over the past decade. As described throughout this book, the Hartford foundation has provided support to prepare social work faculty for research and leadership, support dissertations focused on gerontological social work, bring geriatrics into the curriculum at social work programs, and reengineer the MSW-level practicum to better prepare students for advanced practice with older adults. This support has energized a new generation of faculty and students in aging, fostered innovations in class and field curricula, and developed geriatric social work educational competencies that presage the 2010 implementation of the Council on Social Work Education (CSWE) 2008 Educational Policy and Accreditation Standards (EPAS). The lessons learned over the past decade related to capacity building, sustainability, and working with private funders will be of benefit to leaders in all areas of social work education.

From the inception of the Geriatric Social Work Initiative (GSWI), the principle investigators (PIs), social work deans and directors, and foundation trustees and staff have all recognized that private philanthropic resources cannot become part of the operating costs of professional education. This is true because a foundation's funding priorities may change over time, and because at the recipient level innovations supported solely by external resources are liable to fade if that external support is removed. Private support can only act as seed money, seeking to build a critical mass of faculty, students, and community partners committed to curricular and organizational change and scholarly development.

Throughout its grant making, the Hartford foundation has continually emphasized planning for sustainability. Starting and operating a demonstration program is a significant endeavor, but from a sustainability standpoint it is relatively simple: Projects that do not succeed in the pilot phase are either redesigned or allowed to end. In contrast, mainstreaming a successful demonstration project at its home institution, bringing an innovation to scale via adoption by other educational programs, formalizing curriculum reforms, or building an academic career are much different challenges. In terms of Lewin's (1957) and Lippitt, Watson, and Westley's (1958) models of planned change described in chapter 5, sustainability is vital to freezing the changes made. Central to the last phase of *refreezing* are sustainability strategies, including the continuation of policies, procedures, and deliverable products that support the changes made, to reinforce new behaviors, attitudes, and organizational practices (Burnes, 2004; Cummings & Worley, 2001; Kritsonis, 2004–05; Lewin, 1957).

Recognizing the centrality of sustainability strategies, the GSWI stakeholders have built a range of mechanisms that seek to continue the positive outcomes set in motion by Hartford's support. This chapter reviews a number of sustainability strategies from the perspective of a senior program officer at the Hartford foundation and a grant recipient focused on working with individual social work education programs to sustain curricular and programmatic changes. Examples are also provided from the GSWI programs for faculty scholarly development, doctoral student support, and practicum reengineering. This discussion of national and local strategies is intended to be helpful to social work education leaders across fields of practice who seek to build—and then continue—programmatic components initially funded by "soft money."

These varied grant and program mechanisms are a standard tool of private foundations seeking to create widespread change in a field. Foundations employ a variety of what Prewitt (2006) calls *change strategies* to ensure innovations are adopted and sustained. The Hartford foundation's commitment to the GSWI spans several of those strategies, including creating and applying knowledge, policy analysis and advocacy (within the profession), and social empowerment (of faculty, students, and field instructors interested in aging). Hartford has purposefully not focused on funding delivery of social work services, instead choosing to emphasize gerontological competencies and content in education programs as its point of leverage.

Working toward sustainability of the GSWI programs is particularly challenging because of the wide range of grants funded: demonstration projects, scholar development awards, very small grants for curriculum infusion to individual social work programs, and large multiyear grants to reengineer the MSW practicum. In addition, the Hartford foundation has primarily used a regrant (or subgrant) mechanism to give support to individual social work education programs. Although funding cohorts of programs from a central source at the same time for the same purpose (e.g., funding Geriatric Enrichment in Social Work Education [GeroRich] programs through 67 subgrants) builds a strong peer network among participating organizations, it somewhat isolates the foundation staff from the sustainability challenges faced by individual projects. Instead, Hartford staff has been more involved in working with the leaders of GSWI programs on issues related to sustainability of the overall gero movement set in motion by foundation funding. A further complication is that each type of grant—faculty scholarly development, curricular infusion, practicum reengineering—has its own specific definition of, and paths to, sustainability to be accommodated and supported.

The Different Stakeholders' View of Sustainability

A key challenge faced by the writers of each grant application was forging a proposal that acknowledged the different views of the stakeholders involved and how to obtain their adoption of the changes proposed (Rogers, 1995). Specifically, the challenge has often been to ensure that the broadest possible strategies for sustainability are considered to meet the Hartford trustees' expectations of a long-range plan for the widest possible use of the innovations they are asked to support. This has usually required far more attention to long-range planning than grant applicants have thought necessary to address in their first draft. Over time, Hartford staff have come to realize that this pattern is true for all its grantees across the professions. Reminding program administrators of sustainability expectations occurs consistently, even when working with renewal applications. The following discussion on various perspectives may be helpful to grant seekers in all practice areas.

Foundation Trustees' Perspective

The Hartford foundation is the country's largest private philanthropy with a sustained interest in aging and health, a program focus that is consistent with the goal of many foundations to support innovations in areas that are either ignored or unpopular but seen as important for society to address (Prewitt, 2006). Given the foundation's more than 25 years of funding in geriatric medicine, 12 years of support for geriatric nursing, and 10 years in gerontological social work, applicants are sometimes surprised that the foundation does not fund these areas out of a mission to drive excellence for its own sake in these fields. Rather, Hartford's trustees and staff see sustained support for excellence in those professions as the primary means to fulfilling its mission to increase the nation's capacity to provide effective and affordable care to its rapidly increasing older population (John A. Hartford Foundation, 2006). Hartford's trustees determined that physicians, nurses, and social workers are the keys to quality care of older adults. This difference in perspective has implications for grant development, implementation, and sustainability planning that grant seekers and recipients must constantly address in their communications with the foundation. Similarly, applicants to all private foundations are usually better equipped to prepare successful proposals if they take account of the funder's ultimate goals.

For the foundation's trustees and staff, questions of sustainability and institutionalization of innovations are a natural part of their business. The simple truth is that programs built on soft money, regardless of the specialty area or field of practice, are vulnerable to disappearing once a grant ends. To varying degrees, the staff supported by private funding is no longer available after the funding ceases, or institutions often do not integrate successful programs into policies, procedures, and operations after the demonstration phase is completed. Sustainability of each project, and an initiative as a whole, must therefore be considered at every juncture of development, implementation, and evaluation, with a focus on determining what Bryson (1995) calls *instrumental outcomes* that allow for adaptations to program operations at regular review points. For foundation staff, this entails making the expectations for sustainability explicit and requiring that each proposal address post-grant operations. Yet, as noted earlier, grant applicants are often not oriented to incorporating the full range of mechanisms and strategies for sustainability at the point of proposal development. Effective foundation staff members will often help grantees think through these concepts to incorporate them in the proposal presented to the trustees.

From a private foundation's vantage point, the key to sustainability is having innovations absorbed into a grant recipient's ongoing activities and operations. Tuition-sponsored activities, such as faculty salaries and administrative support for curriculum changes, student education, and career development are the keys for a funder seeking to change the educational enterprise of a profession. For the GSWI, this means seeking to create a stable base for geriatric research by talented faculty and doctoral students' conducting scholarship in aging. It also means trying to ensure that every social work program provides training in appropriate gerontological competencies in classroom and field education. The degree to which these goals become expected normative activities of social work education will be the mark of the ultimate success of the foundation's programs. A complicating factor, of course, is that such an ambitious goal will take more than a decade to accomplish. As Ostrom and Davis (1993) point out, investments in education require a long-term perspective, and the funder must be prepared for changes in the educational environment and commitment to take place over time. As a result, grantees and staff have built intermediate milestones into the funded programs to gauge progress.

The Hartford foundation staff's attempt to create multiple grant programs aimed at institutionalizing gerontology across social work education should also be understood as part of the trend in large American foundations to address their program areas professionally and to give grants strategically to address the root causes of the problems addressed by their programs (Prewitt, 2006). Accordingly, grant seekers benefit by understanding the organizational culture program officers work in so they can create integrated grants programs that try to address the many potential aspects of a strategic initiative.

Issues of sustainability, as opposed to supporting program innovation for the sake of creating new projects and materials, were gaining support in the foundation world just as the GSWI was conceived. This began with Letts, Ryan, and Grossman's (1999) groundbreaking work on the need for foundations to create high-performing nonprofit organizations and copy part of the venture capital model related to clearly defined goals, length of funding, and the grantor–grantee relationship.

From the foundation's perspective, sustainability of the GSWI has two major components, both of which are salient for other important areas of change in the social work profession. First, scholarly and academic leadership must be continued, because through professors' research and teaching they enrich social work's contributions to health outcomes for older people and their families, recruit students into their specialty, and teach future practitioners. In its support of scholarly leaders, the foundation looks to academic productivity in the form of books, peer-reviewed articles, and presentations at scientific meetings as a marker that academic careers are progressing and sustainable. Second, in the classroom and the field, the availability of appropriate images, gerontological competencies, course content and assignments, and hands-on experiences for all students to learn about older adults in foundation and advanced classes and field sites is essential. These measures of progress can be reported on by participating programs through progress reports to the foundation, the CSWE annual statistics, and review of accreditation self-study reports for reaffirmation. From the foundation's standpoint, these components of scholarship and teaching reinforce each other, creating an interlocking set of supports for mainstreaming gerontology into social work education and scholarship. If each component is strong, the entire field will be affected positively, and the funded scholars, fellows, and grant or subgrant PIs contribute not only to their career and individual education program but also to gerontological social work education as a whole. Further, the foundation hopes that the leaders created through these programs will be poised to take advantage of local, regional, and national funding opportunities, promoting further growth and continuation of gerontologically focused educational programming.

The Grantees' Perspective

For grantees, the question of sustainability is often more distant. Addressing what will happen several years in the future is understandably less compelling than launching and maintaining projects in the present. Grantees face the challenges inherent in designing new programs, creating allies, indentifying potential stakeholders, recruiting partici-pants, refining models based on local culture and norms, and pacing activities to budgets. Grantees understand that their ultimate success will be judged on the sustainability of that work, but the competing, im-mediate, and complex demands of launching and operating programs within a short time period often assume higher priority than long-term planning. Partly in recognition of this creative tension, the Hartford trustees' insistence on proactive planning for sustainability has led to annual site visits for Hartford grants, which offer opportunities to assess short-term progress and to reinforce planning for long-term success and continuation.

GSWI grantees have succeeded with sustainability in the short term in one important but easily overlooked aspect. The faculty leaders and staff working on each program have had to prove themselves regularly to the foundation's trustees who have authorized GSWI grants in a step-wise fashion with grant durations of between 1 and 5 years. For exam-ple, six curriculum development commitments that eventually totaled $15.8 million by 2007 started with a modest 2-year $574,988 grant in 1998. Each successive grant, usually larger and of longer duration, was part of an intensive annual review process that resulted in written and oral reports to the Hartford trustees. Those reviews allowed the trustees to monitor and gain confidence in the program's long-term impact. As the trustees approved new strategies over time, the reach of the cur-riculum grants broadened, resulting in a $4.7 million, 5-year commit-ment in 2007. As an annual commitment, the foundation's grants for curriculum have therefore grown from less than $300,000 per year to almost $1 million per year. In all, the $64.5 million committed to the GSWI has come about through 28 separate grant approvals by the Hart-ford trustees.

Similarly, the Hartford Faculty Scholars (HFS) Program, now funded for 10 annual cohorts, began with a grant for just one cohort to allow the foundation and the grantees to determine the extent of faculty in-terest in this approach. The Partnership Practicum Program (PPP), re-named in 2008 to reflect its history and subject matter as the Hartford Partnership Program for Aging Education (HPPAE), and the Hartford Doctoral Fellows (HDF) Program followed similar trajectories. The im-mediate sustainability of the GSWI, therefore, was a strategy developed by the Hartford trustees and staff to use shorter grants at the outset as a means to test whether there was wide demand for the programs and whether these initiatives could be successfully implemented. The success of the leaders of the individual grants in gaining support for their work from within social work education translated into future grants and increased funding.

Sustainability in the GSWI

Sustainability in the GSWI has been approached in the following ways:

1. Creating programs that position gerontology in every point of the development of social work professionals.
2. Requiring matching support and development strategies for grants and subgrants.
3. Planning for the postgrant period to enhance sustainability of program innovations.
4. Crossing institutional boundaries by building communications capacity.
5. Supporting entrepreneurship and grant seeking by explicitly fostering leadership.
6. Creating products for income streams.

Each step and the individual roles played by stakeholders illustrate how sustainability has been conceptualized within the GSWI and to offer examples of the different approaches that can be used by social work faculty and academic administrators seeking to develop or improve relationships with private foundations.

Creating Programs That Position Gerontology in Every Point of the Development of Social Work Professionals

The key to generating social workers ready to provide older adults with effective services is creating educational programming that informs students about the diversity of older Americans and the many service settings where they are found. Given the broad range of social work education programs and the need for students to learn about multiple issues, populations, and interventions for clients of all ages, attaining this ambitious goal has required a multipronged strategy in which each individual grantee or program has had to define sustainability for itself and then again within the larger GSWI. Further, as Ostrom and Davis (1993) suggest, the different organizations involved in the GSWI, either as grant recipients, subgrantees, or sponsors of faculty scholars and doctoral fellows, provided the Hartford foundation with greater opportunities to learn about alternative programs and innovations than would have been the case if all the grants had been made through a single institution.

For example, the HFS program is designed with two goals for sustainability: First, scholars will have successful individual careers through publishing, receiving tenure, and obtaining research grants. Some will eventually become leaders themselves of social work programs. The second measure of sustainability is how well the scholars become engines of research and teaching on gerontological social work, using career activities to recruit students to gerontology and to create new social work practice opportunities to improve the care of older adults. The demonstration of intermediate successes in terms of publications, grants, and tenure by early cohorts of scholars led the Hartford trustees to enthusiastically support the HFS program, whereas the grant leaders and national mentors have been primarily concerned with creating excellent programs to train scholars and leaders. The foci of the two stakeholder groups are different, but each perspective is necessary to ensure long-term sustainability.

In building an initiative that provides examples of excellence in gerontology at every juncture of social work education, Hartford sought to influence the recruitment of students to career and specialization choices, classroom curricula, field education, accreditation of education programs, licensure exams, and continuing education. This multipronged approach focuses on topics in the order students are likely to encounter them (recruitment, classroom, field and career choice) and then issues that are more structural in nature (educational policy, accreditation, licensure, continuing education). However, it would be incorrect to infer that the GSWI was created in this order or that grant dollars were allocated to programs aimed at each of the six areas in any form of rank order. Rather, since 1998 the GSWI has evolved to take into account each of these areas as the field of social work education has proved willing to embrace and institutionalize gerontology. One lesson for sustainability for future initiatives, indeed, must be that once a strategic goal is identified and a community engaged, numerous tactics will become apparent as energized, competent people seek opportunities to reach their goals, and newcomers join the work. For the GSWI, this has meant that the goal of preparing all students for social work practice with older adults has remained constant, but the funded programs have evolved as they acquired experience, increased resources, and discovered new opportunities. For example, although the HDF program quickly began to attract qualified applicants, in 2005 a pre-dissertation travel grant program (the Pre-Dissertation Award Program) was funded to act as a catalyst for over 100 doctoral students early in their academic careers to consider dissertations in aging. Likewise, the Hartford foundation's modest first grant for curriculum led to the CSWE Strengthening Aging and Gerontology in Social Work Education (SAGE-SW) and GeroRich programs, and then subsequent grants to develop the Curriculum Development Institute (CDI) Program of the CSWE National Center for Gerontological Social Work Education (Gero-Ed Center) where individual programs are expected to conceptualize sustainability as institutionalization or formalization of changes within their organizational culture in a range of ways broader than obtaining other funding sources. In each case, programs were targeted according to the availability of Hartford's resources and to changes in the field (some created by other GSWI grantees), but the overall goal of creating a robust gerontological enterprise in social work education never varied.

Recruitment of Students

Student demand for aging is a catalyst for programs to make aging visible and essential and to raise the expectation that gerontological curricular options will be regularly offered. Additionally, mobilized students act as ambassadors among their peers, conveying their excitement about aging to other students. But as noted in chapter 1, recruiting students to gerontological social work careers remains a major challenge nationwide.

In response to this pressing recruitment need, at least four distinct funding strategies have been launched at different times and degrees, spanning three of the GSWI components. To recruit students to aging and social work early in their academic work, a select number of BSW programs have received small grants to create and promote innovative student learning experiences encompassing direct interaction with older adults through the Gero-Ed Center BSW Experiential Learning Program.

Drawing on examples created by faculty participating in the SAGE-SW project, these grants are intended to spur the development of experiential course work to introduce students to older people in their communities and demonstrate the variety of careers available to social workers. In terms of fieldwork, the practicum project reports that the six demonstration programs funded in 2000 produced a 20% increase in the number of students who specialized in aging. Over 600 students participated in a social work rotational model of practicum education across the first 45 schools funded to adopt the model, and each year more than 180 students enroll in these programs. As another example of an effective recruitment strategy, the HDF Pre-Dissertation Awards have drawn nearly 100 doctoral students to learn more about gerontology, a significant shift from 1998 when only 3 people with a new PhD in geriatric social work entered tenure-track faculty positions. A new Gero-Ed Center project to partner with admissions and career counseling personnel is a long-range student recruitment strategy. The aim is to provide these staff with resources about gerontological social work because they work with students at critical junctures in their decision-making process and can profoundly influence students' choice of programs, specialization, and career. Fostering student interest and demand for gerontological social work will ultimately ensure building the gero movement from the bottom up and enhance sustainability of curricular and organizational changes made.

Classroom

Because the classroom is usually the first venue for providing students with knowledge and skills content, the Hartford foundation has consistently recognized the preeminent role of curriculum in preparing students for geriatric practice in its grants in medicine, nursing, and social work. To sustain gerontological content in the social work curriculum, the GSWI has supported the development, implementation, and measurement of geriatric competencies, and the infusion of these competencies along with content and teaching resources on aging in foundation course work and into specialized courses in health, mental health, and substance use.

The first social work grant, the CSWE SAGE-SW project, promoted the development of curriculum standards and the creation of a clearinghouse for geriatric teaching tools. These resources were used by the

GeroRich project to introduce almost 600 social work faculty to topics on aging that could be incorporated in their foundation classes. Later, the GeroRich and Gero-Ed Center programs disseminated gero-infused syllabi, case studies, assignments, and modules, using materials created by faculty participants who understand the daily challenges of teaching and the importance of quality up-to-date curricular materials. Although the emphasis has been on foundation curriculum, a sign of the maturation of the field (and the sustainability of early curricular changes) is a growing interest among faculty and administrators to develop areas of gerontological specialization. This emergent interest will be fostered through an eLearning course and grants to individual programs that are poised to offer gero minors, areas of emphasis, certificates, specializations, or concentrations. Another institutionalization strategy for the CSWE curriculum development projects has been to embed gerontology presentations, curricular resources, and faculty development opportunities in the Gero-Ed Track as part of the CSWE Annual Program Meeting (APM). The formalization of the Gero-Ed Track in the annual conference structure ensures that gerontological content will continue to be part of these national annual gatherings of social work educators, long after foundation funding has ended. It also showcases the ongoing commitment to gerontological social work by the major professional association for social work educators.

An underlying premise of these curricular change initiatives is that creating teaching innovations and modules is not sufficient to ensure their widespread adoption and continuation. The planned change model, designed by the GeroRich project and described in chapter 5, was in itself a primary sustainability strategy. GeroRich leaders recognized that a single faculty member advocating geriatric curricular changes was unlikely to succeed because of the enormity of the task and the potential for aging to be dismissed as a particular professor's issue. Accordingly, each participating program had to nominate a team of faculty to work on curriculum infusion and submit a letter documenting the support, provided by the dean or director, as a requirement of the application process. Sustainability of the curricular innovation was enhanced by embedding the changes in each program's course syllabi, classroom exercises, readings, and assignments; by securing the support of key stakeholders, particularly faculty colleagues; and by formalizing changes through governing curriculum committees, program policies, and other organizational structures. In other words, institutionalizing changes within the fabric of the program—its policies and procedures, library and media holdings, print and electronic documentation, and even artistic representations—was a primary sustainability strategy. Evaluation data showed this systematic approach to be so successful that the planned change infusion model is the defining characteristic of the Gero-Ed Center's multiyear programs that followed the GeroRich project. To embed gerontological competencies in even more curriculum and organizational cultures, Hartford foundation funding was also allocated to create CSWE's first online course on planned curricular and organizational change strategies, which is available to all social work educators.

Several parallel projects were developed to reinforce gero curricular infusion in MSW foundation and BSW required generalist courses. For example, Gero-Ed Center staff consulted with and provided resources to nine authors and two editors of widely used foundation social work textbooks to infuse gerontological content in upcoming editions. Consultation with other authors and editors as they revise their textbooks is ongoing. The Gero-Ed Web site is conceptualized as a sustainability strategy by making extensive resources widely available and easily accessible to all social work educators. The center's Master's Advanced Curriculum (MAC) Project's Gero Innovations Grant is another curricular strategy to embed and sustain gerontological competencies in specialized social work courses on health, mental health, and substance abuse. Last, grants to design specialized gerontological curricula, such as minors, certificates, and concentrations, suggest that the sustainability strategy is coming full circle: The planned change model for foundation courses was adopted in recognition that most social work students were not taking specialized gero courses, but now that gero competencies and content have been embedded and formalized in enough foundation courses, faculty have requested support to create specialized gero curricular structures. In addition, faculty participants in the Gero-Ed Center programs have further strengthened gerontology by interdisciplinary collaboration on their campuses and continuing education offerings for their graduates. Over time, the interplay created by this multipronged strategy between gero competencies infused in foundation curricula and in courses in health, mental health, and substance abuse with gero specialized content and interdisciplinary partnerships will serve to maintain gerontology within the participating programs.

Field Education

The white papers commissioned by the Hartford foundation in 1997–98 to consider how field education could better prepare students for practice with older adults identified two gaps: a general lack of placement sites related to aging and a dominant paradigm in field training, that is, the placement of a student in one agency for his or her entire field experience (Rosenberg, 1998). These gaps meant that students were not exposed to diverse service settings and to older adults with different levels of functional ability. To respond to these gaps, a rotational social work model for the practicum would have to be rigorously tested, and if found successful, would then require substantial resources to be adopted by a critical mass of MSW programs. Only then could the field innovation be considered sustained.

The HPPAE rotational model provides students with field-based curricula that span the fragmented systems of care they will work in after graduation, while introducing them to older adults of varied ages, cultural backgrounds, and levels of functioning. Attracting students with stipends, it then obligates them to participate in a placement in multiple locations where older adults receive services. Funding for a rigorous planning process and a comprehensive implementation phase enabled six sites to develop and test the concept between 2000 and 2003. Working with national leadership and staff at a coordinating center based at the New York Academy of Medicine, the six demonstration sites educated more than 400 MSW students and created new models of training that use the strengths of the academic and practice communities. Evaluation of these demonstration sites showed that all the practicum program stakeholders—students, faculty, field instructors, agencies, deans and directors, and those served (older adults and their families)—benefited from the program, and five of the six local demonstration sites were still in operation 2 years after Hartford foundation funding ended.

Following the demonstration phase, the plan to bring the innovation to scale in social work education was designed for maximum sustainability, with three application cycles established to allow applicants to present the strongest possible application. The coordinating center provided extensive technical assistance on the design of the rotational model and then on implementation and resource development. Each school was required to match the awarded funds with at least an equal amount, and this requirement led many schools and departments to partner with local service providers, government agencies, and foundations at the beginning of their efforts. Each participating program has also been provided with extensive resources, online consultation, and face-to-face training related to fund-raising, marketing, and public relations needed to build sustainability.

Accreditation and Licensure

For outsiders to an educational field, the most direct way to ensure that their concerns are addressed is to place explicit language in the relevant accreditation standards, with the goal of creating a redesigned organizational setting that favors the inclusion of a particular topic or discipline in the academy (Bryson, 1995). However, members of the education community know that the competing demands for attention by accrediting bodies, norms of academic freedom and the profession's autonomy in determining best practices, and the functional limits on a curriculum make such demands from external stakeholders problematic. Balancing this tension is always difficult, but the decennial review of the CSWE 2008 EPAS for its 2010 implementation provided opportunities to comment on draft standards, and gerontological educators were able to organize their comments in ways not possible in prior educational policy reviews. The final language, which requires social work programs to take account of their context, including demographics, in designing student competencies, was viewed by Hartford trustees and staff as a strong lever for programs to regularly review their curricula and field sites in terms of gerontology. As a result of the competency-based approach of the new accreditation standards, another avenue of sustainability was thus opened for gerontology in social work education.

When the GSWI was conceptualized in the late 1990s, it was unclear if licensing exams included content to assess whether social workers were prepared to work with older clients. Attempting to influence these exams became a GSWI priority several years later with the funding of the Gero-Ed Center, but the process of exam writing is, of necessity, closely protected. In addition, questions are not written in terms of specific populations per se. The strategy adopted has been to nominate licensed geriatric social workers to apply to be question writers for the Association of Social Work Boards licensure exam, with the hope that questions that embed gerontology in them and measure gerontological competencies will eventually be included in the exam. This strategy will be continued until an assessment can be made that aging-focused questions have become institutionalized in the exam.

Based on these new developments in accreditation and licensure, GSWI leaders were able to demonstrate to the foundation that there were avenues for creating demand for gerontological competencies and content in social work education. This resonated strongly with the foundation, as most grant seekers offer to increase the supply of some item of their own manufacture, usually making the argument that new and high-quality products will cause potential adopters to choose their materials over existing resources (Rogers, 1995). Given the known difficulties of convincing people to adopt and sustain even simple changes in their regular activities, most external funders are understandably reluctant to accept this argument at face value. In this case, the relatively small amount of staff and faculty time devoted to achieving these developments in accreditation and licensure activities had an inordinate impact on the foundation's decision making for sustaining Hartford's investment on behalf of quality care and services for older Americans.

Continuing Education

Continuing education, although not directly funded by the GSWI, is another area for advancement and institutionalization of geriatric social work resources and skills, particularly through Continuing Education Unit (CEU) requirements for licensure and certification. Participation in the CDI program and the Gero-Ed Track at the CSWE APM provide opportunities for faculty to obtain CEUs. In addition, some social work programs that have participated in the CSWE curricular development programs and the practicum program have sought to expand their reach and sustain classroom and field changes by developing continuing education curriculum in gerontological social work. In fact, some programs used the geriatric eLearning courses and small-grant funding through the Institute for Geriatric Social Work (IGSW) at Boston University, which focuses on training practitioners. Partnerships with IGSW have also created opportunities for GeroEd Center participants to take geriatric social work eLearning courses. In addition, a reciprocal relationship between continuing education and degree-granting programs has enhanced sustainability, because continuing education programs can be a strategy to expand the array of geriatric course offerings, oftentimes through certificate programs. The sustainability of the original Hartford investment has thus been magnified by unanticipated resources that were provided because they offered opportunities for other partners to fulfill their own missions.

Requiring Matching Support and Development Strategies for Grants and Subgrants

A central philosophy of the Hartford trustees is that applicants should demonstrate, in financial terms, a commitment to the programs they are seeking funding for as a means to build success and sustainability. Although a seemingly daunting requirement, especially for social work programs with limited resources, applicants have generally been able to meet this expectation. For sustainability planning purposes, two important lessons have emerged from this practice. First, this requirement has led all GSWI applicants, including subgrantees, to identify the internal supports they can harness in support of gero activities, often by making explicit previously hidden or unmeasured expectations of staff and faculty. As a result, many programs find that they are able to commit to sustaining innovations after Hartford funding ends, because in fact no new operational support is needed. Second, the requirement for matching support has led many grantees to plan for resource development from the earliest stages of their projects, allowing significant lead time for these strategies to come to fruition. The focus on identifying matching support fosters sustainability, not only because it provides evidence of institutional commitment to the original funder but also because it positions the innovator to be able to deliver on its promises.

Planning for the Postgrant Period to Enhance Sustainability of Program Innovations

For a private foundation, ensuring the sustainability of grants to organizations is more difficult than is the case with awards supporting individual professional development. Academics trained to conduct research and teach will be able to perform those responsibilities as their careers evolve, even if they move to different institutions. But it is unavoidable that as other issues and tasks gain attention or if external funds are no longer available to support staff and activities, externally funded programs are at risk of ending. Another risk is that institutional leadership or priorities may change over time, so that an organization's commitment to an area funded by outside dollars may wane as well.

As noted earlier, the Hartford foundation's approach to these issues for the GSWI curriculum and field education components begins with a requirement for matching funds to ensure that the participating faculty and academic administrators understand the resources they are contributing to the project and to motivate them to begin the process of seeking other sources of funding. Another tactic used as part of the competitive application process is to require applicants to propose a project and mechanisms to evaluate it for a specified number of years that are not funded by Hartford. For example, GeroEd Center programs funded schools and departments for 2 years, but each foundation infusion team was expected to complete a 3rd year of unfunded activities and evaluation, and the program director or dean had to specify during the application process how that work would be supported. During this unfunded year, 66 of 67 GeroRich and 58 of 60 Cycle 1 (funded 2004-07) CDI programs sustained activities, including assessing common and project-specific outcome measures. Similarly, during the application process for the practicum program adoption sites, the strongest applicants included plans for continuing their rotational model for 2 years after the end of funding. Among the first 10 sites funded, the majority have been able to maintain the rotational model after Hartford funding ran out. The strong applicant pool for each cycle of practicum funding suggests that the expectation for activities lasting beyond the scope of the funding is not overly burdensome. And for social work education programs seeking support from private foundations, a sustainability strategy that offers specific details—synchronized with their local resources, culture, and demography—can help demonstrate the applicant program's long-term commitment to the proposed innovation and enhance its credibility.

Crossing Institutional Boundaries by Building Communications Capacity

In the three health profession fields funded by the Hartford foundation, geriatrics and gerontology have often been a forgotten or undervalued area of interest among students and faculty. Nor is there adequate private donor support for programs in aging generally. In fact, private foundations' attention to aging and geriatrics overall is much less than an outside observer might expect, considering the demography of the country. Given the relatively low status of geriatrics in the field and among foundations, a communications strategy needed to be implemented (Bryson, 1995). Accordingly, the Hartford foundation views communications, including the capacity to speak convincingly to a wide range of audiences about the need for geriatric health professionals, as a key skill needed by its staff and grantees. Similarly, the foundation recognizes that the GSWI's sustainability would be jeopardized if large segments of the social work education community do not understand gerontology's importance in the training of future social workers. As described in chapter 8, this recognition led to the foundation's direct support of communications for the various GSWI grantees to create venues for skills training in communications, marketing, and public relations.

The need for a communications strategy became even more apparent as the individual grants were launched and the recipients requested assistance in working together with local and national organizations on behalf of their shared commitment to gerontology. Hartford staff understood from the beginning of the GSWI that the initiatives had to function within a set of institutions—the 600 or so colleges, schools, and departments of social work—that operated according to local customs and histories. Institutions varied by structural factors such as their being private or public, enrollment size, external and internal demands for accountability, the roles of faculty in setting policies, and the degree of inclusion of field faculty and staff in decision-making processes. As Gumport and Snydman (2006) note, such varying management structures create a level of complexity that must be explicitly considered by any change effort.

The Hartford foundation allocated additional funding for the GSWI programs to contract with a communications consulting firm specializing in aging to build grantee's marketing capacity, improve print and electronic materials, and increase cohesion and communication between and among grantees. Separately, the foundation provided funding for the GSWI to create a recognizable graphic identity and an integrated set of communications messages for the entire initiative and for each of its four programs (HFS, HPPAE, HDF and the Gero-Ed Center) along with a cross-program display for national conferences and other key meetings. In addition, the GSWI's work devoted to understanding important trends for all of social work education has been shared broadly, such as when data collected for the GSWI provided important insights across all post-master's education at the February 2007 Social Work Doctoral Studies Summit hosted by CSWE at its Alexandria, Virginia, office. Overall, GSWI's communication and dissemination efforts have created a powerful vehicle to build excitement, energy, and cohesion among the multiple grantees and their participating faculty, doctoral students, and community partners. The lesson here for grant seekers in other specialized social work fields of practice is to be specific about their plans to disseminate information and reach target audiences; over time the dissemination and community strategy builds funders' confidence that the grant seeker has carefully thought through how to maintain the core operations of his or her proposal after funding ends.

Among the GSWI programs, communications strategies have been tailored to the distinctive individual program goals and cultures. Faculty scholars and doctoral fellows receive communications training as part of their skill-building activities, as well as structured critiques from the communications staff on poster and oral presentations of their scholarly work. And, especially relevant to an academic audience, a stream of publications has offered regular opportunities for the social work education community to learn about the GSWI and use the resources developed. These include policy briefs, such as *Strengthening the Impact of Social Work to Improve the Quality of Life for Older Adults and Their Families: A Blueprint for the New Millennium* (CSWE, 2001), a monograph on how to build sustainable curriculum and programmatic changes (Hooyman, 2006), and Web site dissemination by the CSWE curriculum development projects, among others. In another example, the MAC Project created literature and evidence-based practice reviews in three specialty practice areas (health, mental health, and substance abuse) for the use of professors teaching in these specialties and for the creation of a document of record for federal agencies that fund research in these areas. The MAC Project's multipronged dissemination strategy, including Faculty Development Institutes at the CSWE APM, is geared toward sustaining their gero competency infusion in social work specialized curricula. The HPPAE, in partnership with the National Association of Social Workers, has sought to build sustainability through the launch of a Web-based aging course called Understanding Aging: The

Social Worker's Role, which has created a mechanism to convey content on aging to over 16,000 social workers from more than 64 countries. Another sustainability strategy through the HPPAE is the implementation of a Leadership Training Academy for deans and directors regarding how to obtain resources to build and sustain practicum partnership models in their individual programs. In these and other instances, the GSWI's communications strategy has been able to continue to expand its standing with the stakeholders of social work education and seek to enlarge the funding base available for geriatric social work research and education.

Although communications and resource development for sustainability are often considered policy and media issues, they are also important in academic development. Since 2004, the annual National Institute on Aging Social Work Research Institute, jointly funded by the Hartford foundation and the National Institute on Aging, has offered participants the opportunity to enhance research skills to be competitive in grant writing, with 30 junior and midcareer social work researchers participating in the first 3 years. Evaluation has found that more than 40% of the participants have been successful in securing research funding from private foundations as well as from state or federal agencies. Although this institute focused on aging, the kinds of methodological and grant development training offered have relevance to other specialized social work areas seeking to build and sustain scholarly capacity.

Support Entrepreneurship and Grant-Seeking by Explicitly Fostering Leadership

The career success of faculty specializing in gerontology is critical to the sustainability of the GSWI. For example, a quality doctoral dissertation can launch a faculty career spanning 20 to 40 years, creating new evidence-based knowledge for practitioners and programs serving older adults, and promoting opportunities to recruit future students to gerontological social work. As noted previously, a hoped-for outcome of the GSWI was to enhance social work faculty's capability to take advantage of emergent funding opportunities—those directly related to aging and those where the case for gerontology needs to be made in response to requests for proposals from social work or human services funders at the state, federal, interuniversity, and private levels. Faculty fund-raising capability has indeed been fostered, as illustrated by the fact that the first seven cohorts of faculty scholars have raised a total of $54.6 million in external research and services funding. This includes traditional research grants from units of the National Institutes of Health, state and regional research projects supported by at least 7 state departments of health or aging, grants from 13 private foundations, and pilot research funds from 9 universities' research regrant programs (B. Berkman, personal communication, August 14, 2008). Additionally, the scholars have widely disseminated their research. For example, 105 scholars and their national research mentors made 154 presentations on their work at the 2006 Gerontological Society of America annual scientific meeting. As another illustration of the continuation of faculty capacity, of the 51 faculty scholars from Cohorts 1 to 5 who have been reviewed for tenure, all but 1 were successful, and 6 have been promoted to administrative leadership positions in their schools and departments. The career trajectory of Hartford faculty scholars clearly suggests that together they are creating an engine to continue to move gerontology forward in the social work academy. With the HFS and HDF programs helping to develop highly qualified faculty, the sustainability of geriatrics and gerontology scholarship in social work seems well on the way. These markers of success and sustainability are also germane to faculty development initiatives in other specialty areas that seek support from private donors.

Similarly, faculty and programs participating in the CSWE curriculum development projects and the HPPAE have been successful in securing other sources of funding, such as local foundation support, university-wide funding, and partner agencies, as well as at institutionalizing changes within their programs' degree requirements and curriculum policies. For social work faculty seeking external support in other substantive areas, these examples suggest that it is possible to make a case for the long-term impact of seed funding, even among programs with relatively limited resources.

Creating Products for Income Streams

Designing products for income streams is another strategy identified by the foundation to build sustainability of innovations. This remains a major challenge for the GSWI programs. Small-scale efforts include the Gero-Ed Center's marketing of individual and institutional subscription rates for its eLearning courses, which will be continued as new eLearning courses are launched. The Gero-Ed Center also experimented with charging a fee for preconference workshops to solidify commitment, decrease attrition, and generate revenue. And filmmakers paid a fee to show their films on aging at the annual conferences. Another relatively traditional income-generating approach was to charge a fee for a national working conference, the Gero-Ed Forum, but in this case, revenue directly supported the center rather than general conference expenses incurred by CSWE. Despite these first steps toward fee-based activities, the income generated to date is currently inadequate to fully fund future center initiatives.

Part of the inherent challenge of this approach is that social work educators in general are not oriented toward marketing and selling products, and in fact may resist the very concept as incompatible with the values of social work and the academy. Another obstacle is that the immediate demands of launching, evaluating, and seeking to sustain projects necessarily take precedence over fee generation. Similarly, an expectation in the social work community is that these foundation-funded initiatives have the resources to make their products available without charge. Given tightening government and foundation funding, this strategy is mentioned here as a necessary direction for sustainability of the GSWI deliverables, especially curricular materials, but one that has not been fully tapped. It also points to the challenges that programs in other specialized social work areas will face if they seek to sell their deliverables.

Conclusion

The strategies toward sustainability described here are transferrable to mission-driven initiatives in other specialized areas that begin with external support but must demonstrate the potential for sustainability to attract significant private funding. These strategies began prefunding, continued as part of the funding requirement, and have been monitored as part of the ongoing evaluation of the GSWI by Hartford staff and trustees. Each grant planned and awarded has required an explicit focus on sustainability to receive approval from the Hartford trustees. This repeated challenge, although often difficult, has proved beneficial: In a 10-year period of constrained state and federal funding and variable availability of support from other private funders, it has nevertheless been possible to design and implement long-term strategies that use the Hartford funds as a base for an expanding movement. The keys to this work have been for applicants and Hartford staff to consistently plan strategically for post-Hartford funding, to frame sustainability as a communications as well as an operations issue, and to provide a variety of funding opportunities targeted at individual and institutional changes. The Hartford trustees, staff, and, most important, the social work education community have created programs so that social work students are being prepared for competent practice with older adults and their families. Together, two agendas have been advanced: The foundation has helped pave the way for better care for older Americans, while social work education has become a leading profession in proactively addressing demographic changes that affect every family and community.

References

Bryson, J. M. (1995). *Strategic planning for public and nonprofit organizations.* San Francisco: Jossey-Bass.

Burnes, B. (2004). Kurt Lewin and the planned change approach to change: A re-appraisal. *Journal of Management Studies, 41*(6), 977–1002.

Council on Social Work Education. (2008). *Educational policy and accreditation standards.* Retrieved August 16, 2008, from http://www.cswe.org/NR/rdonlyres/2A81732E-1776-4175-AC42-65974E96BE66/0/2008EducationalPolicyandAccreditationStandards.pdf

Council on Social Work Education Strengthening Aging and Gerontology in Social Work Education. (2001). *Strengthening the impact of social work to improve the quality of life for older adults and their families: A blueprint for the new millennium.* Alexandria, VA: Author.

Cummings, T., & Worley, C. (2001). *Organization development and change* (7th Ed.). St. Paul, MN: West Publishing.

Gumport, P. J., & Snydman, S. K. (2006). Higher education: Evolving forms and emerging markets. In W. W. Powell & R. Steinberg (Eds.), *The nonprofit sector: A research handbook* (2nd Ed., pp. 462–484). New Haven, CT: Yale University Press.

Hooyman, N. (2006). *Achieving curricular and organizational change: Impact of the CSWE Geriatric Enrichment in Social Work Education Project.* Alexandria, VA: Council on Social Work Education.

John A. Hartford Foundation. (2006*). Annual report.* New York: Author.

Kritsonis, A. (2004–05). Comparison of change theories. *International Journal of Scholarly Academic Intellectual Diversity, 8*(1), 1–7.

Letts, C. W., Ryan, W. P., & Grossman, A. (1999). *High performance nonprofit organizations: Managing upstream for greater impact.* New York: Wiley.

Lewin, K. (1957). *Field theory in social sciences.* New York: Harper & Row.

Lippitt, R., Watson, J., & Westley, B. (1958). *The dynamics of planned change.* New York: Harcourt, Brace.

Ostrom, E., & Davis, G. (1993). Nonprofit organizations as alternatives and complements in a mixed economy. In D. C. Hammack & D. R. Young (Eds.), *Nonprofit organizations in a market economy: Understanding new roles, issues and trends* (pp. 23–56). San Francisco: Jossey-Bass.

Prewitt, K. (2006). Foundations. In W. W. Powell & R. Steinberg (Eds.), *The nonprofit sector: A research handbook* (2nd Ed., pp. 355–377). New Haven, CT: Yale University Press.

Rogers, E. M. (1995). *Diffusion of innovations* (4th Ed.). New York: The Free Press.

Rosenberg, G. (1998). *Identifying and improving effective gerontological social work practice and service models.* White paper commissioned by the John A.Hartford Foundation, New York.

CHAPTER 10

Concluding Comments

Nancy R. Hooyman

The Geriatric Social Work Initiative (GSWI) is presented throughout this book as one example of a national model for capacity building among faculty, students, community partners, and social work programs. Lessons learned that could be translated to other substantive areas and fields of practice within social work as well as other disciplines have been identified throughout. Although the GSWI is generously funded by the John A. Hartford Foundation, many of these strategies could be implemented without external funding, albeit on a smaller scale. This chapter summarizes effective strategies within the four initiative components of (1) faculty development and leadership capacity building, including faculty from culturally diverse backgrounds; (2) student recruitment and leadership development, including students from historically underserved populations; (3) community partnerships with agencies serving a diverse range of older adults; and (4) institutional change and sustainability.

Underlying all of these strategies is the vision of the Hartford foundation and of the GSWI principal investigators (PIs), along with 30 years of documented need for geriatric social work capacity building. Each of the PIs brought to the initiative extensive gerontological and administrative experience, a clear direction for change, and different national organizational affiliations in social work, health care, and gerontology that broadened the GSWI's reach. The PIs also recognized that traditional approaches, such as offering aging courses or specializations and relying on a small number of gerontological social work educators and scholars to recruit and teach a modest number of BSW, MSW, and PhD students committed to aging, were not working (Scharlach, Damron-Rodriguez, Robinson, & Feldman, 2000; Wilson, 2006). A multipronged, systematic, long-term approach oriented to sustainability and programmatic-level capacity building was essential to ensure that the social work profession as a whole is prepared to meet the growing workforce needs created by the aging of the baby boomers.

Faculty Development and Leadership Capacity Building

Building leadership capacity among social work faculty as scholars/researchers and educators has been a central component in all the GSWI's programs. The primary strategies used to promote such leadership are described in the following sections.

Mentoring

Mentoring, at both national and programmatic/institutional levels, is a distinguishing characteristic of all the GSWI programs and central to the success of participants in the Hartford Faculty Scholars (HFS) and Hartford Doctoral Fellows (HDF) Programs and the Council on Social Work Education (CSWE) National Center for Gerontological Social Work Education (Gero-Ed Center). The HFS program has designed, implemented, and evaluated a distinctive model of providing a national research mentor and an institutional sponsor for each of the faculty scholars; this model recognizes that junior and midcareer faculty members need assistance with scholarly development and with negotiating the organizational structure of the scholar's home institution. The primary mentor in the HDF program is the fellow's dissertation chair, but this mentoring is supported by supplemental consultation and assistance by the faculty leaders on the HDF selection committee, who often assume mentoring functions. In both programs, priority is placed on ensuring the cultural competence of mentors as they interact with an increasingly diverse group of mentees.

National mentors also have been central to the CSWE Geriatric Enrichment in Social Work Education (GeroRich) and the Gero-Ed Center's Curriculum Development Institute (CDI) programs for curriculum and programmatic change. In both instances, faculty mentors are prior participants in CSWE curricular change projects (2001–06), who draw upon their own experience of bringing about sustainable changes in their foundation curriculum. Based upon feedback from GeroRich participants, attention has been given to ensuring the cultural diversity of the national mentors in the CDI programs. Mentors are assigned to a group of faculty participants who typically come from institutions with similar characteristics in terms of size, geographic location, cultural diversity of their student body, and program degree level (BSW only, MSW only, joint). A striking benefit of the group mentoring approach is the networks created among faculty participants who provide peer support to each other during and after funding; in fact, most Gero-Ed Center faculty have continued to collaborate with each other and their mentors on issues related to problem solving and dissemination through conference presentations and peer review articles, even after Hartford funding has ended.

The national leaders associated with the HFS program and the GeroRich and Gero-Ed Center have learned over time the importance of providing faculty mentors and mentees with specific written recommendations for effective mentoring relationships. They have also systematically created opportunities for mentors to discuss openly some of the challenges of long-distance mentoring relationships that rely primarily on phone calls, e-mail communication, and meetings at the annual meetings at national conferences. And they ask program participants for feedback on the effectiveness of their mentoring relationship. Based on these data, the HFS program and the CSWE curriculum development projects regularly evaluate their mentoring approaches and make changes for future cohorts.

Training/Professional Education

Most of the professional development opportunities, such as workshops prior to national conferences or regional and national meetings of program participants, have not focused on gerontological content per se. Instead, attention is given to the development of skills that can strengthen faculty's long-term capacity as researchers, teachers, community partners, and organizational change agents. It has been generally assumed that program participants already have some gerontological knowledge and skills, or could obtain such content through didactic training opportunities at their home institutions, national gerontological conferences (including the Gero-Ed Track at the CSWE Annual Program Meeting [APM]), or online courses (such as those developed by the Institute for Geriatric Social Work at Boston University and funded by the Atlantic Philanthropies, see http://www.bu.edu/igsw/). To illustrate, the HFS and HDF programs have typically offered workshops on methodological skills or proposal writing. But they also have provided travel expenses to major gerontological and social work conferences where scholars and fellows can expand their gerontological knowledge as needed. The CSWE curriculum development projects and the Hartford Partnership Program for Aging Education (HPPAE) have designed opportunities to present didactic content on strategies for the implementation and measurement of geriatric social work competencies; curricular change approaches to infuse geriatric competencies at the BSW and MSW foundation level or geriatric specialization at the advanced graduate level in health, mental health, and substance use; building and sustaining community partnerships; and evaluation, dissemination, and institutionalization of changes made.

Training in conjunction with professional education is a necessary component for the effectiveness of the GSWI programs but is not sufficient in itself. Social work faculty members have typically had individualized opportunities to advance their expertise through national conferences, continuing education, topically oriented meetings, and workshops, and to operate as individualistic entrepreneurs, particularly within research-oriented social work programs. The GSWI training model is differentiated by the collaborative opportunities to learn from and collaborate with peers/colleagues, to build ongoing networks of support and assistance across a wide range of diverse social work programs from the inception of funding, and to plan for sustainability of changes made.

Collegial and Collaborative Networking

Peer problem solving and mutual learning are central to the GSWI programs. The HFS and HDF programs have identified the benefits of collegial networking at several levels: among the scholars and fellows; across the scholars, fellows, and pre-dissertation fellows; and among the national mentors or dissertation chairs, institutional sponsors, scholars, and fellows. Building a strong cohort of participants who socialize and work hard together is promoted by the HFS program; this occurs through the numerous learning opportunities where scholars meet, not only at national conferences but also at the fall orientation meetings and a national teaching institute attended by fellows in their second year. The HDF program also fosters peer networking among the pre-dissertation and dissertation fellows, as well as across the HFS and HDF programs. The HDF networks continue to provide support and assistance as fellows move into faculty positions where they may be mentored by scholars in their new home institution.

Participants in the HPPAE and the CSWE curriculum development programs gather at least once a year at national meetings just prior to the CSWE APM or the Gerontological Society of America (GSA) meeting. These programwide gatherings are structured to promote peer problem solving and networking, within and across mentor groups. In fact, evaluations of the GeroRich and the Gero-Ed Center programs consistently point to the value of learning from peers at national meetings and recommend that didactic content be presented either in short segments at such meetings or via eLearning that can be completed outside these formal gatherings. This preference among faculty participants for ample time for networking and peer problem solving reflects how informal collegial support systems strengthen each individual's ability to overcome obstacles and achieve his or her goals.

Financial Support

Without a doubt, the fiscal resources available through the Hartford foundation have been pivotal in creating a national gero social work movement. An important lesson learned for other programs, however, is that some effective strategies, such as peer networking and problem solving and engaging key constituencies in the change process, can be conducted without extensive resources.

Fiscal support, whether in the form of grants directly to individual scholars and fellows or to the home institutions of the HPPAE and Gero-Ed Center faculty participants, has been essential to jump-start and accelerate the pace of change. For the scholars and fellows, direct financial support has ensured adequate workload time for them to conduct high-quality research as well as to seek other sources of external funding to further their research careers.

Because of the Hartford foundation's expectations of institutional commitment and sustainability of changes, the amount of funding available to participating schools and departments in the HPPAE and Gero-Ed Center programs has intentionally declined since their inception in 1999 and 2001. This shift has necessitated that academic administrators increase their programs' allocations of resources to ensure the success of the faculty who participate in HPPAE and Gero-Ed Center initiatives. Some social work programs have chosen not to participate because of the reduced funding. However, programs generally have recognized the necessity of the targeted field and classroom curricular changes to ensure the adequate preparation of their students for 21st-century practice. They also have valued the opportunity for their faculty to participate and the recognition accorded their program by Hartford funding, and they have allocated the fiscal and in-kind resources to ensure the success of these curricular initiatives. In other words, as the need for *gerontologizing* the field has become highly visible, programs are willing to step up to meet this demand, despite limited external funding and increased expectations of program matching funds.

Student Recruitment, Development, and Capacity Building

Recruiting students to geriatric social work, even when funding is available, remains a major challenge for the field (Cummings, Alder, & DeCoster, 2005). Accordingly, national leaders and faculty participants associated with the HDF, HPPAE, and the Gero-Ed Center programs have actively designed strategies to engage students within their programs and through national venues. Throughout, attention has been given to outreach to students from historically underserved populations. Student recruitment is, of course, central to the HDF program. It was recognized early that despite the extensive branding and marketing of the GSWI, simply distributing HDF recruitment materials to deans and directors was not an effective strategy for reaching doctoral students. Instead, personalized outreach to doctoral students is essential and is accomplished at national conferences, through visits by the HDF PI or advisory board members to some doctoral programs, and by electronic and hard copy distribution—at multiple times—of the program application to doctoral students and doctoral faculty. The HDF PI's accessibility to student applicants at national meetings and via e-mail and phone consultation has been vital to encouraging students to apply successfully for HDF funding. The pre-dissertation fellowship component of the HDF program, described in chapter 4, arose directly from a lesson learned early in the HDF program; the HDF leaders recognized the importance of reaching students early in their doctoral work, well before they have settled on a topic for their dissertations. This timely outreach has been effective in recruiting students from historically underserved backgrounds as well as those who were not initially planning to conduct dissertation research in aging; it has also served to expand the pipeline of applicants to the HDF Pre-Dissertation Award. Faculty mentoring by the leaders associated with HDF and program faculty, such as the chairs of doctoral programs, supervisory exam committees, and dissertation committees at students' home institutions, are also critical to recruitment across the wide range of doctoral programs in social work.

Recruiting students to HPPAE and the Gero-Ed Center participating programs takes place at the level of the individual program supported by these initiatives and thus depends largely on the faculty participants at the funded schools and departments. In most instances, having a cadre of faculty mentors tends to be more effective at coaching and recruiting students than having just one lone faculty member with a commitment to gerontological social work (Marimaldi et al., 2004; Schuster, 1993). Both curriculum development initiatives have thus encouraged the hiring of a "critical mass" of gero faculty as a way to recruit more students and ensure sustainability of changes in the classroom and field curriculum. HPPAE's recruitment effectiveness has been fostered by the following factors: funding for stipends (albeit at reduced levels since 2004), the distinctive learning experiences of the rotational model through which students are exposed to more than one service delivery system and varied functional levels of culturally diverse older adults, and the recognition and status accorded students who are associated with this distinctive national program. Most programs participating in the HPPAE offer special geriatric learning opportunities for their students, such as tailored seminars and colloquia that aim to foster students' leadership capacity. Additionally, the faculty and field supervisors associated with HPPAE programs provide extensive mentoring for their students in their advanced-year field placement. In some HPPAE programs, prior student participants and alumni are particularly effective recruiters, conveying their enthusiasm for working with older adults and for participating in the rotational model of field education. Last, HPPAE, in collaboration with the National Association of Social Workers, has designed a competency-based online course in aging, which is available without charge to anyone.

An underlying premise of the GeroRich and the Gero-Ed Center planned change model is that infusion of gero competencies in foundation and advanced nonaging curricula (e.g., the Master's Advanced Curriculum project's targeting of health, mental health, and substance use specializations) is the most effective long-range strategy to educate students and eventually recruit some of them to gero specialized classes, field placements, and careers. This approach would undoubtedly be similar for faculty who are seeking to embed content on other substantive areas or populations in required curricula. When faculty participants in these CSWE curriculum programs seek to recruit more students to specialize in aging, they nevertheless frequently encounter low student interest in attending gero-specific learning opportunities, such as colloquia, special lectures, or electives. The Gero-Ed Center has initiated two new strategies to promote student recruitment.

Recognizing that experiential learning opportunities are effective in changing students' attitudes toward aging and increasing their interest in working with older adults (Cummings & Galambos, 2002; Kropf, 2002), the Gero-Ed Center has launched a program to design experiential learning activities early in students' academic careers at the BSW level. This strategy was targeted to BSW programs with highly diverse student bodies. A hoped-for outcome of this strategy is that more students will pursue a field placement, graduate degree, or career working with older adults. In addition, the Gero-Ed Center is reaching out to social work admissions and career counseling staff, because these personnel can profoundly influence students' attitudes and interests in gerontological social work. Even though many admissions staff received the publication *Experience* (described in chapter 7) in the past, the Gero-Ed Center is developing lower-cost and easily accessible career materials, such as colorful bookmarks and fact sheets, to try to reach more students. Overall, admissions and career counseling personnel have welcomed the additional information about geriatric social work and workforce demands as a way to recruit students to course work, placements and careers in aging. The challenge with this strategy, however, is that admissions functions vary widely among social work programs and home institutions, and hard copy materials need frequent updating. Both HPPAE and Gero-Ed Center programs are now providing recognition to students at the national level through awards presented at the CSWE APM, anticipating that this will foster a buzz about geriatric social work among students.

In sum, early outreach in a students' academic career, whether at the BSW level or the pre-dissertation level for doctoral work, opportunities to interact directly with older adults in a wide range of practice settings, recognition awards, and mentoring by faculty at students' home institutions are promising strategies for student recruitment and leadership development. Strategies to engage admissions and career counseling staff are targeted toward students at point of entry and graduation from social work education program. As more students enter the geriatric social work field, they are expected to become the best recruiters as well as future local and national leaders, thereby expanding the reach of the GSWI national gero movement.

Community Partnerships

Building partnerships with practitioners and agencies is central to the success and sustainability of the HPPAE field rotation model; it has also been important, though not primary, for GeroRich and the Gero-Ed Center initiatives, which have aimed to infuse gerontological competencies into the BSW advanced generalist and MSW foundation field. Community partnerships have also been pivotal in the development and testing of the two sets of geriatric social work competencies, foundation and advanced. HPPAE-funded programs have creatively designed expanded roles for field supervisors, which have served to strengthen their essential function in students' education. Even though field learning is viewed as the signature pedagogy of professional social work education (CSWE, 2008), far too often in the past, field supervisors have felt unrecognized and alone in their training of students (Reisch & Jarmon-Rhode, 2000). The expanded roles, the training, and the peer support inherent in the HPPAE model have promoted the leadership capacity of field supervisors in aging-focused settings throughout the country, with most field supervisors expressing enthusiasm for the HPPAE rotational matrix. The strategies for community partnership building developed by HPPAE do not require extensive fiscal resources and are transferrable to numerous settings, as shown by HPPAE's training of social work deans and directors in this partnership model.

Although field experience is not central to the CSWE curriculum development projects, many participating programs put into practice the widely agreed upon premise that field and classroom learning must be integrated and support one another (Liley, Mellor, & Ivry, 2002; Rogge & Rocha, 2004). They did so by working with field supervisors in nonaging-focused settings to ensure that all students in their foundation field placements had opportunities to interact with older adults and their families. As noted previously, positive personal interactions with elders can profoundly change students' attitudes toward aging and increase their receptivity to gerontological social work field placements and careers (Cummings et al., 2005).

Obtaining the support of field supervisors and practicum faculty who are based in academic settings has been essential to the implementation of gero competencies in required generalist or foundation field placements. To illustrate, as a result of the infusion of geriatric competencies in BSW senior or MSW 1st-year placements, more students interning in child welfare placements have systematic opportunities to work with grandparent caregivers and learn about the age-associated challenges facing these primary caregivers of children. Similarly, more students placed in mental health settings are learning about issues of mental well-being for older adults.

Program Development and Capacity Building for Sustainability

Building capacity for sustainability is inherent in all GSWI programs. Strategies for capacity building occur at a number of different levels: in the home institution of the participating faculty and doctoral students, including partnering with community agencies, other social work programs, and other disciplines; across GSWI programs through collaboration among PIs, including working together to influence federal legislation related to loan forgiveness and implementation of recommendations from the Institute of Medicine (IOM; 2008) report; the virtual team building of the operational or administrative staff for each program; and systematic training of GSWI PIs and project directors related to communications, branding, marketing, and dissemination of deliverables within a cross-disciplinary context involving medicine and nursing.

Capacity building in the GSWI participants' home institutions takes place in the HFS program through engagement of institutional sponsors and on-site meetings with the national mentor, institutional sponsor, academic administrators, and individual scholar; in the HDF program through communication with the fellow's dissertation chair and other mentors; and in the HPPAE and Gero-Ed Center through ongoing support and technical assistance of faculty participants who are working to institutionalize geriatric competencies in the classroom and field curriculum. In particular, the HPPAE model includes partnership-building strategies that are systematically disseminated to deans and directors through training by the New York Academy of Medicine (NYAM) Leadership Academy in Aging. A distinctive capacity-building aspect of the leadership academy is that deans/directors are encouraged to select a senior mentor with expertise in an area in which the participating dean wants to perfect his or her skills. The mentor offers guidance via a written contract that outlines mutual expectations and visits the participating dean to shadow him or her to offer additional insight into strengthening leadership skills. Capacity building is also promoted by the requirement of all GSWI programs for an institutional match and letters of support and memoranda of agreement from academic administrators. From the point of application to the HPPAE and Gero-Ed Center programs, faculty participants and academic administrators are required to begin planning for the sustainability of the changes made in the classroom and field curriculum and the programmatic structure. The systematic approach of the planned change model, in particular, has been found to be conducive to ensuring the sustainability and institutionalization of changes made by the Gero-Ed Center programs.

Geriatric social work capacity building has also been strengthened by GSWI programs' collaboration with other professions to influence federal and state legislation. For example, several of the GSWI programs worked with other disciplines and with the office of California's U.S. senator Barbara Boxer to write the bill that would forgive school loans of health care providers who specialize in geriatrics (Caring for an Aging America Act of 2008). More recently, the GSWI programs and their affiliated professional organizations (the CSWE, GSA, and NYAM) have been participating in the National Eldercare Workforce Alliance of more than 30 organizations to move forward the recommendations of the IOM (2008). Collaboration related to policy-making initiatives is crucial because united cross-program legislative efforts are likely to have more impact than individual programmatic representation and agendas.

The centrality of collaboration among operations staff for each of the GSWI programs was not initially recognized by the GSWI PIs or their staff, but became readily apparent as the GSWI grew in size and scope. The strategies GSWI staff used to build effective virtual teams are certainly transferrable to any programmatic initiatives that involve multiple sites, geographic locations, and organizational auspices.

Similarly, the communications and dissemination strategies to develop a common vision and message that have been adopted by the GSWI PIs and program directors and the ongoing assistance and availability of communications resources through the Hartford-funded communications consultant, described in chapter 8, are central to the depth and sustainability of changes. Individual participating programs have been assisted in their communication and marketing efforts. For example, in HPPAE and the Gero-Ed Center, program faculty are provided with press kits and suggestions for working with their home institution's public relations unit to give visibility to their change efforts.

Branding has been a central component of the communications strategy. The GSWI ripple logo, designed by the communications consultant with the PIs' input, captures the concept that gero changes in faculty and students, in academic home institutions, and in field supervisors and partnership agencies can reverberate across systems, building the geriatric social work capacity of the profession and promoting sustainability of changes made. Our hope is that this book serves to expand the ripple's reach to influence faculty in other social work practice or specialized areas as well as other disciplines committed to expanding gero capacity. We encourage you to try out the strategies found to be effective in the GSWI; adapt them to fit your area of specialization, discipline, or home institution, and maintain the focus that unites all of us to ensure the highest-quality professional preparation of BSW, MSW, and doctoral social workers across all areas of practice, as well as that of students from other disciplines committed to the care of older adults and their families.

References

Caring for an Aging America Act of 2008, H.R. 6637, 110th Cong. (2008).

Council on Social Work Education. (2008). *Educational policy and accreditation standards.* Retrieved November 12, 2008, from http://www.cswe.org/NR/rdonlyres/2A81732E-1776-4175-AC42-65974E96BE66/0/2008EducationalPolicyandAccreditationStandards.pdf

Cummings, S. M., Alder, G., & DeCoster, V. A. (2005). Factors influencing graduate social work students' interest in working with elders. *Educational Gerontology, 31,* 643–655.

Cummings, S. M., & Galambos, C. (2002). Predictors of graduate social work students' interest in aging-related work. *Journal of Gerontological Social Work, 39,* 77–94.

Institute of Medicine. (2008). *Retooling for an aging America: Building the health care workforce committee on the future health care workforce for older Americans.* Washington, DC: The National Academies Press.

Kropf, N. P. (2002). Strategies to increase student interest in social work. *Journal of Gerontological Social Work, 39,* 57–67.

Liley, D. G., Mellor, M. J., & Ivry, J. (2002). Bridging the gap between classroom and practicum: Graduate social work students in health care with older adults. *Advancing Gerontological Social Work Education, 39*(1), 203–217

Maramaldi, P., Gardner, D., Berkman, B., Ireland, K., D'Ambruoso, S., & Howe, J. L. (2004). Mentoring new social work faculty: A gerontological perspective. *Gerontology & Geriatrics Education, 25*(1), 89–106.

Reisch, M., & Jarmon-Rhode, L. (2000). The future of social work in the United States: Implications for field education. *Journal of Social Work Education, 36,* 201–213.

Rogge, M. E., & Rocha, C. J. (2004). University-community partnership centers: An important link for social work education. *Journal of Community Practice, 12*(3), 103–121.

Scharlach, A., Damron-Rodriguez, J., Robinson, B., & Feldman, R. (2000). Educating social workers for an aging society: A vision for the 21st century. *Journal of Social Work Education, 36,* 521–538.

Schuster, J. H. (1993). Preparing the next generation of faculty: The graduate school's opportunity. In L. Richlin (Ed.), *Preparing faculty for the new conceptions of scholarship* (pp. 27–38). San Francisco: Jossey Bass.

Wilson, N. L. (2006). Educating social workers for an aging society: Needs and approaches. In B. Berkman (Ed.), *Handbook of social work in health and aging* (pp. 1041–1050). New York: Oxford University Press.

Index

Asian/Pacific Islander, 4, 67, 94
competencies and, 42
debt and, 9
of geriatric social workers, 87
of Hartford doctoral fellows, 94
of Gero-Ed Center, 102-103
infusion approach within curriculum and,
102, 103
Latinos, 4–5, 94
mentoring and, 53, 67–69
Native Americans, 4, 94
poverty rates and, 5
of Pre-Dissertation Award recipients, 94
in university–community partnerships, 149–
50
in virtual teams, 159
in workforce, 4, 5–6, 7
Diwan, Sadhna, 99
Doctoral studies. *See also* Education; Hartford
Doctoral Fellows program (HDF)
barriers to, 80–82
dissertation proposal seminars, 93
dissertations, 12–13, 82
grants for dissertations, 83–84
mentoring and, 81–82, 85, 90
need for programmatic support for, 79–80
research emphasis in, 91
supplemental academic career advising, 85–86
support for, 200

E
Education. *See also* Classrooms; Curriculum;
Field work
Bachelors. *See* Bachelors of social work (BSW)
classroom vs. field, 34, 40–41, 44, 209–13
competency-based, 21–49. *See also*
Competency-based education
continuing, 7, 30, 84–85, 214–15
curriculum for field, 39
doctoral students, 79–97. *See also* Doctoral
studies
eLearning, 15
Master's. *See* Master's of social work (MSW)
mentoring and, 54
postgraduate, 30
specializations, 8
training/professional, 227–28
Educational Policy and Accreditation Standards
(EPAS), 14, 23–24, 101
CBE, 25–26
competency-based education (CBE) and, 38,
41, 42, 44, 109–10
field education and, 134–35
infusion approach of, 101
practice behaviors and, 36
sustainability and, 199, 213
Educational Policy 1.2 (CSWE), 25
Educational Policy M2.2 (CSWE), 26
eLearning courses, 221, 232

Electronic communication and virtual teams,
160, 174
E-mail
curriculum change and faculty
communications, 112
in mentoring relationships, 66
virtual teams and, 171, 174
Empathy, 56
E-newsletters, 193
Entrepreneurship, 219–20
EPAS. *See* Educational Policy and Accreditation
Standards
Ethnic minorities. *See* Diversity
Evaluation, 115–16, 121–22. *See also* Feedback
of mentoring, 70
phase of planned curricular and organizational
change, 106, 115–16, 121–22
Evidence-based practice, 22, 37, 44

F
Face-to-face interactions for virtual teams, 168,
172
Faculty Development Institutes, 218
Faculty hiring of Hartford doctoral fellows, 86–
90
Feedback. *See also* Evaluation
from mentors, 63
in planning stage of curriculum change, 107
Field work
as signature pedagogy, 39
CBE training, 39–40
classroom vs. field education, 34, 40–41, 44,
209–13
curriculum for education, 39, 40–41, 43
importance of, 134–35
instructors' expanded role, 142, 146–48
placement, 34
rotational field models, 13–14, 23, 137–38,
144–46
sustainability and, 212
university–community partnerships and, 140,
233
Financial support. *See* Funding; Grants and
grantees
Fisher, R., 133
Focus groups for community support, 113–14
Foundations. *See* Private foundations
Funding, 12–13, 16. *See also* Grants and
grantees
HFS program attaining, 71
Pre-Dissertation Award, 92–95
sustainability and, 219–20, 229–30

G
Geriatric Enrichment in Social Work Education
Project (GeroRich)
background, 10, 15, 99
collaborative networking and, 229
competencies and, 26, 31, 37, 99–100, 109